The Cold War and the University

The Cold War & The University

TOWARD AN INTELLECTUAL HISTORY
OF THE POSTWAR YEARS

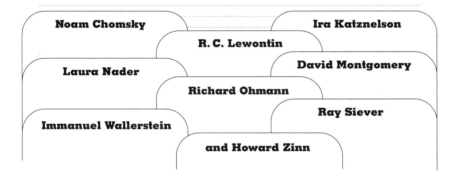

Noam Chomsky

Ira Katznelson

R. C. Lewontin

David Montgomery

Laura Nader

Richard Ohmann

Ray Siever

Immanuel Wallerstein

and Howard Zinn

THE NEW PRESS ★ NEW YORK

LIBRARY OF CONGRESS CATALOGING-IN-PUBLICATION DATA
The Cold War and the university; toward an intellectual history
of the postwar years / Noam Chomsky...[et al.].
    p.   cm.
Includes bibliographical references.
ISBN 1-56584-005-4
    1. Education, Higher—Political aspects--United States—History—20th century.
    2. Cold War. 3. Education, Higher—United States—History—20th century.
    4. United States—Intellectual life—20th century. I. Chomsky, Noam.
    LC89.C565   1997
    378.73'09044—DC20   96-25426
    CIP

Published in the United States by The New Press, New York
Distributed by W.W. Norton & Company, Inc., New York

Established in 1990 as a major alternative to the large commercial publishing houses, The New Press is a nonprofit American book publisher. The Press is operated editorially in the public interest, rather than for private gain; it is committed to publishing, in innovative ways, works of educational, cultural, and community value that, despite their intellectual merits, might not normally be commercially viable. The New Press's editorial offices are located at the City University of New York.

Book design by Smyth and Whiteside (BAD)
Production management by Kim Waymer
Printed in the United States of America

9 8 7 6 5 4 3 2 1

Contents

Editor's Note

Historians agree that the Cold War was the most important fact in all of our lives during most of the second half of this century. It dominated our politics, transformed our economy, and affected the lives of people throughout the world in a myriad of ways. It also radically changed our perspectives in a number of crucial areas, from the way we think about history to the way we approach the culture and societies of other countries. Yet there has been no thorough study of its impact on intellectual life. How were the universities affected by the Cold War tensions? By personnel policies during and after the McCarthy period? By the massive influx of government funding for certain kinds of research? How were the very disciplines affected?

These were the questions that led us to begin work on this project. At the time, we expected to find a vast bibliography of sources on the subject. Much to our surprise, we discovered that very little had been written beyond the excellent studies of the effects of the McCarthy investigations on the universities. Vast areas—including the crucial question of how changes in government funding of scholarly work during the Cold War helped to determine and alter the pursuit of knowledge—lacked even basic statistical data.

Personal experiences of the period had doubtless long been exchanged in private, but the universities had yet to encourage any of the basic data gathering and exchange of views that enable historical discourse. How then to begin this discussion, so long overdue?

Over several years, The New Press initiated a series of discussions at various universities about these very questions. As we met with scholars from different fields, it seemed clear that, given the lack of sources, a traditional, research-based work of history would not yet be possible. Rather, the discussions suggested that much could be gained from gathering autobiographical reflections, from some of the country's most distinguished scholars, on the impact of the Cold War on their own intellectual and professional lives. Indeed, one of the most striking results of the seminars was the consensus, after all of them, that this was the first time that a group of scholars from a given university had actually sat down together to discuss these crucial issues.

The present volume is the result of these discussions. It is meant to be a collection of individual and, in some cases, very subjective accounts of the affect of the Cold War on various disciplines. Two of the authors, Ira Katznelson and Immanuel Wallerstein, have chosen to concentrate on key documents in their respective fields. Others have chosen to write along more general lines, evoking both their own student days and the ensuing Cold War years, in which they began to play a role in their professions.

As a result, the essays in this volume are very disparate. No attempt has been made to impose uniformity of tone or of content. Each author was encouraged to write in whatever form they felt most comfortable, in the hope that their evocations of these crucial years would begin to define the parameters of the future debate.

This will be the first of several volumes discussing the ramifications of the subject. The next volume, edited by Christopher Simpson, concentrating on the impact of U.S. military and intelligence agencies on the American university, is to be published shortly after this one. Future volumes will look in greater detail at the impact of governmental spending on the directions taken by research, and examine parallel developments in Europe and elsewhere during these crucial years.

This first volume, with those to follow, will encourage a new generation of scholars to begin the research that is still needed for a history of the period. We hope that this first volume will give those who lived through the Cold War, as well as those lucky enough to have avoided it, some idea of the intellectual climate that prevailed and the changes it wrought, often unnoticed and unexamined, in the very ways we think.

—André Schiffrin

$\left(\text{David Montgomery}\right)$

Introduction
Prosperity under the Shadow
of the Bomb

During the last weeks of May 1946, Philip Morrison and
other members of the Association of Los Alamos Scientists recorded
a series of radio broadcasts designed to inform the American public
about the nature of atomic bombs and the importance of placing
atomic energy under civilian and international control. Special
urgency was added to their effort when their friend Louis Slotin was
subjected to a lethal dose of radiation while bringing two hemi-
spheres of plutonium together during a test essential for assembly
of a new bomb to be set off at Bikini Atoll a few weeks later.

Two rooms in the corner of Fuller Lodge (a former school
building that had been commandeered by the Manhattan Project)
housed the studio and control room of Station KRS. Speaking into
the station's microphones, the scientists described in grim detail,
not only information on the manufacture of bombs which had
already been released the previous September in the official report
Atomic Energy for Military Purposes, but also the damage inflicted
on the people of Hiroshima and Nagasaki, which had conspicuously not been mentioned in that report. Their observations were
spiced with caustic, though deliberately obscure, references to
plans for experiments aboard ninety-eight warships during the

explosions scheduled for Bikini.¹ These men whose work had helped create the first atomic bombs believed that only an informed citizenry could make the political decisions necessary to protect the world's future from their handiwork.

To the best of my knowledge, no one outside Los Alamos ever heard those broadcasts. Not a single commercial radio station in the land would touch them. I heard them all, because I was the soldier who had been assigned by Station KRS to operate the controls in the room adjacent to their studio, cutting the transcriptions that they hoped would be played over other stations around the country. That solitary encounter with earnest scientists trying in vain to impart their knowledge to an imperiled world was my introduction to the Cold War.

The Cold War reshaped university structures and the content of academic disciplines, just as it penetrated the whole fabric of political and intellectual life. The essays in this volume traverse such varied topics as the transformation of research in physical and social sciences, the redefinition of liberal democracy by political theorists, the intellectual arrogance encouraged by the exercise of world power, and the role of academic dissenters in national life. My own contribution will devote more attention to the national political and economic environment within which universities functioned than to the academy itself. It takes this path in part because my own half century of experience as a soldier, student, trade union activist, and historian did not find me on a university faculty until the 1960s, and in part because the Cold War transformation of intellectual life was not confined to the academy.

The Hill

I had arrived in the Los Alamos control booth by a series of almost chance occurrences. Because of my young age I was among the last Americans called up under the World War II draft. In fact, I was inducted in March 1946—one week after Winston Churchill had delivered his speech at Fulton, Missouri, under the approving eye of President Truman, calling for an Anglo-American alliance to repel the "growing challenge and peril to civilization" posed by

"Communist Fifth Columns."[2] Although his message stirred widespread public controversy, the army in which I was enrolled lost no time adapting to it. Despite the fact that German prisoners of war were still conspicuously engaged in labor at Camp Lee, Virginia, and discipline was kept slack by the many combat veterans awaiting discharge, Information and Education courses for basic trainees were promptly refocused on the menace of Communism, and sergeants assured us that the figures in German uniforms on which we practiced bayonet drill were really Russians.

Most recruits, however, were preoccupied with other concerns. The roommate of my accelerated freshman year at Swarthmore College had been among the first black students ever admitted to that institution. After we were drafted, I could converse with him only through the wire fence that separated the white soldiers of Camp Lee from the black. The rash of racist violence, which claimed the lives of at least five black war veterans in the first six months of 1946, produced an assault by the national guard on black veterans, homes and businesses in the Mink Slide district of Columbia, Tennessee, and would bring death to twelve other African Americans in the Deep South before August was out, inspired intense and often angry debates among recruits housed on both sides of that fence.[3] Within our segregated barracks, a couple of southern whites boasted of their personal roles in lynchings back home.

We were also aware, however, that measures had been proposed in Congress to outlaw segregation in employment and to make lynching a federal offense—only to be defeated by a solid phalanx of southern opposition. Later, in September 1946, a delegation of prominent African Americans, led by Walter White and Paul Robeson (who could then still publicly act together), visited President Truman to demand that he take action against the outrages that had shaken the land. That effort bore fruit in the President's appointment of a Committee on Civil Rights, whose report in October, 1947 proposed a federal antilynching law, a permanent commission on fair employment, and an end to segregation in the armed forces and public accommodations.[4] We watched and discussed intensely every development in this struggle.

Moreover, the assault on the edifice of overt white rule was not confined to the United States. Its global nature had much to do with my going to Los Alamos. None of the soldiers among whom I was trained wished to go into combat in order to hold colonial peoples in obedience to their European or American rulers. The independence struggle uppermost on our minds at the time was neither that unfolding in Vietnam nor its counterpart in the Philippines, but in Indonesia. Indonesia's declaration of independence, in the immediate aftermath of Japan's surrender, had been challenged not only by the Netherlands, which had not yet recuperated the military power it would need to mount its three-year "police action," but also by the United States and especially by England. British forces had opened fire in Indonesia less than a month before Churchill's Fulton speech about the need for joint defense against the "growing challenge and peril to civilization." Moreover, the American press frequently drew attention to the prominence of Communists in Indonesia's independence forces.

There was not a man in my company eager to fight for the Dutch empire. Our apprehension mounted when we were drilled in tactics of controlling civilian crowds (though the immediate prospect we faced for use of that training was that of going into action against American railroad workers, who then threatened a national strike). When, therefore, an officer asked who would volunteer for a secret mission "somewhere in the United States," many hands flew eagerly up, in flagrant violation of the old soldiers' admonition never to volunteer. Within days we were on a troop train bound for Los Alamos.

Earlier in the year the army had sent out a call, at the request of the military and civil directors of the Manhattan Project, General Leslie R. Groves and Dr. Norris E. Bradbury, for new troops to keep the project going, while soldiers with wartime service there were being discharged. I was not to learn of that request until forty-seven years later, when I paid a return visit to Los Alamos, and in the Lodge, which once had housed the radio station and now was the only building from my experience still standing in the totally rebuilt town, I read the letter in a folder of historical documents on display for tourists. Neither was I to learn until later years that Bradbury's mission, from the day he had replaced Robert Oppenheimer as project director, was to keep bomb production going despite Japan's surrender. By the time of his death, Louis Slotin had performed the "crit test" to prepare bombs for use not three times, but at least twenty-four times.

Bombs were then stored unassembled at Los Alamos, so that completing them and transporting them to awaiting B-29s required at least two days. By the end of 1949, a stockpile of 200 bombs was operational, developmental work was underway for a bomb weighing less than one ton, which could be delivered by rockets, and a crash program to create hydrogen fusion bombs had begun. A steady routine of open-air testing helped the stockpile grow to a peak of 32,500 weapons in 1967. It also involved experimentation on both military and civilian populations, which grew totally reckless during the 1950s, and which was not to be acknowledged by high government officials until Hazel O'Leary became President Clinton's Energy Secretary.[5]

At the Bradbury museum, which exhibited the project's scientific work for visiting tourists in 1993, this frenzied experimentation and developmental work went unrecorded. Moreover, neither the museum displays nor the documentary film about Los Alamos' early years so much as mentioned Hiroshima or Nagasaki. The film ended with scenes of the test detonation of the first bomb at Alamogordo, followed by an unidentified flash of light and swelling music. Slotin's death was also absent from the historical museum, as was only appropriate: in December 1946, all personnel at Los Alamos had been forbidden to testify about the subject of radiation.[6]

Two Camps

As the essays in this collection make clear, the Cold War, and in particular the commitment of both the United States and the Soviet Union to rapid development of massive stockpiles of weapons with which they could exterminate each other, fueled a rapid expansion of business and academic activity, which continued for thirty years. From the start that expansion was blighted by the silence and deception which surrounded nuclear weapons and blended neatly with officially inspired fears of "the enemy within." At the very time the Los Alamos broadcasts were being consigned to oblivion, A. J. Muste wrote to John Foster Dulles:

> You speak of "the secrecy which surrounds what is going on in the Soviet Union." What but secrecy surrounds the atomic stockpile? Are we not asking Russia to raise the "iron curtain" at the same time that we keep the atomic curtain down tight?[7]

That question pursued me upon my resumption of Swarthmore College, through my days inside the labor movement, and ultimately into the historical profession.

It would be hard to imagine a better education than Swarthmore offered me between 1947 and 1950. Seminars were enlivened by veterans, who did not isolate their studies from their own experiences with life and death. Our discussions were oriented not simply toward understanding the world, but toward changing it, in contrast to the celebration of "cultural freedom" in the 1950s, which favored minds that purred like finely tuned engines, while the gears that might connect them to popular struggles remained in neutral. We devoured books, stuffed many carbons into the typewriters on which we banged out papers late into the night, and argued incessantly about economic planning, civil rights, labor's new power and the Taft-Hartley Law, the United Nations, and the triumphs of the Chinese Red Army.

The economics seminars were especially memorable. They resounded with controversy over fundamental principles and assumptions. Although no student then cringed before the authority of professors, to say the least, our instructors had just returned from government agencies that investigated the concentration of corporate power or administered economic controls. Capitalism, socialism, and the quest for a future that might borrow wisely from all existing systems were matters of immediate, practical concern to us.

Campus political activity revolved around the American Veterans Committee (AVC), which at one point had over 300 members in a student body which the GI Bill had swollen to 1600. A wide range of views animated its debates, as members challenged the institutionalized hazing of new women students, "flexible geographic targets" which limited the admission of Jewish students, and racial segregation in town facilities, as well as the policies of the federal government. All of us took heart from the ringing denunciation of segregation and of the "separate but equal" doctrine embodied in the 1947 report of Truman's Committee on Civil Rights and cheered the next year when the Democrats—the historic party of White Supremacy—adopted a comprehensive civil rights program, prompting the secession of Strom Thurmond and his fellow Dixiecrats, who wished to preserve the party's most deeply rooted tradition.

A majority of members supported the Marshall Plan, but also opposed the formation of NATO, the revival of the draft, and the division of Germany by America's promotion of a Federal Republic in the western occupation zones. The hopes of most of us rested on the wartime call of the Congress of Industrial Organizations (CIO) for "a substantial downpayment on the Four Freedoms," starting with interracial democracy in the American South and national planning for postwar prosperity.[8] The fact that 77 percent of the 805,000 workers who voted in 5,194 NLRB elections between June 1946 and May 1947 cast their votes for unions (more than any other year since enactment of the Wagner Act) buoyed our optimism. We studied closely the coalition governments that seated Communists together with other recent foes of the Nazis in France, Italy, and Hungary until the spring of 1947, and in Czechoslovakia until February 1948. The sweeping changes promised by Britain's new Labour government held special fascination for the AVC. Whatever the views of members on other subjects, and whatever their opinions of Secretary of Commerce Henry A. Wallace, all agreed when he responded to Churchill's 1946 "iron curtain" speech by deploring "any recrudescence of imperialism even under enlightened Anglo-Saxon atomic bomb auspices."[9]

By the spring of 1949, however, our AVC chapter was disintegrating (under my chairmanship!). The cause was not simply that the last large contingent of veterans was about to graduate. Most members had already dropped out of the organization, while the remainder divided into deeply antagonistic Right and Left factions. The political middle ground on which the organization had rested disappeared. President Truman had dismissed Wallace from his cabinet, when Secretary of State James Byrnes, an advocate of military and diplomatic confrontation with the Soviet Union, declared that he would quit the government unless Wallace was removed. In 1947, Truman had proclaimed the containment of communism the core of American foreign policy and taken over from the British the mission of defeating the Communist insurgency in Greece, and he had followed that declaration with a loyalty screening of all federal employees. That purge produced the Attorney General's List of Subversive Organizations, which Americans learned to consult before they joined organizations or signed petitions. The national executive board of the AVC began to adhere more closely to Truman's policies, and it removed Communist editor John Gates from its own ranks, over the protests of the Swarthmore chapter.

Two events of 1948 swung the country decisively behind Truman's measures. The first was the massive February mobilization of strikes and street demonstrations in Czechoslovakia, which put its government exclusively under Communist control. Student veterans had been especially attentive to Czech politics, and their division over that development left no middle ground. Then, in June, the USSR tried to halt the formation of a separate West German state by blockading the Allied outpost of Berlin. For almost a year, virtually every newsreel, which preceded all movies in those days, featured shots of American military aircraft carrying supplies to the beleaguered city. Berlin had been transformed in the popular imagination from Hitler's citadel into the bastion of freedom, and pollsters found a majority of Americans believing that another great war was at hand.[10] Eleven leaders of the Communist Party were indicted under the Smith Act in July (to go on trial a year later). Henry Wallace's campaign for the presidency, which had held considerable promise the previous year, mustered less than 2.5 per cent of the popular vote in November.

Within two more years, the anticipated war had materialized in Korea. The military budget leapt from $13 billion to $54 billion over the year 1950, and remained at more than ten per cent of the gross national product for following decade. As R. C. Lewontin, Richard Siever, and Noam Chomsky make clear in their contributions to this volume, military expenditures not only became the driving force of economic growth for the next forty years, but also provided a shelter for research grants, fellowships, and the cultivation of new fields of study in higher education. We had come a long way since the late 1930s, when President Franklin D. Roosevelt had felt it necessary to hide appropriations for the Two Ocean Navy in budgets for public works.

Nuclear weaponry proved to be a dull instrument of diplomacy. American policymakers seriously considered unleashing their deadly arsenal in Korea and in every subsequent crisis, and they persuaded themselves that the sums spent on developing and maintaining that possibility (sums totalling $3.9 trillion in 1995 dollars over the half century following Japan's surrender) "deterred" aggression by the Soviet Union. When the Russians developed their own massive arsenal, that doctrine was formalized as the pursuit of peace through Mutually Assured Destruction (MAD).[11] Soviet military power, however, was employed almost exclusively within the terrain controlled by Communist governments, while American bombers, missiles, and infantry ranged freely over the rest of the world, most violently in Korea, Vietnam, Lebanon, Panama, and Iraq. In all, 194 wars have been recorded since the United Nations secured victory and peace in 1945, most of them ravaging Asia and Africa and supplied with weapons by one or both of the Great Powers.

Although the "ultimate weapon" has brought more anxiety than peace, the protracted world confrontation under its shadow maximized the pressures for secrecy, suspicion, and conformity within both the United States and the Soviet Union. Scarcely had security clearances been required for government employment in 1947, when the Washington legislature instituted the first of many searches for subversive teachers in the state universities. Academic administrators, with a few notable exceptions like Horace Mann Bond and Alexander Meiklejohn, hasten to volunteer their services in removing faculty members identified by investigating committees. Yale's president Charles Seymour explained his commonplace policy of refusing employment to Communists and making one administrator campus liaison with the FBI, as a way of securing independence from government control. "There will be no witch hunts at Yale," said Seymour," because there will be no witches."[12]

But witch hunts were the order of the day, especially between 1949 and 1954, the epoch named after Senator Joseph McCarthy. Essays in this collection stress the almost serendipitous targeting of individuals by investigating committees and observe that scientific researchers were subjected to less scrutiny than their colleagues in humanities and social sciences. At Yale, untenured faculty, graduate students, and interns in law and medicine suffered the most dismissals. Nevertheless, the legal prosecutions most effectively used (then and now) to justify the search for subversives were those of "atomic spies." The charges brought against Klaus Fuchs after the Soviet Union had exploded its first bomb, were followed by a rash of lesser cases, and then by the trial and execution of Ethel and Julius Rosenberg. Admonitions of 1945-46 from scientists at Los Alamos and at the University of Chicago that the only remaining "secrets" were "scientific and engineering details," which "could be duplicated in other countries within a few years," were drowned out by the judicial pronouncement that the espionage of the Rosenbergs had made possible not only the Soviet bomb but also the war in Korea.[13]

On the night the Rosenbergs were executed, I stood among thousands of people, who were packed into side streets off of New York's Union Square, to protest and to hope for a last-minute reprieve from the White House. When official confirmation of the executions was announced, we turned westward, sweeping down a dark and deserted Fifth Avenue in a mass of silent, enraged humanity. For the first time in my life I saw New York police flee in terror. But our fury was futile. The era of conformity was upon us.

Simultaneously, in lands where Marxist theory had become the reigning ideology, it was being reduced to catchphrases and official apologetics. While Soviet authorities asserted truthfully that their foreign policy "proceeded from the fact of the long-time existence of two systems—capitalism and socialism," and sought formal arrangements stabilizing relations between the two political spheres of influence, the Soviet cultural leader, A. A. Zhdanov led a systematic and relentless assault within his sphere against "kow-towing to the West" in the sciences, humanities, or economics, from the summer of 1946 through the following year. *The History of the Communist Party of the Soviet Union/Bolsheviks/Short Course,* originally written for the occasion of the Moscow Trials, became the obligatory textbook for all students in eastern Europe. In September 1947, Zdhanov himself delivered the keynote speech at the founding convention of the Communist Information Bureau. He proclaimed the division of the world into two camps: a Camp of War, Imperialism, and Reaction led by the United States, and a Camp of Peace, National Independence, and Socialism led by the Soviet Union. The parties invited were governing parties, so that even the important and embattled Communists of China, Greece, and Germany were left out. Leaders of the large French and Italian parties were invited, only to find themselves castigated by Zdhanov for their "parliamentary illusions" and especially for the Italians' notion that they could find their way to socialism through the expansion of democracy into every sphere of life.[14]

Less than a year passed before the Yugoslav party, which had occupied a special place of honor at the founding convention, was expelled and denounced by the Cominform. There followed a wave of trials, imprisonments, and executions of alleged "Titoists" across eastern Europe. Among them were Rudolph Slansky, Laslo Rajk, Josef Grosz, and Traicho Kostov, all of them Communists renowned for their parts in the wartime resistance to Nazi con-quest. In the Soviet Union itself between 1949 and 1952, the heyday of McCarthyism in the United States, thousands of people were jailed or executed on such charges as "rootless cosmopolitanism" and "worship of things foreign."[15]

The Korean War secured the permanent ascendancy of military budgets in Eastern Europe, as well as in the United States. Nikita Krushchev was soon to denounce the "metal eaters" of armed forces for their distortion of the postwar Five Year Plans.

Persecuted and defamed by their own government and press, and ardently resisting Truman's bellicose policies, American Communists and their dwindling numbers of allies found it hard to resist the temptation to discern only hope and progress in their own camp. They rejected the unflattering reports on the Soviet Union that emanated from the mouths of their enemies, and believed the most fantastic charges leveled by Communist governments against their dissidents.[16]

Consequently, the psychological blow to American leftists was especially devastating when, in 1956, Nikita Krushchev told the Soviet party congress that a legacy of rule by coercion and deception had undermined his own country's development. Supplementing his argument was a secret speech recounting Stalin's crimes against his own people and party, a speech soon know around the world. Many American leftists concluded that their lives of struggle had been in vain.

Planning vs. Productivity

The American Association of Universities responded to the global confrontation by declaring that the main threat to academic freedom was "world Communism." No one who aided that cause had a place in the academic world. The association's statement, *The Rights and Responsibilities of Universities and Their Faculties,* which a committee chaired by Yale's President A. Whitney Griswold took three years to write, was endorsed by the administrations of thirty-seven universities. It described the university as "an association of individual scholars," who are "united in loyalty to the ideal of learning, to the moral code, to the country, and to its form of government." It added: "free enterprise is as essential to intellectual as to economic progress."[17]

By the time Griswold's committee issued its declaration, it was of no immediate concern to me. I had long since decided that the decisive battle for the hopes and ideals around which we had organized, argued, studied, and acted at Swarthmore was being waged in America's factories and its unions. I was learning the machinist's trade.

Congressional majorities had been hostile to the union movement since 1938, and had been restrained from passing restrictive legislation primarily by the persistent threat of presidential vetoes. After the Republican sweep of Congressional elections in 1946 under the banner of fighting "Communism, Controls, and Chaos," all of which they identified with "Big Labor," they were able to override President Truman's veto of the Taft-Hartley Law.

Nevertheless, workers continued to flock into unions. Union membership reached all-time peaks in the movement's historic strongholds, such as construction (87 percent of all workers), mining (65 percent) , and railroads (76 percent). In manufacturing, where "open shop" policies had long cultivated the "loyal employee," workers continued to vote for union representation in such numbers that the historic high point of 42 percent was not reached until 1953. Most of the new members in manufacturing were affiliated with the Congress of Industrial Organizations (CIO), which had proven itself a formidable mobilizer of workers' votes in 1944. The size, dynamism, and strategic location of the CIO at the heart of American urban-industrial life made it the agency to which all aspirations for social reform attached themselves.

Despite the vast expansion of government's economic role during the war and despite almost universal expectations of renewed depression, once military production was cut back, the range of policy options seriously considered within the Truman administration was actually narrower than what had been proposed at the end of the thirties. As Ellis Hawley has argued, policy advisors of the late New Deal included advocates of national economic planning, of systematic anti-trust action to dismantle concentrations of corporate power, and of heavy governmental expenditures to encourage economic growth. Because none of

DAVID MONTGOMERY

these alternatives enjoyed clear ascendancy, there was little con-
sistency in federal economic policy. As early as 1943, however, two
of the three policy courses had been ruled out. The anti-trust
approach was an early casualty of war mobilization. All agencies
dedicated to economic planning except those directly related to
wartime controls were shut down, and the Works Progress
Administration (WPA) disappeared along with them. Despite the
formal commitment to "full employment" proclaimed by law in
1945, the only path to achieving that goal that was left standing
was a limited version of Keynesian fiscal policy: manipulation of
government expenditures and of money supplies to encourage
sustained economic growth.[18]

The CIO had much more than that in mind. Its convention in
November 1946, was held in the wake of a wave of strikes far
larger than anything seen in the 1930s, and in which workers won
major wage increases and fended off employers' demands for
reduction of union authority in the workplace. Turning their attention to the future role of the government, the delegates demanded
national health insurance, national child care facilities, the legal
prohibition of racial or sex discrimination, public ownership of all
installations related to atomic energy, a Missouri Valley Authority,
federal construction to relieve the housing shortage, voting rights
for African-American and Chicano citizens, and the reinstitution of
government controls over prices, inventories, and the distribution
of vital economic resources, in order to "direct materials to the
right places" and "avoid a serious depression."[19]

The CIO's program met with complete defeat in Congress
during the next four years, leaving the United States with a welfare state whose functions were sparse in comparison to those
then being enacted in Europe and in Canada. The effective campaign mounted by business leaders to reinvigorate managerial
authority in the workplace, curb unions by law, end government
economic controls, and retain pension and medical benefits within
the domain of compensation designed to cultivate workers' loyalty to the firm (rather than universal benefits provided by government) laid the basis for a new style of stabilized contractual

relations within the unionized sectors of manufacturing. The crusade against Communism provided the rolling barrage behind which the campaign advanced.

Beginning with the highly publicized 1948 "Treaty of Detroit" between General Motors and the United Auto Workers, wages were commonly pegged to the index of productivity improvement for the economy as a whole, in return for union acknowledgement of management's prerogatives in the quest for ever-higher output. Productivity, long the Holy Grail of management, became, in Charles S. Maier's apt phrase, "a principle of political settlement in its own right."[20] The Marshall Plan shared with the Treaty of Detroit the principle that stability would be secured through steady growth. For more than twenty years per capita output in industrialized countries grew at a pace rivalled only by the expansion in North Atlantic countries of 1848 to 1875. Thanks to the ability of labor and urban Democrats to improve both the wage standards set by industry and transfer payments fixed by legislatures, incomes at the bottom levels of the population grew almost as rapidly as those of the top echelons. Median family earnings rose by 85 percent, while even working-class teenagers were no longer expected to contribute to those family earnings. Despite the prominence during those years of commentary about "poverty in the midst of affluence," the 1950-70 epoch is used by liberals today as the standard against which trends of the last twenty-five years are criticized.[21]

Trade unionists who continued to espouse class struggle had difficulty surviving investigations by the FBI and Congressional committees and the IRS audits that routinely followed subpoenas, non-communist affidavits required of union officers, deportations, Smith Act indictments, contempt and perjury prosecutions, state insurance commission actions against their fraternal organizations, hostile hearings by the Subversive Activities Control Board, and NLRB rulings that flagrantly favored their less controversial union rivals. Companies with military contracts were required to have security officers, and personnel managers were frequently hired on the basis of their FBI experience (starting with Ford's employment of the Detroit FBI director, John Bugas).

Although R. C. Lewontin has noted the lack of systematic attention to the political sympathies of researchers in the government's
lucrative extra mural contract programs, the scrutiny of industrial
workers was official and often draconic. The Atomic Energy
Commission ordered both General Electric and the University of
Chicago not to deal with left-wing unions. On the eve of a crucial
1953 union election at its Lynn works, General Electric announced
a national policy of dismissing any employee who "refused to
cooperate fully" with Senator McCarthy's committee. Before the
policy was quietly abandoned in 1966, 28 workers, many of them
shop stewards and other local officers, had been fired at the Lynn
works alone. The Coast Guard was authorized in 1950 to conduct
a nation-wide port security program, and it soon put 2,700
seamen and dockers out of their jobs.[22]

Despite this political cleansing, workers' demands for economic improvements remained irrepressible, just as did their
informal challenges to the pace of production and to managerial
authority on the shop floor (often in defiance of union contracts).
New technologies, new markets, and incentives offered by state
and local governments encouraged corporations to respond to
that persistent militancy by moving operations out of industrial
cities to the suburbs or to regions like the Southwest that offered
both fewer unions and potential customers. My own beleaguered
United Electrical Workers (UE) local in Brooklyn captured national
attention by a sit-down strike against American Safety Razor in
1954, but could not stop the firm from moving its plant to Virginia.
Because an effort to prevent plant-closings involved a frontal challenge to managerial authority, "runaway shops" and red-baiting
frequently became entangled with each other.[23] The economic
geography of the United States was being rapidly transformed
along with its political life.

Modernization Theory

By the time such screening had black-listed me out of the
machinist trade and made me begin graduate study in history
(1959), I found that the triumphant cult of productivity had

reshaped the intellectual climate of the university as well as factory life. Although important changes in the dominant methods and concepts could be encountered in all disciplines, I was especially taken by the new way in which the labor movement was discussed. In my Swarthmore days my fellow students and I had wrestled with the question of why labor in the United States had not developed socialist objectives and class-based political parties, as European movements had done: the hoary problem of "American exceptionalism." I returned to find that industrial relations in the United States were discussed as the model toward which the whole world was moving.

Alexis De Tocqueville's conceit of America as humanity's future was lurking behind every page of the most recent publications among my readings. In the behavioral sciences, where my attention was focused, the new approach was summed up in the volume *Industrialism and Industrial Man*, first published in 1960. Its authors, Clark Kerr, John T. Dunlop, Frederick Harbison, and Charles A. Myers, were prototypical men of their times. They were equally at home lecturing, writing up their research, arbitrating industrial disputes, serving on (or heading) government policy boards, and presiding over departments, if not universities—living embodiments of the intellectual, as he was celebrated in Richard Hofstadter's profoundly influential book, *Anti-Intellectualism in American Life* (1962). These men had not only investigated contemporary industrial life; they had helped to fashion it, and were still doing so.

In their view, both the predominant John R. Commons school of labor history and its Marxist critics had been asking the wrong question, by focusing analytical attention on the evolution and handling of labor "protest," when in reality " the labor problem in industrial development" was "the structuring of the labor force." That task had historically been assumed by various "industrializing elites," among whom they specified "political leaders, industrial organization builders, top military officers, associated intellectuals, and sometimes leaders of labor organizations." Within the contexts of "specific cultures and environments," such people pursued a "logic of industrialization," which was universal.[24]

Here was rising productivity presented not simply as a formula for political settlement, but also as the definitive theme of history. Moreover, this conceptual framework unceremoniously deflated Soviet claims to represent a superior way of life by applying the same style of analysis to all industrial countries, regardless of their ideological pretensions.

The hegemonic influence formerly exercised over the writing of American history by Mary and Charles Beard was gone, and with it the Beards' economic determinism, and their unfolding of the dialectic of Hamiltonians versus Jeffersonians through sectional conflict and through clashes between "the people" and "the interests." Indeed the Beards had been the prime target of denunciations by rising historians since 1945. Marxist influence had always been meager among Americans writing their own country's history (though it had left a clear mark on the writing of European and ancient history).[25]

By 1960, the "logic of industrialization" had eclipsed the conflict of economic interests. Richard Hofstadter's magisterial *Age of Reform: From Bryan to F.D.R.* (1955) had displaced Beard's beloved Populists from the role of heralds of reform in an age of ruthless Robber Barons to that of confused and reactionary foes of modernity. Daniel Bell's compelling arguments in *The End of Ideology: On the Exhaustion of Political Ideas in the Fifties* (1961) insisted that postwar politics aligned not social classes against each other, but elites with cosmopolitan outlooks against protests of parochially-minded "publics." Bell's conceptual framework was quickly adapted to the past by historians on the intellectual cutting-edge. A new wave of writings on political history, for example, replaced the Beardian quest for economic motives with the study of "ethno-cultural" antagonisms, as illuminated by negative reference group theory. McCarthyism itself came to be envisioned as a form of "anti-intellectualism."

But the "logic of industrialization" was not applied only to the United States and the USSR. It also provided a way of interpreting the roles of the new states of Asia and Africa, which had dramatically proclaimed from their conference in Bandung, Indonesia, in

1955, that they had no intention of surrendering their hard-won independence to either of the Great Powers. While the Soviet Union rushed to associate itself with the aspirations of Bandung, and the People's Republic of China had been a major participant, Secretary of State John Foster Dulles repeatedly denounced "neutralism" as an unspeakable dereliction of political morality.

Modernization theory offered a somewhat more creative approach. The Third World was "developing." It was comprised of "traditional" societies on the verge of "modernity." Walt Whitman Rostow, another commuter between Washington and the academy, wrote *The Stages of Economic Growth: A Non-Communist Manifesto* (1960) in search of "take-off periods," after which economies enjoyed self-sustaining acceleration in productivity. For economic historians, who had an increasingly quantitative bent, the challenge was to locate such take-offs historically and explain their appearance in different countries. For policy makers the task was to stimulate their materialization in the Third World, so that both its newborn states and older sovereign entities which had long been ensnared in poverty might gravitate toward the logic of industrialization and the outcome that the United States represented.

After Modernity, What?

The political order in the major Western countries shifted subtly but perceptibly toward liberal reformism about the time I exchanged the daily class confrontations of the factory for assigned readings about modernization. Despite steadily rising per capita income, Michael Harrington's discovery of *The Other America* (1962) struck a very receptive chord in public debate. The severe unemployment of 1958-60, which made my blacklisting easy and saw many thousands of other industrial workers search for new forms of employment, raised alarms about the potential impact of automation. It was then that I first discovered the ominous words Norbert Wiener had written in *Cybernetics* (1948) that although some highly trained experts would be needed by an economy whose production was guided by electronic control of information, "taking the second revolution [automation] as accomplished, the average human being of mediocre attainments or less has nothing to sell that it is worth anyone's money to buy." A few participants in the ensuing debate, among them John Kenneth Galbraith in *The Affluent Society* (1958), even questioned the cult of productivity and espoused reconstructing society in ways that would shrink the labor force and dry up the supply of "crude manpower at the bottom of the ladder." The words with which Wiener himself had followed his stark prediction brought back to me the intellectual openness of the postwar years, in which he had written them: "The answer, of course, is to have a society based on human values other than buying and selling. To arrive at this society, we need a good deal of planning and a good deal of struggle, which, if the best comes to the best, may be on the plane of ideas, and other-wise—who knows?"[26]

The automation debate ended abruptly with the inauguration of John F. Kennedy and his proposal of tax cuts to stimulate growth and an increased arms budget to "close the missile gap." Despite his bellicose rhetoric and conduct in office, however, Kennedy took power after Nikita Krushchev had toured the United States talking peace with Eisenhower and corn and hogs with Roswell Garth; after the Midwest had come alive with popular protest against atmospheric testing of atomic bombs, which was putting enough Strontium 90 in our food to kill us all before the Russians even had a chance to bomb us; and after Pope John XXIII had opened American (and world) Catholicism to peace, social justice, and a renewal of the Church. Above all, in the wake of the Bandung con-ference Algeria and central Africa had challenged European rule, and Third World countries had undertaken a quest for measures that would end their roles as suppliers of raw materials for the West—policies sometimes called import substitution, sometimes labeled African socialism or Arab socialism. Within the United States the attack of African Americans on segregation had not only won stunning victories in the courts, but also become a mass movement, guided by the gospel of civil disobedience.

The response of presidents Kennedy and Johnson to this new environment was to supplement their unswerving adherence to the politics of productivity with civil rights legislation and the use of transfer payments to lift the incomes of the poor. For a decade or so the incomes of the poorest 20 percent of Americans actually rose faster than those of the wealthiest 20 percent. Although the deep structural inequalities in labor markets triggered a frontal attack by black workers on union as well as company practices by the end of the decade, union members in the richest corporations also demanded major pay increases and an end to their subordi- nation in routine work. After 1968 what E.H. Phelps-Brown called "a pay explosion" in both Western Europe and the United States drove up wages faster than productivity could rise, provoking a contraction in returns to capital invested in production and trade by 1973, and producing a season of wage freezes and incomes policies. A scholarly panel on the problems of blue-collar workers assembled by President Nixon proposed that the government issue national awards for outstanding craftspeople and a postage stamp celebrating skilled workers.[27]

By that time, however, the Vietnam War had shaken the acad- emic world to its very foundations. This was the war the engaged scholars had made. Its measured responses and controlled escala- tions of destruction not only horrified rapidly growing numbers of students, but also echoed the lectures on modernization, which they endured in the company of hundreds of fellow note-takers. They took to the streets and occupied administration offices to protest (and/or drop out from) the war and also the role of their universities and academic professions in directing and sustaining it.

The torrent of social criticism unleashed by the anti-war move- ment broke through the intellectual levies which had been erected around the modernization paradigm. Initially historians' new intel- lectual currents made their way to the surface at the University of Wisconsin. Three brilliant disciples of the Beards had kept the crit- ical edge of that older school of thought well honed through the 1950s: Merle Curti, Howard K. Beale, and Merrill Jensen. Many of the best known graduate students they attracted to Wisconsin during the Eisenhower era were children of New York leftists. The atmosphere at Wisconsin sheltered them from McCarthyite attacks (in the Senator's home state!), tempered their outlook with the legacy of Midwestern radicalism, and encouraged them to found, in 1959, the influential journal *Studies on the Left*.

Their attention turned first to critical reassessment of this country's diplomatic history, and then to recasting the history of African Americans and of popular culture. Unlike those rebels of 1968 who often repudiated their teachers, such Wisconsin students as James Weinstein, Martin Sklar, Lee Baxendall, Ira Berlin, and Warren Sussman enjoyed rigorous intellectual nurturing at Wisconsin and drew heavily upon both older traditions of American historical writing and the newer concepts of the fifties. The images of the expansionist foreign policy impulses supported in various ways by all echelons of society, of the distinctly non-radical quality of twentieth-century cultural and intellectual life, and of the dominance of the century's politics by "corporate liberalism," retained the consensus emphasis of modernization theory but replaced the celebratory tone of the latter with a sharply critical evaluation.

The strong impetus provided the study of African-American history by the civil rights movement received creative guidance from John Hope Franklin, who taught at leading black universities in the South before coming to Wisconsin, on the way to becoming department chair at Brooklyn College. Most significantly, Franklin's book *Reconstruction, After the Civil War* (1961) was the first systematic denial of the ubiquitous legend of tragedy and corruption under black rule in the South to published by a major academic press. Under his tutelage, and that of Kenneth Stampp at Berkeley, young scholars began to move black history into the prestigious journals and publishing houses of the profession.

By the late sixties graduate students around the country took the initiative in pressing new fields of study and new styles of understanding history upon their departments. Black Studies departments took shape quickly, when student agitation merged with ghetto uprisings triggered by the murder of Martin Luther King Jr. in 1968. Moreover, those departments shifted the scholarly angle of vision from the role of blacks in the history of the United States to the African diaspora as a global phenomenon. In the subsequent development of women's studies and Chicano studies the initiatives of graduate students were even more prominent. Students edited the first historical journals; they devised, taught, and persuaded deans and departments to authorize the first courses. As Immanuel Wallerstein points out, unlike officially sponsored area studies programs, black studies, Chicano studies, ethnic studies, and women's studies "had bottom-up origins. They represented the (largely post-1968) revolt of those whom the university had 'forgotten.'"[28]

My own experience related especially to the abrupt catapulting of working-class history from oblivion to major historical journals and even Ivy League universities. Once again I had managed to be away from American university life at a crucial moment in its development. During the upheaval of 1967-69 I was introducing American labor history to a newly established university in England, so that I participated in the vehement dialogue over academic life as it was spoken in a different accent. Upon my return to the University of Pittsburgh, however, I found that many of the ablest and most committed graduate students had discovered the working class. They were aroused especially by the 34 major strikes of 1970 (the most the country had experienced in 18 years), and especially by the way those strikes breached the established parameters of collective bargaining. Walking picket lines with miners, teachers, postal workers, auto workers, and teamsters, they had heard personal narratives which gave new meaning to the animosity toward "the logic of industrialization," which the carnage in Vietnam had inspired. They sought to incorporate into their vision of history the insight which was reasserted pungently by Reg Theriault:

> The curious thing about the "logic" of not just General Motors but the entire industrial production process is that no one questions whether or not it is logical, except the workers in their own unorganized, human ways. No one, to my knowledge, has ever attempted to define 'logic' in human terms. Is it logical that technological advance—that is, more efficient production— should always take place ?[29]

Students flocked to Pittsburgh, Rochester, and Binghamton to pursue this historical interest with an intellectual energy reminiscent of the veterans of 1946-47. They extracted the critical potential suggested by the scholarly generation of Kerr and of Hofstadter, by aiming their research at the workplace, rather than movements, and teasing out the submerged meanings and tensions of popular culture. They found boundless inspiration in the work of E. P. Thompson, who revealed a Marxist style of analysis that was not crippled by Zhdanov's cant and casuistry.

Despite the zealotry and posturing that accompanied the new enthusiasms, the era of struggle against the war in Vietnam generated an unprecedented quickening of historians' imaginations and a reorientation of historical research toward people, styles of life and meaning, and possibilities for human development, which had long been excluded from the profession's purview.

By the 1990s, scholars trained in the paradigms inspired by that epoch are to be found in history departments around the land, on the editorial boards of major journals, and in the elected leadership of professional organizations. What they have encountered there, however, is a political and cultural environment very different from the days of their graduate studies.

The Cold War is over, ended by the abrupt disintegration of the Soviet Union and the People's Democracies. The immense antimissile struggle of the early 1980s had brought together people with common aspirations but very different experiences from both sides of the Berlin Wall, before that wall itself came down. Possibilities of renewed intellectual life, out from under the menace of the bomb and the official secrecy that went with it, were personified by Jiri Dienstbier, who had become Czechoslovakia's foreign minister by way of his prominence in the popular struggle against nuclear missiles, and who had committed his country to ending its lucrative export of arms.

> We should probably have the courage [Dienstbier said,] to
> return to the year 1945, to the principles of the Atlantic Charter
> and the anti-Hitler coalition, to connect ourselves with the idea

of postwar cooperation in building a free and democratic
Europe, as if these intervening 40 years didn't exist.[30]

Those words were soon drowned in the tumult of free-market triumphalism and genocidal nationalisms. Dienstbier was dismissed
from his post and his country divided. The United States still has
9,250 operational nuclear warheads, and the curtain has been low-
ered on Secretary Hazel O'Leary's brief but unprecedented
moment of official candor. As if in mockery of Norbert Wiener's
advice, the public sector faces dismantling in every industrialized
country, and all social activities are made the subject of buying
and selling. The most innovative historians have turned to de-cen-
tered narratives, while their professional opponents, heavily
funded by new foundations created for ideological struggle against
scholarship seen as "hostile to capitalism,"[31] engage them in
Culture Wars.

If "the intervening forty years" of political history cannot be
undone, however, neither can the extraordinary reconstruction of
the scale, style, and content of academic research. The university
is now an institution of decisive importance in the shaping of intellectual and social life. It provides political space of critical importance in the quest for ideas than can help shape a more humane
existence—space, which in the worst days of McCarthyite repression was the envy of men and women battling in other sectors of
society. The Cold War experience of universities needs to be
reviewed, not only to teach us how the human imagination has
been contained, but also how it has broken through the veils of
secrecy and deception.

Notes

1. Henry DeWolf Smyth, *Atomic
Energy for Military Purposes* (U.S.
Government Printing Office, 1945,
republished with some
modification by Princeton Univer-
sity Press in 1945, and reissued by
Stanford University Press in 1989,
with a new foreword by Philip Mor-
rison). The death of Slotin is dis-
cussed well in Clifford T. Honicker,
"America's Radiation Victims. The
Hidden Files," *New York Times*,
Nov. 19, 1989, Sec. 6, p. 39; Martin
Zeilig, "Dr. Louis Slotin and 'The
Invisible Killer,'" *The Beaver:
Exploring Canada's History*,
August/September, 1995, 20-26;
and Dexter Master's novel *The*

Accident (New York, 1955). It was grotesquely distorted in the 1947 movie *The Beginning or the End,* in which a young scientist sacrificed his life to prevent tens of thousands of Pacific Islanders from being blown up.

2. D. F. Fleming, *The Cold War and Its Origins* (2 vols., Garden City, N.Y., 1961), I, 349.

3. John Egerton, *Speak Now Against the Day: The Generation before the Civil Rights Movement in the South* (New York, 1994), 361-9.

4. Ibid, 413-6.

5. Honicker, 39; report on U.S. Nuclear Weapons Cost Project, *New York Times,* July 13, 1995.

6. On the 1946 order, see Honicker, 41.

7. Quoted in Gregg Herken, *The Winning Weapon: The Atomic Bomb in the Cold War,* 1945-1950 (New York, 1980), 149.

8. "What Are We Fighting For?" *Steelabor,* May 28, 1943, pp. 6-7.

9. Wallace quoted in Herken, 144.

10. For a chronicle of these events from the perspective of the times, see Fleming, I, 489-510.

11. *New York Times,* July 13, 1995.

12. Quoted in Sigmund Diamond, *Compromised Campus: The Collaboration of Universities with the Intelligence Community,* 1945-1955 (New York, 1992), 42.

13. The scientists' statements are reproduced in Fleming, I, 522.

14. Ivo Banac, *With Stalin against Tito: Cominformist Splits in Yugoslav Communism* (Ithaca, NY, 1988), 24-8; Wolfgang Leonhard, *Eurocommunism: Challenge for East and West* (New York, 1978), 47-50; Roy A. Medvedev, *Let History Judge: The Origins and Consequences of Stalinism* (New York, 1973), 474-85.

15. Medvedev, 474-85.

16. See, for example, Derek Kartun, *Tito's Plot against Europe: The Story of the Rajk Conspiracy* (New York: International Publishers, 1950).

17. Quoted in Deborah Sue Elkin, "Labor and the Left: The Limits of Acceptable Dissent at Yale, 1920s to 1950s" (Ph.D. Dissertation Yale University, 1995), 266-8.

18. Ellis W. Hawley, *The New Deal and the Problem of Monopoly: A Study in Economic Ambivalence* (Princeton, 1966).

19. *Final Proceedings of the Eighth Constitutional Convention of the Congress of Industrial Organizations... 1946* (n.p. n.d.). The quotations are on p. 42.

20. Charles S. Maier, *In Search of Stability: Explorations in Historical Political Economy* (Cambridge and New York, 1987), 123.

21. See, for example, "Here We Go Again," *The Nation,* 263 (Aug. 26/Sept. 2, 1996), 18-9.

22. Ellen W. Schrecker, "McCarthyism and the Labor Movement: The Role of the State," in Steve Rosswurm, ed., *The CIO's Left-Led Unions* (New Brunswick, N.J., 1992), 139-158; Michael J. Bonislawski, "The Anti-Communist Movement and Industrial Unionism: IUE vs. UE" (M.A. Thesis, University of Massachusetts at Boston, 1992), 70.

23. The interplay is captured vividly in two plays by Emanuel Fried, *The Dodo Bird* (Buffalo, 1963), and *Drop Hammer* (Buffalo, 1977).

24. Kerr, Dunlop, Harbison, and Myers, *Industrialism and Industrial Man* (second edition, New York, 1964), 8, 8n, 10.

25. In my Swarthmore readings, Louis Hacker, Oliver Cromwell

Cox, Herbert Aptheker, and C.L. R. James (deported in 1953) had been the exceptions.

26. Norbert Wiener, *Cybernetics: or Control and Communication in the Animal and the Machine* (Cambridge, Mass., 1948), 28; John Kenneth Galbraith, *The Affluent Society* (Boston, 1958), 334-48. Wiener's mental anguish over the social implications of his scientific work is evident in his later book, *The Human Use of Human Beings: Cybernetics and Society* (New York, 1950).

27. Giovanni Arrighi, *The Long Twentieth Century: Money, Power, and the Origins of Our Times* (London and New York, 1994), 304-5; Nixon's panel is discussed in Aaron Michael Brenner, "Rank and File Rebellion, 1966-1975" (Ph.D. dissertation, Columbia University, 1996), 77.

28. See below, p. 228.

29. Reg Theriault, *How to Tell When You're Tired: A Brief Examination of Work* (New York, 1995), 120.

30. *New York Times*, January 25, 1990.

31. The phrase is from William E. Simon, *A Time for Truth* (New York, 1978), 231.

$\left(\text{R.C. Lewontin}\right)$

The Cold War
and the Transformation
of the Academy

"War consisteth not in battle only, or the act of fighting: but in a tract
of time, wherein the will to contend by battle is sufficiently known."
—Hobbes, *Leviathan*

Depending upon their politics, intellectuals remember the
Cold War badly for different reasons. When liberal and Left academics think of the Cold War, they think of research agendas warped
by the ideological fervor and political pressures of American foreign policy, and of professional and personal lives ruined directly
and indirectly by anticommunist witch-hunts and pusillanimous
academic administrations. Other essays in this book document the
damage inflicted on scholars and scholarship by those events. For
neoconservatives, the bad memories are very different. Some, of
course, are former Trotskyists who were delighted to see the
Communist Party and its sympathizers routed, and were even active
participants in the campaign. For them, however, and for the larger
conservative constituency to which they became assimilated, the
still-itching scars of the Cold War are from the wounds of Vietnam.
Neoconservatives still relive the major struggles with rebellious students over the legitimacy of academics to rule the classroom and to
subject students to their intellectual prejudices without challenge.

1

Still, twenty-five years after academics reasserted their uncontested authority, the academic Right continues to worry about its injuries.¹ Only an unusually candid member of a Russian Research Center or physicist at the Lawrence Livermore Laboratory will admit to thinking that maybe the Cold War was not so bad after all.

Yet what will be disdained as raw self-interest on the part of Kremlinologists and ballistic-missile scientists, is, in fact, the big truth about the Cold War and the academy. Both by its material manifestations and through the ideological atmosphere that it was instrumental in creating, the Cold War was responsible for an unprecedented and explosive expansion of the academy. Moreover, by making entrepreneurial professors the conduits through which extraordinary sums of public money have flowed into the universities, the Cold War has provided academics as a profession with a potent weapon in their struggle for power within their institutions and thus has given them an extraordinary degree of control over the conditions of their employment. Although it is a severe blow to their sense of moral righteousness and self-esteem, academics must face the fact that the Via Dolorosa along which many of their colleagues, friends and comrades were dragged to their crucifixions was also the high road to professional prosperity for the great majority.

The Economics of the Cold War

The Cold War was a solution to a major dilemma of American economic development. It has been obvious to all makers of national policy in Europe, North America, and Asia since the end of World War II, and even to most economists, that the prosperity of modern capitalism is critically dependent on massive state intervention in the economy. That intervention is not simply in the form of control of the supply of money and in the redistribution of wage goods through taxation and welfare programs. It involves, as well, a vital role of the state as a provider of subsidies to production and employment by three routes. The primary one is for the state to become a major purchaser of goods and services. A second is to provide capital directly to undercapitalized sectors, enabling them to modernize at public expense, as, for example, by temporarily nationalizing railroads, rebuilding their material infrastructure, and then reselling them on the market. The third is to assume the cost, unbearable even by the largest individual enterprises, of creating new technologies and the trained cadre required both for the implementation of technology that already exists and for creating further innovations.

The first large-scale state intervention in modern times was during World War I, when both in Europe and North America, the state, through its armed forces, became a major employer of labor and a purchaser of their wage goods, a principal purchaser of capital goods, and the instigator of scientific research for war purposes. Immediately after that war, all such state investment ceased, and after a brief two years of postwar boom to fill an accumulated demand for consumer goods, there was a widespread slump. Even during the temporary "boom" of the mid-1920s, preceding the catastrophic collapse of 1929, European unemployment averaged more than 10 percent in England, Germany, and Sweden, and a catastrophic 17 to 18 percent in Denmark and Norway.[2] It is hardly necessary to review the economic events in Europe and North America from 1929 through 1939, except to remind ourselves that despite a variety of redistributive efforts to create consumer demand, these economies remained in a severe depression with unemployment rates between 10 percent and 20 percent until World War II.

With the coming of the new world war, there was again a major intervention of the state into the economies of Europe and America on yet a grander scale than twenty-five years before. In the United States, immense plant capacity in chemical, electrical, machine tool, automotive, and aeronautic industries was created at public expense. Scientific research became a state enterprise, of which the Manhattan Project was only the most visible example, and the universities were incorporated into the training apparatus of the military. But the experience of World War I and of the interwar years had formed the consciousness of economists and planners. Paul Samuelson wrote in 1943 of the possibility, after the war, of "the greatest period of unemployment and industrial dislocation which any economy has ever faced."[3]

How could economies, deprived of the immense purchasing and capitalizing power of the state, maintain their high level of activity? In fact, they could not, and the solution to the problem in Europe was for the state to remain in place after the war, intervening directly in the economy where it was most needed. Social democratic regimes or social democratic policies in the hands of nominally conservative governments have been the rule in Britain and Europe since the war. Beginning with the Labor Party victory in Britain barely two months after the surrender of Germany, major sectors of industry that were in danger of failure, such as steel, mining, and railroads, were simply nationalized. In other cases, as in France and Italy, the state became a co-owner of enterprises. Scientific research became primarily a state function through institutions such as the Centre National des Recherches Scientifiques in France or the Research Councils in Britain, and direct state support of the universities became the unvarying rule.

For the United States, the European (and Japanese) solution was not possible. The entire ideological history of the United States stands in opposition to a major overt state role in the economy beyond its power of taxation and a modest redistributive power. The political rejection of a general socialization of health costs in the United States, despite the successful demand for it in other rich capitalist countries, is the most obvious example of that opposition. The power of this ideological stance extends even to meaningless symbols. Although conservative European parties can carry the name "Socialist" and a Mexican party of capitalist oligarchs can rule under the banner of the party of "Revolution," apparently without the slightest embarrassment, the idea of an American president attending, like Willy Brandt, the meeting of the Socialist International belongs to fiction. It is only in the crisis of war, when the very survival of the nation and of civilization at large are threatened that serious state intervention in production and consumption becomes a political possibility in the United States.

The history of state purchases of goods and services since 1929 is shown in Figure 1. At the beginning of the depression, federal purchases consumed a little more than 1 percent of the gross national product (GNP). As a consequence of New Deal policies, this increased in the prewar years to about 6 percent and then, with the beginning of a war economy, federal purchases rose to an extraordinary peak of 42 percent of GNP. Within two years of the end of the war these purchases had fallen to their 1936 level, as military expenditures all but disappeared. But then, beginning slowly in 1948, and accelerating as a result of the military expenditures during the Korean War, the federal government became a major consumer. Since 1951, purchases by the federal government have been at an average of about 10 percent of GNP, with a peak of 16 percent toward the end of the Korean War. Even the extraordinary economic crisis that followed 1929, which was met by the New Deal's policy of federal expenditure, did not induce a level of government purchase of goods and services equal to that created by the Cold War. As Figure 1 shows, an important fraction of the federal purchases since the beginning of World War II has been for

FIGURE 1 Proportion of the Gross National Product constituted by all governmental, local, federal and military purchases.

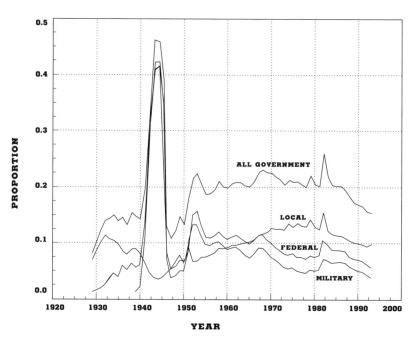

military purposes. The advantage of "war," whatever its tempera-
ture, is that it creates an immense demand for hard goods which
cannot be saturated, either because the goods are being destroyed
constantly, or because, in the imagination of military planners, it
is always possible to create a better weapons system independent
of its actual use in battle. People can eat only a limited amount,
but the appetite of the state for bombers is insatiable.

Although it is trivially true that military preparedness creates a
direct demand for production, a more subtle yet, in the long run,
more important economic consequence for the United States has
been a legitimation of a high level of state expenditure on goods
and services. As Figure 1 shows, military expenditure has
decreased markedly and progressively as a proportion of total federal purchases, dropping from over 60 percent at the beginning of
the Cold War in 1951 to less than 30 percent at present. There has,
moreover, been a transfer of state purchases from the federal government to the local authorities. A great deal of public purchasing,
chiefly for roads, education, sanitation, police, and similar infrastructure, has always been regarded as legitimate for local and
individual state governments. Figure 2 shows that the proportion
of GNP purchased by all governmental authorities has been constant since 1951, but that the proportion ascribable to the federal
government as opposed to local authorities has changed from 70
percent to less than 40 percent. By 1993, the role of government
and the relative parts played by local and federal authorities in purchasing the national product had reverted to the situation at the
entry of the United States into World War II. The Cold War may
have ended, but the role of the state has become permanent. It is
important to understand that all of the values in Figures 1 and 2
are for the *purchases of goods and services* and exclude redistributive
functions and transfer payments such as welfare or Social Security.
Despite the antisocialist theme that remains dominant in
American political ideology, the state has become a major and permanent consumer of the GNP.

State capitalism is like abortion: even for those for whom it is
anathema, it is permitted in cases of rape. For the American

FIGURE 2 Total federal expenditures on research and development in millions of constant (1983) dollars.

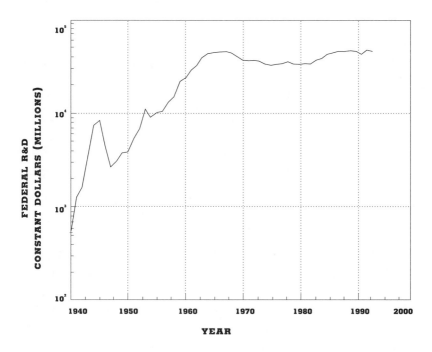

economy, the Cold War declared by Churchill in his famous Fulton, Missouri, speech of 1946, was a godsend. Beginning in earnest with the Truman Doctrine and the Marshall Plan of 1947, and passing through bouts of hot war in Korea and Vietnam, a consciousness of a state of national military emergency has been maintained continuously for 50 years, and with it an uninterrupted period of relative economic stability without precedent in American history. Although it would be foolish to say that the Cold War was created in order to justify a role for the state in supporting the economy, for it certainly was a manifestation of a larger struggle over world political and economic power, it became the instrumentality of a vital national economic policy. If the Cold War had not existed it would have had to be invented.

But what has all this to do with the academy?

R.C. LEWONTIN

The Socialization of Intellectual Production

Before the World War II, technical innovations on which economic expansion depended were the product of individual entrepreneurs working at a low technological level. Agricultural and industrial mechanization, automotive traction power, aeronautics, electrification, and early electronics were developed by "backyard workshop" inventors or in small industrial enterprises. Only chemical innovation, which required a relatively high degree of technical training and laboratory infrastructure, was a regular feature of major corporate enterprises, as for example in the development of synthetic rubber, dyes, and lubricants.

Beginning with World War II, however, innovation became increasingly dependent on a very high level of scientific and technological expertise, and on a corresponding investment in an extremely expensive capital plant to carry out research and development so that only very large enterprises could undertake such programs. The problem for innovation then was to produce a large body of scientifically trained experts with an orientation toward research as a career, and to provide those research workers with libraries, laboratories, technical assistants, equipment, expendable supplies, and channels for communication of preliminary results. Although the aggregate resources in the hands of corporations are more than sufficient, those resources cannot be mobilized by the usual anarchic and competitive mechanisms of capitalism. First, capital in excess of what is available even to the largest individual enterprises is needed both for the education of scientists and engineers and for many research projects. Although the American Telephone and Telegraph Company could fund the most successful corporate research enterprise in existence, Bell Laboratories, it could not also create the universities, their faculties, laboratories, and libraries in which Bell Laboratory scientists were formed. Second, investment in research is not only risky, but even if successful will not usually produce a return for ten or more years, while the typical corporate investment horizon is two to three years. At times of reduced profit, the research and development laboratories of a corporation are the first departments to be cut. Third, successful innovation usually depends on a wide sharing of preliminary results in an international community of scientific workers with similar interests. But the proprietary interests of corporations prevent that sharing.

Some method must be found to pool the individually limited resources of private producers while resolving the contradiction between the individual competitive demands for immediate profit and market advantage on the one hand, and the long-term cooperative nature of research on the other. That is, both the cost *and the conduct* of research and technological education must be socialized. It is not sufficient that some money be found to carry out a piece of engineering development required for the production of a particular commodity. Pharmaceutical companies can add the costs of development to the price of a proprietary drug. To produce the spreading effect of innovation on the economy, both the patrons and the performers of research must initially be outside the system of proprietary interest. Only when an innovation comes close to taking a concrete form, as an actual commodity, can an individual firm be allowed to appropriate it as property. Before that point, the process of innovation must be socialized. It is obvious that only the state can be the instrument of that socialization. One hardly needs to be a follower of Marx to recognize the deep truth in his claim that the state is "a committee for managing the common affairs of the whole bourgeoisie."

For the state to socialize research and technical education requires more than that it simply bear the costs. It must also employ institutions as performers of the research, institutions whose survival does not depend on acquiring a property interest in the outcome. That is, the performers of the research must be producing it as a process or service rather than as a competitive market commodity. Private research and development companies such as Arthur D. Little can serve this function. Manufacturing enterprises also can carry out developmental work on a cost-plus, fixed-charge basis, when the state is the customer, as when aerospace manufacturers are awarded development contracts by the National Aeronautics and Space Administration. The state, too, can produce research in its own laboratories. About one-fifth of the $9 billion in research funds now expended by the National Institutes of Health (NIH) is spent internally. For research that is not directly connected with production, however, the universities and research institutes under their control are the obvious candidates. They already have investments in infrastructure such as libraries and laboratories; they are the workplace of professional intellectuals devoted to research as a career; they are the institutions that produce the engineers and scientists in the first place; and they are not constrained by the necessity to produce commodities for sale and to make a profit for their shareholders. Thus, there is an easy partnership between the state and the academy in the patronage and performance of research.

The question has been how to socialize the cost and process of innovation in the face of American antistate ideology. The answer has been war.

War as a Condition for the Socialization of Research and Education

Before World War II, the federal government established relationships with the national scientific community on two occasions, both during wartime. During the Civil War, Abraham Lincoln created the National Academy of Sciences (NAS) to enlist the expertise of elite natural scientists in the service of the state. The NAS's honorary membership, however, was too small (and too old) to serve the technical demands of a modern war machine, so during World War I, Woodrow Wilson considerably augmented and modernized the expertise of the NAS by creating the National Research Council (NRC). The NRC, which operates under the general direction of the NAS, co-opts a large body of scientists and engineers, most of whom have not been elected to the NAS but only dream of their apotheosis, to carry out investigations of scientific problems of interest to various government agencies. The fiction is that the NAS and NAC are autonomous, nongovernmental entities, but, in fact, they are obliged to pursue investigations that are requested and paid for by any agency of the state.

At first sight there would seem to be a major exception to the rule of war. Agricultural education and research have been a commitment of the state since the middle of the nineteenth century. But the exception is only apparent. The Organic Act, which founded the Department of Agriculture and established its research function, and the Morrill Land Grant College Act, which established the State Colleges of Agriculture and Engineering and provided for experimental farms, were both passed in 1862, in the middle of the Civil War. The earliest research carried out by the Department of Agriculture emphasized the replacement of southern by northern crop production, especially the possibility of northern cotton production, sugar from maize and sorghum, and the cultivation of silkworms.

More revealing for our understanding of the ideological problem is the history of state support of agricultural research since 1865. Agriculture is an extreme case of a productive sector in which there is a low concentration of private capital and production of value. There have always been more than two million petty producers of farm commodities and even at present the largest 16,000 farms produce only 30 percent of total output. Some attempt is made to socialize research costs by the producers themselves, who form self-taxing producers groups to support research, but this support is in the form of grants to state agricultural experiment stations which have the necessary capital, plant and staff to carry out the research. The providers of farm inputs are as highly concentrated as other industrial sectors, but even the oligopolized seed industry, much of which is owned by pharmaceutical and other chemical companies, depends absolutely on state agricultural experiment stations for its basic genetic material.

The way in which the socialization of research and educational costs in agriculture have been legitimated is by a division between the *source* of funds and the *control* of their disposition. The entire history of the state support of agricultural research and training has been a struggle between local and national forces for the control of the money appropriated by Congress, with the unvarying victory of the individual directors of state agricultural experiment stations over the U.S. Department of Agriculture. The original Hatch Act of 1887 that created the state agricultural experimentation system provided federal money to be given directly to individual state experiment stations to carry out "researches and experiments bearing directly on the agricultural industry of the United States, *as may in each case be deemed as having due regard to the various conditions and needs of the various States and Territories*" (emphasis added).

Repeatedly, Congress has appropriated money and created institutions for agricultural innovation and then turned over complete control of the funds and institutions to their local constituencies.[4] The "block grant" was in operation in agricultural research before any member of the 104th Congress was born. But the avoidance of the specter of state socialism that has been possible in agricultural research has not been a possibility in other sectors. Agriculture is unique in its essentially local character, in the necessity of regionally differentiated research and training programs geared to local commodities produced under local conditions to meet the demands of local producers. Moreover, because so much of the output of agricultural research must ultimately be tested in an actual local setting, the research must be physically decentralized and research decisions must be made in a local context. North Carolina corn does poorly in Minnesota but a space shuttle launched in Florida can land in California. To justify the centralization of research on a large scale, it is hard to see how one can dispense with war.

The State Becomes the Patron of the Academy

Before World War II, state support of research in institutions of higher education was effectively confined to individual state funding of the land grant universities and the use by the state agricultural experiment stations, which were integrated into the state university system, of both federal and state funds for agricultural research. The total federal funding for research and development in 1940 was a mere $74 million, of which agriculture accounted for 40 percent. The rest, chiefly for military research, was carried out in government and industrial laboratories. There was no model of centralized government support for a broad array of scientific projects, or for a leading role for universities in providing research and development for national objectives. The atomic bomb changed all that. The remarkable success of a single focused project under government sponsorship and control had a powerful effect on the consciousness of both academics and political planners. It was not simply that a centrally planned and funded scientific project worked so well, but that it integrated various branches of science and, most significant from the standpoint of the academy, was completely dependent on the efforts of university scientists. Project research before the war was an industrial or government enterprise carried out by industrial and government scientists in industrial and government installations. In contrast, although Oak Ridge and Los Alamos were indeed government reserves, their culture was made by professors, many of them Europeans. It is not General Groves at his desk in the Los Alamos laboratories that has provided the symbolic image of the atom bomb project's iconography, but an Italian professor building an atomic pile under the spectator's stands of the University of Chicago's athletic field. It is there, not in the Nevada desert, that Henry Moore's ambiguous fusion of a mushroom cloud and a death's head memorializes the Bomb.

As early as November 1944, with Allied troops on the Rhine and Americans back in the Philippines, Roosevelt showed his concern with the role that state-funded science was to play in the postwar economy. He asked Vannevar Bush, head of the Office of Scientific Research and Development, to make recommendations on how to continue the wartime relationship between the state and science. Bush, acting as spokesman for the scientific establishment, responded with the manifesto, *Science — The Endless Frontier*, that makes a close argument.[5] First, research is claimed as the foundation of a prosperous and secure nation:

> New products, new industries and more jobs require continuous additions to knowledge of the laws of nature...Similarly, our defence against aggression demands new knowledge...[which] can be obtained only through basic scientific research.[6]

Second, the state can do nothing more important than to be the patron of that research, *and of the training of scientific workers*:

> The most important ways in which the Government can promote industrial research are to increase the flow of new scientific knowledge through support of basic research and to aid in the development of scientific talent.[7]

Third, although the state should provide the money, the control of who gets it and how it is spent should be effectively in the hands of those to whom it is given. An agency to give away the money should be made up of

> persons of broad interest in and understanding of the peculiarities of scientific research and education.
>
> The agency should promote research through contracts or grants to organizations outside the Federal Government. It should not operate any laboratories of its own.
>
> Support of basic research in the public and private colleges, universities and research institutes must leave the internal control of policy, personnel, and the method and scope of the research to the institutions themselves.
>
> This is of the utmost importance.[8]

What Bush does not say is that to leave the "internal control" to the "institutions themselves," is, in fact, to leave it to the individual recipient scientists who originally asked for the money and are the only ones in the institution who know what it is all about. Since the responsibility for giving the money in the first place is delegated to people who understand the "peculiarities" of scientific research and education, that is, representatives of the same people who get the money, *una mano lava l'altra*.

It is a sign of the immense prestige that military science and scientists had acquired during the war, not only from the Manhattan Project, but from the development of radar, of miniaturization of electronics, of rocket propulsion, that Bush had the nerve to ask openly for the establishment of this manifestly self-serving system. It is said that a particularly insulting and aggressive *schnorrer* once accosted Rothschild, who admonished him, saying that he might be more successful at getting money out of people if he were more accommodating. "Rothschild," the man replied, "Do I tell you how to be a banker? So don't tell me how to be a *schnorrer.*"

Congress, however, was skeptical. Legislation to establish the National Science Foundation (NSF), the agency envisaged by Bush, was first introduced by Truman in 1946, but the attempt failed, although not only on the grounds that scientists would have their hands in the public pocket. As in the case of agriculture, the Congress has never had a serious ideological reluctance to turning over the expenditure and control of federal monies to independent agents. What was also expressed was the classic fear of government control of education and scholarship. As a promising young science student, I was personally involved, if only briefly. The Westinghouse Electric Corporation had initiated a national research competition for science students and I was a winner. It was arranged by Westinghouse that my fellows and I would be invited to testify in favor of the NSF legislation before the congressional committee considering the bill. We were asked by committee members whether we were not afraid that accepting public money would make us unfree. Whatever the Congress thought of the wisdom of government support of research, the Westinghouse Electric Company had no doubts. That same tension is still a major issue in the politics of educational support. Local school systems are supported by local property taxes, but have increasingly accepted federal subsidies. However, these subsidies have carried with them certain federal mandates, as, for example, the requirement of special education programs for emotionally or physically handicapped children. These mandates are a serious source of conflict and resentment at the local level, precisely because the school authorities feel trapped by the need for the money.[9] The NSF was not finally established until 1950, when the Cold War was in full operation and had already become considerably hotter in

Korea. Its original 1951 budget of $100,000 grew to $100 million in ten years, 85 percent of which went to universities and research institutes under university control.

It should not be supposed that congressional reluctance prevented federal support of academic research under the very conditions described by Bush. While the NSF and the extramural programs of the NIH were still in their initial stages, the Atomic Energy Commission (AEC), the Office of Naval Research (ONR), and similar agencies were funding research in universities and university research institutes by a system of contracts. The term "contract," conveying the notion of the procurement of a determined product specified by the purchaser, hides the reality. The "contracts" with academic institutions were, in fact, grants to individual investigators or small groups to carry out research projects generated by intellectual forces internal to the disciplines, provided only that some general relevance to the mission of the federal agency could be established. As a young assistant professor at the University of Rochester in the late 1950s, I was approached, first by the ONR and then by the AEC, which had heard that I was using large digital computers to simulate population genetic processes, and offered contracts to support my work. The ONR was generally interested in developments in computers and the AEC's mission included research on the effect of mutations in human populations. The AEC contract was administered by a succession of program officers drawn from the academic biology community, none of whom, in the fifteen years of the contract, ever intervened in any way except to remind me annually that it was time to send in my renewal application for money that had already been put aside for the next contract year. Even major government facilities, such as the Oak Ridge National Laboratory which was run for the AEC by the Union Carbide Corporation, included groups of scientists whose research and whose work culture was indistinguishable from that of the universities. Their employment in Oak Ridge was partly the historical remnant of the small number of academic positions available in the early 1950s, and partly because a national laboratory provided easy access to research funds and no obligation to teach undergraduates. As federal funds available for research in universities grew, with the accompanying dramatic increase both in the number of university scientists and their power to control the conditions of their work, there was a steady migration of these scientists into academia.[10]

With the final establishment of the NSF and the immense expansion of the extramural programs of the NIH, Bush's model of the federal funding of research became established. Blocks of research funds are appropriated, which, for the most part, are not tied in the appropriation process to particular research proposals. Some large national facilities such as astronomical observatories and particle accelerators may be separately budgeted, but even for these, there is no specification of the research itself. Research to be carried out with federal grant money is proposed to individual state agencies like the NSF or NIH by individual investigators. The decision about which proposals are to be funded and suggestions about the specific budget are effectively made by committees of fellow academics who are appointed on the recommendation of their predecessors and who, themselves, have federal grant funds. In the NIH system the committees (study sections) assign numerical scores to proposals, and awards are finally made, almost without exception, according to these scores. In the NSF, the committees (advisory panels) are formally only advisory to scientifically qualified program officers who have more leeway than their NIH counterparts, but an NSF program officer cannot flagrantly disregard clear recommendations for or against a proposal. In effect, then, Congress appropriates money that is ultimately given out to academics by "persons of broad interest in and understanding of the peculiarities of scientific research and education," that is by their academic colleagues. Although the money is given, legally, to the academic institutions in which the investigators work, in practice these institutions exert only fiscal and not substantive control. In seeking and expending research funds, academics are acting as independent entrepreneurs.

R.C. LEWONTIN
State Patronage and Anticommunism

There was another important divergence between legislative and executive policy that is central to our understanding of the effect of the Cold War on the academy. Despite the persecution and purging of radical intellectuals that we associate with the Cold War, there was never a coherent state security policy. The Cold War witch-hunts were the continuation by state legislators and the Congress of a history of attack on radicals by ambitious politicians that began with the Palmer Raids of 1920 and that was only interrupted briefly by World War II. Far from being an expression of a general governmental attack on academic radicalism, legislative anticommunism was, in part, a politics of opportunism to provide notoriety for some members of Congress and state legislators, and, in part, an instrument by which one party in Congress could carry on a political struggle against another party in the executive branch. The work of attacking the academic Left was carried out either by university administrations under pressure from trustees and state legislators, or by a succession of legislative committees, which could, on occasion, frighten governmental departments into symbolic actions. The notorious House Un-American Activities Committee was in operation before World War II under Martin Dies and then continued after the war under J. Parnell Thomas. The Senate Internal Security Subcommittee (the McCarran Committee and then the Jenner Committee) was explicitly modeled after the prewar Rapp-Coudert Committee that purged the Left from higher education in New York State. It should not be forgot that the major emphasis of McCarthy's Permanent Subcommittee on Investigations was to show that the executive branch was hopelessly "soft on" Communists and riddled with radicals. The opportunistic pursuit of radicals, even when manifested in an occasional self-protective action by an executive agency, should not be confused with state policy.

In contrast to a highly visible legislative attack on academic radicals, there was a widespread indifference to political ideology in the research supported by agencies of the state. The most telling example is the agency that, at first glance, should have been most sensitive to security concerns, the AEC. Security clearances were, of course, necessary for entry and employment in the production and technological development facilities at Hanford, Los Alamos, and Oak Ridge. But the entire biology division and even the computing center at Oak Ridge were outside the security area and freely accessible without clearance, as were the facilities at Brookhaven and Argonne National Laboratories.

The extramural contract program seemed to pay no attention to the known political sympathies of its contractors. A striking case is that of L.C. Dunn, a professor at Columbia University. Dunn was an organizer or officer of a number of Soviet-American cooperation and cultural exchange organizations. He was highly visible on the letterheads and at the rallies of Left and pro-Soviet groups and, although he was not a member of the Communist Party, he was active in many organizations supported by the party. He was the classic "fellow traveler" of the McCarthyites and his application to be scientific attaché in the American embassy in Paris was denied, presumably for political reasons. Nevertheless, during the entire period of his political activity, his research was supported by an AEC contract. My personal experience in the 1960s was similar. While on the faculty of the University of Chicago, I worked with the Black Panther Party, gave public speeches attacking the war policy of the government, was on the committee, together with officials of the Socialist Worker's Party and the Communist Party, that organized peace marches through downtown Chicago, had open relations with the representative of the Vietnamese National Liberation Front, and helped to organize scientific support for them, including submitting a research grant proposal to the Republic of North Vietnam. These activities were closely monitored by the Federal Bureau of Investigation, as shown by the responses to my request for files under the Freedom of Information Act, yet during this entire period and afterward, my research was supported by a long-standing contract from the AEC and its successor agencies, ERDA and the Department of Energy. The famous removal of security clearance from J.R. Oppenheimer in 1954 was not evidence of a state policy, but the consequence of a personal struggle between Oppenheimer and Edward Teller who had powerful political allies. The greatest direct enemy of the Left in the academy was not the coherent policy of the state, but the opportunism and cowardice of boards of trustees and university administrators.

The History of Cold War Patronage

The Cold War provided the instrument for the state to become a major stimulus for American production, but the level of its intervention has been more or less constant since the end of World War II. Since 1950, state and federal purchases have been roughly 20 percent of the GNP, although they have decreased somewhat over the last half dozen years as the Cold War has disappeared. Indeed, federal purchases have been cut in half since the Korean War, partly as a result of a reduction in military expenditure. The role of the state in research and education, however, has had a very different history. First, as Figure 2 shows, there was a period of considerable growth, in constant dollars, of federal expenditure on all research and development for twenty-five years beginning in 1940. Putting aside the big investment during World War II, expenditures on research and development grew at an exponential rate until 1964, reaching a value ten times the average wartime level before leveling off. Second, although total government spending on research and development has not increased for the last thirty years, the proportion and, therefore, the total amount spent in universities has continued to rise, as shown in Figure 3, and has risen at a constant exponential rate of about 2 percent per year since 1965. In 1954, universities received about 5 percent of total federal expenditures for research and development, whereas now they get about 22 percent. This figure is all the more striking because it includes not only basic research but applied research and development. The dividing lines between these categories are necessarily vague, but the NSF regularly categorizes all expenditures under these rubrics.[11] Using the NSF tabulation, universities and their associated research institutes account at present for about 60 percent of federal expenditures for basic research (but only 60 percent!), 30 percent of applied

FIGURE 3 Proportion of federal research and development funds received by colleges and universities including federally funded research and development centers.

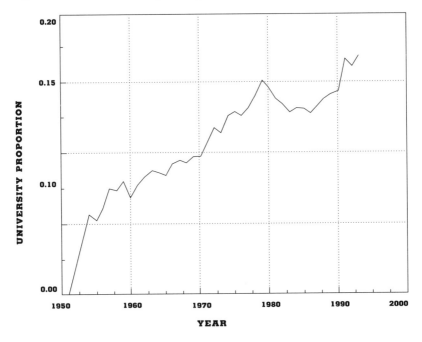

research and, as expected, only about 7 percent of development which is largely an industrial function. The figures twenty-five years ago were 50 percent, 23 percent, and 4 percent, respectively, so the university share has grown for all kinds of investigations, but at a greater rate for applied research and at a much greater rate for development than for its traditional sphere of basic research.

The Cold War or the War on the Cold?

While it cannot be disputed that ever-increasing amounts of state expenditure have gone into the academy since the end of World War II, it does not follow necessarily that the waging of the Cold War was the driving force. It might be that the public consciousness of the potential for state intervention in managing social problems was raised by the wartime experience so that when new social demands were made after the war, the state was seen as the agent of their satisfaction. To the extent that research and

21

development were necessary to meet these demands, the universities were the clear candidates for the institutions that might do the state some service. An obvious sphere to look for evidence for this alternative explanation is in health.

It cannot be doubted that public consciousness of health problems and the demand for health services have become a major public and political preoccupation. Perhaps universities are simply the beneficiaries of the demand for health. From the point of view of the professor of English in a large research university, the medical school seems an ever-expanding tumor on the academic body, consuming a disproportionate amount of the university's resources of space and endowment and paying obscene salaries to its professors. In the middle of the Cold War period, at the end of the 1960s, the Division of Biological Sciences at the University of Chicago, which included the medical school, dominated the university both physically and fiscally. It accounted for half of the entire instructional and research budget. When the president of the university wanted to build a new university library, he had to "borrow" the medical school's richest patron from its dean, promising to return her for later benefactions.

When the history of the state's expenditures on research and development in the academy is displayed alongside the history of its expenditure on health research, as in Figure 4, there is a remarkable similarity. The curves for federal expenditure on health research and on all university research and development follow each other not only in their general upward trend but also in remarkable detail in their shorter-term undulations. But the claim that the demand for health is driving academic research budgets will not work. First, health-related research costs account for only about one-third of university research and development, and this proportion has been constant for at least thirty years. As Figure 4 shows, university research expenditures on both health and on all other subjects have shown the same historical pattern, and are both manifestations of some other driving force. Second, if there were a successful public demand for the socialization of health costs, it would surely manifest itself in the demand for the socialization of the immediate

FIGURE 4 Total federal expenditures for health-related research and development, total federal expenditures for all research and development in colleges and universities, and federal expenditures in colleges and universities for health and nonhealth-related projects.

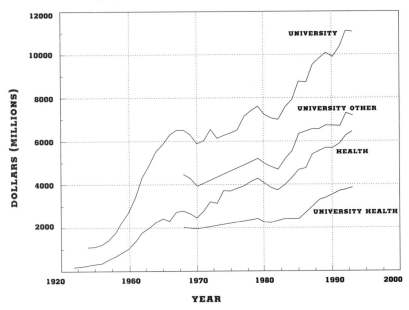

material costs of *care*, rather than in the more nebulous and distant costs of research. However much Americans may worry about sickness and death, it has not been sufficient to overcome their ideological antipathy to socialization.

The legitimation of state economic intervention provided by the Cold War is both an example of and reinforcement for the more general effect on consciousness that can be produced by a state of war.[12] A major push for expenditure on health research has been justified by the metaphor of the "war" on cancer, and the need to "forge weapons" to "defeat the enemy." The "war" on disease, the "war" on poverty, the "war" on drugs are the easy metaphors for a general consciousness that has been formed in the midst of a fifty-year war. Kennedy's inaugural address in 1961 expressed the national consciousness and created all the links:

> Now the trumpet summons us again—not as a call to bear
> arms, though arms we need; not as a call to battle, though

embattled we are; but a call to bear the burden of a long twilight struggle, year in and year out....a struggle against the common enemies of man: tyranny, poverty, disease, and war itself.

The Effect on the Academy

It hardly seems necessary to document in detail the immense increase that has occurred in the size of the academic enterprise in the United States since the end of World War II. In constant dollars, the total budgets of colleges and universities increased by twenty times between 1946 and 1991 and the value of their physical plants by a factor of six in the same period. During those years the average full-time compensation of faculty increased by two and a half times. The annual number of college and university degrees increased ninefold. The question is how much of this immense increase in size and prosperity of the academy can be attributed to the Cold War. It is impossible to give a direct answer because it is impossible to say what portion of general economic growth is owed to it. Of course, if the fears of Samuelson and other economists during World War II were justified, then the *entire* growth of the economy was enabled by the Cold War, without which we would have repeated the events of the 1920s. We can, however, ask more modestly what the role in the political economy of the universities has been played by the direct payments of the state to higher education.

Before World War II, and immediately after it, in 1946, income from the federal government constituted 5 percent of college and university income, but it rose rapidly after 1946 and fluctuated considerably from 12 percent to 26 percent, settling down in the 1980s to about 15 percent of general academic revenues. There is, however, an immense variation among academic institutions both in the proportion of the total federal expenditure they receive, and the proportion of their own budgets that come from the state. In general, big, rich institutions get most of the money and a much larger fraction of their income comes from federal sources. These inequalities have been constant over the entire history of the Cold War period. Ten universities accounted for 28 percent of all federal obligations for research and development in 1968 (24 percent in 1990), and fifty universities received 68 percent of the money (64 percent in 1990). Each of these fifty largest recipients currently gets between $60 million and $500 million annually of research and development funds from the federal government. Over 95 percent of federal expenditures for research and development are distributed to 10 percent of four-year colleges and universities. Moreover, there has been a great deal of stability in which institutions are major recipients of federal funds. Table 1 shows that the list of fifteen largest recipients of federal research and development funds in 1990 had hardly changed from the list in 1975 (Berkeley and Chicago, which were eleventh and fifteenth in 1975, had dropped to sixteenth and eighteenth in 1990). Reciprocally, these large academic recipients also depend heavily on the state for their income. Table 2 gives the proportion of total institutional income that came from federal research funds for institutions at different levels of support in 1967 and the equivalent expenditures in 1991. The sixty largest performers of research were deeply dependent on the federal government for their income, as they still are.

TABLE 1

The fifteen universities that received the highest amount of support from federal research and development funds in 1990 and their rank in 1975.

INSTITUTION	RANK 1990	RANK 1975
Johns Hopkins University	1	10
Stanford University	2	3
M.I.T.	3	1
University of Washington	4	2
University of California—Los Angeles	5	4
University of Michigan	6	14
University of California—San Francisco	7	18
University of California—San Diego	8	8
University of Wisconsin—Madison	9	5
Columbia University	10	7
Harvard University	11	6
Cornell University	12	13
University of Pennsylvania	13	9
Yale University	14	16
University of Minnesota	15	12

TABLE 2

Proportion of total institutional income from Federal research funds.
(From "The Dynamics of Academic Science," 1967, NSF 67-6)

Level of Federal Support in 1967	Approximate 1991 equivalent	Number of Institutions	Ratio of research support to total budget
$ above 20,000,000	above $140,000,000	14	.355
10,000,000–20,000,000	80,000,000 to 40,000,000	15	.303
5,000,000–10,000,000	35,000,000 to 80,000,000	31	.241
500,000–5,000,000	4,000,000 to 35,000,000	106	.187
100,000–500,000	700,000 to 4,000,000	129	.054
1,000–100,000	10,000 to 700,000	416	.018

It may be objected that these figures badly overestimate the dependency of large institutions on research funds. After all, much of this money is for direct costs of the research, so if it were not available, the university would simply go on with its business of teaching. But it is not so simple. At present, 40 percent of the total value of a federal research grant is in "indirect costs," money that goes into the general funds of the institution to be spent for its general purposes. Obviously, carrying out research does involve infrastructure expenses such as heat, electricity, and administration, some fraction of which would not have to be borne if there were no research. On the other hand, direct costs are typically heavily weighted toward salaries, including stipends for graduate students and general secretarial costs. Faculty salaries are also paid from direct costs either as "summer salary," a kind of subsidy to regular salary, or, in some institutions, as a proportion of academic salary.

The income to colleges and universities from research and development funds represents only part of their subsidy from the federal government. Student grant and loan programs administered by the institutions, fellowships, work-study programs, funds for construction and other forms of subsidy beyond grants and contracts for research and development account regularly for between 40 percent and 55 percent of total federal expenditures in institutions of higher learning. In 1970, of the total federal expenditure of $3.24 billion in higher education, $1.76 billion was for purposes other than research and development. In 1990, the total was $15.21 billion of which $6.06 billion was for these other educational purposes. The major expenditure of federal funds for higher *education* rather than for research represents a major challenge to the American antistate ideology. It might be argued that the socialization of research and development was driven by the direct need for the production of new military technology and that the academy happened to have the pool of technologically trained people necessary for the research. But the devotion of large resources for nonresearch purposes transcends this narrow purpose. The state has deeply penetrated higher education as a means for the production of the large managerial and technical cadre without which a successful economy is not possible. Just as for research, the resources for education cannot be made available by individual firms, no matter how large. The radically expanded, higher-educational infrastructure needed after World War II could only have been provided through the socialization of educational costs, and the state has responded. Without a war mentality, that response would have been politically unacceptable.

One consequence of the pouring of federal money into academia both for research and training has been a change in educational structure and self-image of institutions that were previously serving a local constituency. North Carolina State College of Agriculture and Engineering became North Carolina State *University*, as research money from state-controlled funds for agriculture came more and more to be replaced by NIH, NSF, Department of Energy, and Department of Defense grants and contracts, allowing the broadening of the intellectual range of departments and expansion in numbers. Pennsylvania State has turned its back on the town of State College and now is to be found in University Park with its own zip code. Scores of women's colleges, agricultural and mechanical institutes, and teacher's colleges that were once looked down upon by elite institutions have become state universities with graduate programs and research enterprises. The biology program at Butler University, without graduate students, carries on an active and high-level research program with its undergraduates, using federal funds. The opportunity exists in almost any institution for a faculty member to "buy time" from teaching with a small federal grant designed to allow college teachers some opportunity for scholarship. Given the very uneven distribution of federal support, the majority of four-year institutions, of course, still can provide little or no opportunity for their students and faculty to carry out research; however, there has been an immense increase in the number of institutions in which some significant amount of scholarship can be pursued.

A Shift in Power

The growth in wealth and size of academic institutions as a result of the socialization of the cost of scholarship has had a second, contradictory effect on institutional power. A peculiarity of universities and colleges is that their academic staff have the education, social status, and special intellectual craft knowledge of self-employed professionals such as doctors and lawyers, while at the same time are salaried employees who are required to work for periods and under conditions set by their employing institution. There has been a continuing struggle of academics to increase their power over their own conditions of work. They have attempted to free themselves as individuals from institutional constraints by appeals to the principle of academic freedom, and to protect themselves from reprisals by strengthening the rules of promotion and tenure. At the same time they have attempted collective control of the conditions of their employment by taking over institutional governance.[13] The weapons available to academics in this labor struggle before World War II were not very powerful. They were barred by their sense of their own status, and by the cultural and class milieu in which they were formed, from the usual kinds of labor action and organization. Academics depended on repeated reassertions of their rights by their representative organization, the American Association of University Professors (AAUP). In the absence of any real threat to withhold their labor, academics could only hope that public opinion and the desire of university authorities to have a reasonably contented faculty would work in their favor. In joint meetings with representatives of the Association of American Colleges representing management, the AAUP produced several documents between 1915 and 1940 outlining basic concepts of academic freedom, and of the regularization of appointment and tenure. Only the 1940 statement was sufficiently detailed to serve as an effective model, however, and the coming of the war made the issue temporarily irrelevant. It was not until 1958 that a final agreement on procedural standards for dismissal proceedings was reached.

The Cold War changed all that. Beginning at the end of the 1950s and in the early 1960s, before the major wave of the postwar baby boom created a huge demand for places in colleges, there began a major expansion in the size of university faculties, especially in science, as a result of the inflow of money from the state. The result was a labor shortage that, at least in science, lasted for twenty-five years. At the same time, research universities became dependent on the subsidy from the state in the form of grants and contracts, but the channel for that subsidy has been through individual entrepreneurial professors. The combination of a short supply of academics and the conferring on them of a unique power to bring large amounts of money into the university transformed the balance of power between the employer and the employed in setting the terms of the bargain. Professors in natural and social sciences could now choose among institutions who vied for their services by offering lower teaching loads, larger and more lavishly equipped physical space, a liberal leave policy, some research support, and very attractive fringe benefit packages. Professors no longer worked *for* universities, but *in* universities, fully conscious of the fact that they could move the site of their operations if they got a better offer elsewhere.

The advantages of federal funds were felt not only by established scholars, but also in the recruitment of beginning faculty and in the conditions of graduate study. In the mid-1950s, in biology, a graduate student at an elite university typically supported him- or herself (usually himself) by teaching, working part time at non academic jobs, borrowing, or by being married to a working spouse. On receiving a degree, there was a small chance of finding an academic position that allowed time, space, and funds for research, but the most likely employment was in full-time teaching.

Beginning, however, in the mid-1960s, a new pattern was established. A biology graduate student is now offered a full tuition scholarship and graduate fellowship from university funds from several competing universities, or an NIH or NSF predoctoral fellowship or training grant stipend. After the Ph.D., there follows a two- or three-year postdoctoral fellowship from the NIH or NSF, or a postdoctoral research associateship in an established research laboratory on government grant funds. Until about 1990, nearly every young biologist who spent two or three years as a postdoctoral fellow could count on a job as an assistant professor with a laboratory remodeled to order, and start-up research and equipment funds from the university in anticipation of an NIH or NSF research grant. Often, no teaching was required for the first year of work so that the new faculty member could get his or her research program under way. For newly hired faculty members at research universities, these conditions still apply.

Although the power to command these favorable conditions of employment accrues at first-hand to established academics in the natural and some of the social sciences, primarily at large research universities, it has changed the relationship between institutions and academics generally. Some discrepancy in teaching obligation is tolerated between tenured and nontenured faculty members and between molecular biologists and literary critics, but there is a limit to how much discrepancy can be maintained within an institution. Lower teaching loads in science have meant lower teaching loads in the humanities. There is also a limit to how much discrepancy in salary scales will be tolerated between disciplines, and research income from grants and contracts provides general university funds for raising salaries. Higher salaries for biologists have meant higher salaries for biographers, and improvements in fringe benefits affect all faculty members.

Increases in the collective power of faculty governance that have resulted from the financial power of individual recipients of research money have, in fact, gone disproportionately to humanists and social scientists because of the social organization of scientific work. When academic scientists speak of "the laboratory," they do not mean simply a physical place but a small community of graduate students, postdoctoral fellows, and technical workers who share common physical and social space and who are in daily social interaction. The intellectual and fiscal administration of even a small "laboratory" occupies a good deal of the psychic energies of the academic who is responsible for it. Moreover, the "laboratory" is not a democracy or even an oligarchy, but a small kingdom. The privilege of debating the academic calendar or degree requirements for undergraduates is left willingly to the humanists in the faculty senate.

It is not only in the conditions of work but in the conditions of scholarship as a whole that the academy has benefited from state subsidy. The National Endowment for the Humanities, whose budget is only $140 million (8 percent as large as the NSF), only one-sixth of which goes to research grants, nevertheless makes a significant contribution to scholarship. It is part of a halo of legitimation surrounding the socialization of research costs that illuminates intellectual matters far from questions of international economic and military power.

Old Wine in New Bottles

The Cold War is over, at least for the moment. At the same time, a public demand for a reduction in state expenditure has been successfully created by conservative political forces, based on the undoubted increase in economic anxiety that has flowed from a reduction in the real wage and in job security. The problem for economic policy has been to reduce total expenditure while maintaining the level of state intervention that all political forces recognize as essential to the stability of modern capitalism. Finding popular ways to reduce expenditure has been easy, attacking entitlements and redistributive programs that benefit marginalized groups without political power, who are, in any event, the objects of resentment and anger for their "free ride." The problem has been to prevent the demand that has been generated for retrenchment from spilling over onto the state subsidy for production, without overtly admitting the role of the state.

The old method is still in use. "The will to contend by battle is sufficiently known." New enemies continue to be uncovered and some old ones are kept in the public consciousness by periodic renewals of the rhetorical and political campaigns against them. Yet none of these national enemies individually can make up for the loss of the Soviet Union as a source of anxiety. Not even the most paranoid exile, musing in his golf cart while riding between holes in Palm Springs or Key West, imagines that the forces of el Barbudo are about to attack him. There is, of course, an attempt by the state, reflected by the creators of public consciousness, to appeal to a more diffuse sense of world instability, as exemplified by Bosnia, Chechnya, Lebanon, and Korea. And as these are insufficient in themselves, there are periodic reminders of Tiananmien Square, the invasion of Tibet, and the Achille Lauro. Yet, it remains unclear whether unfocused appeals to "national security" can do the necessary political work for the indefinite future.

There is a substitute for military security that has come to occupy an increasing part of the creation of a "will to contend." Economic wars are replacing armed struggle as a major impetus for state intervention in the economy. The threat that Japan or Western Europe will continue to displace American production cannot be met by boycotts and import restrictions because of the dependence of American capital on its own export market. It is obvious to all that the advance of other state-subsidized economies cannot be resisted by a withdrawal of the American government from its role as a patron of production. An important part of that patronage is, as always, in the socialization of the costs of research and training. There are two, partly contradictory elements that provide a force to maintain that patronage. First, it is well known that basic and applied research and the first development of new technology are mostly American because no other economy is remotely large enough to support the large-scale socialization of innovation costs. Attempts by Europeans to pool their contributions to these costs in institutions such as CERN for research in nuclear physics or EMBO for research in molecular biology are still much too small in scale to challenge the American hegemony in research and development. At the same time, there are repeated claims, given wide publicity, that American students are badly behind Japanese and Europeans on scientific and mathematical tests, and that a major effort in education in the sciences is desperately needed if the flow from the font of innovation is not to dry up.

Unlike clashes of arms, the economic war is self-renewing and unending. There is no danger that the state will run out of external enemies that justify its economic role. And central to that role is the subsidization of research and higher education. Whatever attacks are made on federal subsidies for scholarship or even for the arts outside of the academy, they must now be made either because economic catastrophe forces a wholesale reduction in state expenditure, or because the content of particular programs makes them especially vulnerable, but not on the grounds that for the state to subsidize them is contrary to the basic nature of the American polity. The Cold War may have ended, but the socialization of intellectual work is here to stay.

Notes

1. Two recent examples are Gertrude Himmelfarb's *On Looking Into the Abyss: Untimely on Culture and Society* (New York: Alfred Knopf, 1994), and Paul Gross and Norman Levitt's *Higher Superstition: The Academic Left and Its Quarrel with Science* (Johns Hopkins Univ. Press, 1994).
2. See E. Hobsbawm, *The Age of Extremes* (New York: Pantheon, 1994), 90–93. I am indebted to Hobsbawm's discussion not only for these statistics, but also for pointing me to several primary references from which I have taken quotations.
3. Paul Samuelson, "Full Employment After the War," ed. S. Harris.

Post-war Economic Problems (1943), 27–53.
4. The details of this history are treated in a forthcoming book *The Political Economy of Agricultural Research*, by R.C. Lewontin, S. Baker, F. Valente, and N. Makhoul.
5. Vanevar Bush, ed., *Science — The Endless Frontier* (Washington, D.C.: Office of Scientific Research and Development, 1945).
6. Ibid., 5.
7. Ibid., 7.
8. Ibid., 33.
9. This ideological demand for local autonomy even extends to resistance against state authorities, despite serious economic costs.

So, two years ago, in Vermont, local towns rejected a plan for a statewide redistribution of school tax revenues that would have relieved the property tax burden on poorer school districts at the expense of districts whose revenue came largely from nonresident vacation property owners. The voters of my town, Marlboro, who would have greatly benefited, rejected the plan openly in the town meeting on the frankly ideological ground that it would give the state government an excuse to interfere in school affairs.

10. For example, in the mid-1950s, working in the Biology Division at Oak Ridge were W. Baker, D. Lindsley, E. Novitski, and L. Sandler, who then dispersed to the universities of Chicago, California, Oregon, and Washington, where they became prominent national and international leaders of genetics.

11. The NSF defines basic research as gaining "more complete knowledge or understanding of phenomena and observable facts," while development is "systematic use of the knowledge or understanding gained from research, directed toward the production of useful materials, devices, systems or methods, including design and development of prototypes and processes." Applied research somehow falls between these and is devoted to "meeting a recognized need."

12. I am indebted to Elinor Barber of Columbia University for the realization that the metaphor of "war" does powerful work in public policy, outside the direct consciousness of the Cold War.

13. For a variety of viewpoints on this history, see the essays in W.P. Metzger, ed., *Reader on the Sociology of the Academic Profession* (Arno Press, 1977), and the reprinted documents in W.P. Metzger, ed., *The American Concept of Academic Freedom in Formation* (Arno Press, 1977).

$\left(\text{Howard Zinn}\right)$

The Politics of History in the Era of the Cold War:
Repression and Resistance

The academy is "no ivory tower," to borrow the title of
Ellen Schrecker's fine study of McCarthyism and the universities.
The practice of history, therefore, has been affected by the various
currents of postwar America, by McCarthyism in the 1950s, and
the rise of "radical history" in the 1960s. During the decades that
followed, there was a persistent conflict—in politics, between
repression and resistance; in the historical profession, between a
spurious objectivity disguising conservatism and an openly
declared commitment to social change.

What I hope to do in this essay is to describe that conflict, as I
experienced it, as observer and participant, in the fifty-year postwar
period through which I have lived. During World War II, I was a
shipyard worker who enlisted in the Army Air Corps and became a
bombardier flying missions over Europe. After the war, I worked as
a ditchdigger, waiter, city employee, and brewery worker. In 1949,
with my tuition paid by the G.I. Bill of Rights, I began formally to
study history, then to teach and write as a professional historian.
All through those years, whether outside the academy or in it, I
was involved in political activity, from organizing shipyard workers
to participating in the civil rights and antiwar movements.

At the time I enlisted in the air force, I had read a smattering of works in history: Charles Beard's *The Rise of American Civilization*, the journalist George Seldes's account of Mussolini's rise to power (*Sawdust Caesar*), and enough on German Naziism to make me yearn to fight in "the good war."[1]

The political nature of history was at that time a concept foreign to me. I did not learn until much later that historians often have their work distorted by national loyalties. This is always most evident in wartime, when historians are invited to enlist their professional talents for the goal of military victory.

When the United States declared war on Germany in 1917, some of the nation's leading historians (Frederick Jackson Turner, J. Franklin Jameson among them) gathered in Washington to discuss "what History men can do for their country now." One of the things they did was to produce over 33 million copies of pamphlets distributed by various government agencies. In a study of historical propaganda during "the great war," George T. Blakey concludes that many historians "succumbed to the pressures of national bias and placed war aims above scholarly restraint."[2]

The same writer says that later historians were sobered by that experience. But, as Peter Novick shows in his extraordinary study of the claim to historical objectivity,[3] World War II brought another burst of patriotic fervor by distinguished scholars.

Harvard University's Samuel Eliot Morison, in an essay written during the war, affirmed his traditional commitment "to explain the event exactly as it happened." Yet, in the same essay, Morison criticized those historians who had expressed disillusionment with World War I. He said that they made the World War II generation of youth "spiritually unprepared for the war they had to fight.... Historians...are the ones who should have pointed out that war does accomplish something, that war is better than servitude."[4]

On the opposite side of the World War II controversy was Charles Beard, who bitterly denounced Roosevelt for bringing the nation, through deception and manipulation, he asserted, into the war. Beard was more forthright than Morison in acknowledging the inevitably political nature of historical writing. In his prewar presidential address to the American Historical Association (AHA), Beard quoted the philosopher Benedetto Croce that history is "contemporary thought about the past," and stressed that history involves the selection and arrangement of facts. The historian, he said, "helps to make history, petty or grand."[5]

It was only after the war that I began to think about the political character of the history I read with total acceptance as a teenager. It was the troubled state of the postwar world that made it more and more impossible for me to separate the study of history from the conflicts, different ones, that were under way.

I had been an enthusiastic bombardier, but, returning home, the promises of a different postwar world were soon emptied of meaning. Fascism was defeated in Germany and Italy but was displaced to other areas of the world. The imperial powers of the West, despite the pledge of self-determination in the Atlantic Charter, were waging war in Malaya, Africa, Indochina, the Philippines to hold onto their old colonies. Militarism, so hateful as embodied in the Fascist states, was rising again, now on a nuclear scale, with the start of the Cold War between the United States and the Soviet Union.

As I began my formal study of history in 1949 at New York University, and soon at Columbia University, while living with my wife and two children in a low-income housing project in Manhattan, and loading trucks in a warehouse on the four-to-midnight shift, I was very much aware of the new old climate of ferocious anti-Communism. The political and ideological clashes in the world were coming home.

That very year, 1949, my wife, six-months pregnant, our two-year-old daughter Myla, and I traveled in our antiquated 1932 Buick to Peekskill, New York, to attend an outdoor Paul Robeson concert. Robeson was, for so many radicals, old and young, a cultural and political hero. The concert was being held in defiance of threats by right-wing veterans groups in the Hudson Valley to prevent the concert from taking place, as they had done successfully not long before. But we assumed, naively, that because of the earlier publicity, and the huge crowd now going to Peekskill in a picnic atmosphere, that it would be safe.

We were wrong. Robeson sang. Pete Seeger sang. But as they did, a boisterous mob gathered on the periphery of the concert ground, and as the audience moved out on the one dirt road, the mob attacked vehicles and individuals with rocks and sticks while the police stood by without interfering. My wife and daughter crouched down in the front seat. A fusillade of rocks smashed every window in the car. I felt more fear, mingled with anger, than I felt flying bombing missions through German flak. A rock smashed the head of a young woman who was riding with us, fracturing her skull.

Various events in the world were creating a climate of fear and hysteria in the United States: the Soviet occupation of Eastern Europe, the victory of Communism in China, the explosion by the Soviet Union of its first atomic bomb, the start of war in Korea. At home, there were the trials of communists and suspected communists, whether for "perjury," as in the case of Alger Hiss, or for "conspiracy to teach and advocate the overthrow of the government by force and violence," as with the leaders of the American Communist Party.

Walking out of our "project" apartment one evening in 1950, I came upon a tumultuous scene in a nearby building. Men and women, bleeding from face and head, were staggering down the street. They had just attended a Quaker meeting protesting U.S. involvement in the Korean War, and had been attacked by superpatriots.

Another time, walking home to our project apartment with a bag of groceries, I was stopped by two men in trenchcoats (they knew how to dress, having watched many movies) who flashed their FBI credentials and asked if I would talk to them about communists I knew. I refused. The next day, in an impulsive move that I have regretted ever since, my wife and I gathered the box of letters we had written to one another during the war, in which we had sometimes mentioned friends in the Communist movement. We walked out into the hall and threw them down the incinerator chute in the hall. They were historical documents, it is fair to say, and became victims of the Cold War.

The intensity of the conflict between the two postwar superpowers was soon matched by the unabashed partisanship of some of the most eminent American historians. Peter Novick writes:

> It was the community of diplomatic historians who contributed most wholeheartedly and directly to the support and defense of the American cause in the Cold War. These scholars' principal contribution was providing a version of recent history which would justify current policy, linking America's struggles with the Axis and with the Soviet Union as successive stages in one continuous and unavoidable struggle against expansionist totalitarians.[6]

National policy defined historical tasks for some leading historians. After Winston Churchill's "Iron Curtain" speech in 1946, came the promulgation of the Truman Doctrine of March 1947, offering military and economic aid to Greece and Turkey to protect their governments from Communist insurgency. That same month, Truman's Executive Order #9835 established loyalty-security criteria for all federal employees, with even "sympathetic association" with Communists a ground for dismissal.

In the early 1950s, William L. Langer and S. Everett Gleason wrote a two-volume history of American entry into World War II, to chronicle, as they put it, "the tortured emergence of the United States of America as leader of the forces of light in a world struggle which even today has scarcely abated." Although they were given access to privileged government documents, they claimed that no government official "has made the slightest effort to influence our views."[7] However, the connection between these two scholars and the government was not a subtle one. Langer was director of research of the Central Intelligence Agency, and Gleason was deputy executive secretary of the National Security Council.

Perhaps the most widely used college textbook in the history of U.S. foreign policy, *A Diplomatic History of the American People*, by Thomas Bailey, concluded: "Not all Americans...are prepared to recognize that their very way of life is jeopardized by the communist menace. Many are grumbling over defense expenditures, not realizing that to Moscow the most eloquent language is that of force."[8]

The 1949 presidential address to the AHA, by Conyers Read, declared: "Total war, whether it be hot or cold, enlists everyone and calls upon everyone to assume his part.... [W]e can never be altogether free agents, even with our tongue and our pen."[9]

The presidential address of diplomatic historian Samuel Flagg Bemis to the AHA in 1961 was equally blunt:

> Too much self-study, too much self-criticism is weakening to a people.... A great people's culture...begins to decay when it commences to examine itself.... [W]e have been losing sight of our national purpose...our military preparedness held back by insidious strikes for less work and more pay.... How can our lazy social dalliance and crooning softness compare with the stern discipline and tyrannical compulsion of subject peoples that strengthen the aggressive sinews of our malignant antagonist.[10]

The Cold War against the Soviet Union was seen as a continuity of the war against fascism, of democracy against totalitarianism. But I think it is fair to say that these historians, during the rise of Fascism in Europe, had not lent their scholarship with such fervor to the antifascist struggle. The "other" totalitarianism occupied them much more strenuously—matching the record of the Western powers, who were loathe to confront fascism until it began to challenge their imperial standing in the world.

As I took courses in "Western Civilization," it did not occur to me that this very choice as a basic university curriculum came out of a nationalist bias that fitted the requirements of the Cold War. In 1945, Harvard's General Education Committee issued a report (*The Reforming of General Education*), which was described by Daniel Bell as reinforcing "the principles of a free society...the definition of democracy in a world of totalitarianism...the need to provide a 'common learning' for all Americans as a foundation of national unity."[11]

The phenomenon of McCarthyism—a frenzied searching for communists, defined broadly enough to include any strong critic of American society or of U.S. foreign policy—went far beyond the work of Senator Joseph McCarthy of Wisconsin. But McCarthy carried the Communist hunt to the point of hysteria. He burst upon the national scene early in 1950, when he created a sensation by announcing that he possessed lists of communists high up in the U.S. government. It turned out that his "lists" were spurious.

Nevertheless, in a series of hearings before the Senate Committee on Government Operations, specifically, its Subcommittee on Investigations, both of which he chaired, he attacked as Communist-influenced not only the State Department but the Voice of America and the Government Printing Office.

The crusade against communists spread, and historians suspected of Communist connections were among its victims. At hearings in 1952 of the Senate Committee on Internal Security, headed by Senator Pat McCarran of Nevada, historian M.I. Finley was named by two witnesses as having organized a Communist study group while a graduate student at Columbia University in the 1930s. Called before the committee, he denied membership in the Communist Party, but refused to answer questions about people he knew.

Now at Rutgers University, Finley was considered an outstanding teacher and scholar, and a university committee, after its own investigation, concluded that both Finley and another faculty member who had refused to answer questions by the McCarran Committee (Simon Heimlich, a mathematician) were within their constitutional rights in their responses to the committee.

The Rutgers University Board of Trustees, however, decided, in a unanimous vote, to fire the two men. One of the trustees referred to the faculty report: "What the Committee has done is to treat this whole thing as an abstract situation in which the niceties of the law...are given preeminence. It seems to me that we lost sight of the fact that we are at war with Communism." Another trustee pointed out that with 60 percent of its budget coming from the state, the university "cannot offend public opinion."[12]

Indeed, the statement on public opinion was accurate. The congressional investigations, the muted response of the American press, the increasingly heated atmosphere of the Cold War, were reflected in American public opinion. Whereas, in 1946, a Gallup Poll found that 44 percent of respondents favored making it a crime to join the Communist Party, by 1949, the figure was 68 percent. By 1954, a survey conducted by social scientist Samuel Stouffer of Harvard found that 52 percent of those polled were in favor of imprisoning all communists.[13]

Although some historians defied the congressional committees and lost their jobs (Finley left the country and went on to a distinguished career in England, being knighted by the Crown), others cooperated with the inquisition. Historian Daniel Boorstin testified before the House Committee on Un-American Activities in 1953 that he had briefly been a Communist Party member in the late 1930s, but now said that no communist should be allowed to teach in an American university. He agreed that the committee "had not in any way impinged on [his] academic freedom."[14]

Boorstin, asked by the committee to show how he had expressed his opposition to Communism, said: "First, in the form of an affirmative participation in religious activities, because I think religion is a bulwark against Communism....The second form of my opposition has been an attempt to discover and explain to students in my teaching and in my writing the unique virtues of American democracy."[15]

McCarthy, at the height of his public notoriety, puffed up with success, overreached himself. While investigating what he claimed were communist influences in the U.S. Army itself, McCarthy attacked the widely respected General George Marshall. Soon after, his credibility declined rapidly, his support disappeared, and finally in 1954 the U.S. Senate voted to "condemn" him.

The senator had gone so far as to become embarrassing to the Establishment, but the crusade against communists continued in other forms, and historians suspected of communist connections were among its victims. Presidents and chancellors of the leading universities in the country rushed to declare their opposition to Communism. In 1953, their organization, the Association of American Universities (AAU), declared that membership in the Communist Party "extinguishes the right to a university position."[16] The heads of Harvard, Yale, Columbia, Princeton, MIT, Chicago, Caltech, and thirty other institutions subscribed to that statement.

The effect of the anticommunist inquisitions on the work of historians went far beyond the dismissal of suspected radicals. And went beyond the work of McCarthy himself. Ellen Schrecker notes "the political reticence that blanketed the nation's colleges and universities." She writes:

> Marxism and its practitioners were marginalized, if not completely banished from the academy. Open criticism of the political status quo disappeared.... [T]he full extent to which American scholars censored themselves is hard to gauge. There is no sure way to measure the books that were not written, the courses that were not taught, and the research that was never undertaken.[17]

In the very year Daniel Boorstin was testifying before Congress, I was finishing my graduate course work at Columbia and choosing a topic for my doctoral dissertation. When I suggested to a senior member of the Columbia history faculty, himself a distinguished defender of civil liberties, that I might write something in that field, he cautioned me to try another area. Civil liberties were too controversial and might make it more difficult for me to get my degree.

But was this caution the result of the specific phenomenon of 1950s McCarthyism, or was it part of the ongoing situation in the United States—before and after McCarthyism—of "books that were not written...courses that were not taught...research that was never undertaken." Has there not been a persistent conservatism in American culture, including the practice of history, which is challenged significantly only in times of social protest— the 1930s, the 1960s?

Richard Hofstadter wrote his book *The American Political Tradition* before the Cold War atmosphere took hold. In it he characterized the boundaries of American political leadership: "property and enterprise...the economic virtues of capitalist culture," a culture which he described as "intensely nationalistic."[18] Those boundaries have also marked the limits of respectable historical scholarship throughout our national history, before and after the specific phenomenon of McCarthyism.

When Charles Beard stepped firmly outside those boundaries with the publication in 1913 of his ground-breaking *An Economic Interpretation of the Constitution*, the *New York Times* went to the trouble of writing an editorial denouncing his book. When, in the 1930s, a history text by Harold Rugg, which showed a degree of consciousness about class, became widely used, the National Association of Manufacturers launched an attack on Rugg's work. They succeeded in pushing his work out of the schools, thus sending a cautionary warning to writers and publishers of historical texts in the 1940s.[19]

As for Marxist historians, they were certainly beyond the pale, even before the McCarthy period. Thus, the pioneering historical work of Herbert Aptheker and Philip Foner could only be accepted by houses on the margin of the publishing industry. Aptheker's classic *A Documentary History of the Negro People in the United States*, a collection immensely valuable, indeed indispensable to anyone doing research in African American history, was published by the small Citadel Press. Foner's multivolume *A History of the Labor Movement in the United States*, an extremely useful resource for anyone doing work in labor history, was published by the left-wing International Publishers.

Both of those works could have been done by non-Marxists, in the sense that they did not represent "Marxist" interpretations of American history, but it seems that Marxist historians were simply more conscious than others about the importance of the history of black people and of working people. It is a revealing commentary on American society that mainstream historians paid so little attention to African American history. Judging from the titles of approximately 450 articles in the *American Historical Review* from 1945 to 1968, only five dealt with African American themes.

To find extensive work on African American history, one had to go to the venerable *Journal of Negro History* and other publications stimulated by the Association for the Study of Life and History, which was founded by Carter Woodson in 1915, shortly after the formation of the NAACP. A small body of published books by black historians did exist: Woodson, John Hope Franklin's *From Slavery* to Freedom, W. E. B. DuBois's Black Reconstruction, and Rayford Logan's The Betrayal of the Negro: From Rutherford B. Hayes to Woodrow Wilson.

What was available to me, a young aspiring historian, entering the profession at the outset of the Cold War, in the early 1950s? No overview of American history written from a radical point of view. No critical history of American foreign policy—not until the end of the decade would William Appleman Williams publish the book which would initiate an era of "revisionist" history, The Tragedy of American Diplomacy.

It was a time when high praise was given to historians like Arthur Schlesinger, Jr., whose book, The Age of Jackson, won a Pulitzer prize. Colorfully written, it presented Jackson as a hero of the democratic tradition, a forerunner of Franklin D. Roosevelt. But, even after a war that should have made scholars more sensitive to issues of racial hatred, Schlesinger's book, emphasizing Jackson as an opponent of national banking interests, overlooked him as a racist, a slaveholder, a mutilator and killer of Indians. (I must say that I was oblivious to those omissions myself at that time, and read Schlesinger with enjoyment and admiration.)

Mainstream history of the 1950s has often been described as "consensus" history—in which conflicts in American society are seen as muted, kept within a narrow band, not subject to the violent upheavals found in societies where class lines are drawn more sharply. The so-called consensus historians agreed on this as a description of the American past, but disagreed on the merits of this consensus.

Daniel Boorstin reveled in this consensus, this continuity, considered it "the genius of American politics" (in a series of lectures at the University of Chicago in 1952, and a book of that title published in 1955). Daniel Bell, in his book The End of Ideology, also welcomes this lack of conflict, both ideological and actual, as a sign of the maturing of American society.

On the other hand, Richard Hofstadter was critical of the ideologies—capitalism, nationalism—that bound the political leadership of the country in that consensus. Louis Hartz, while tracing the lack of class conflict to the absence of feudalism in the origin of the American colonies, clearly was unhappy with the narrow boundaries within which American discourse was kept.[20]

While doing my graduate work at Columbia, I found the boundaries that both Hofstadter and Hartz described—in my courses, in the literature offered to me. I did find liberal scholars: Henry Steele Commager, teaching constitutional history, David Donald, Mississippi-born but clearly an admirer of the abolitionists. Their work fit well within the liberal tradition.

On the conservative side of the consensus was their colleague, Allan Nevins, a prolific writer, who, while writing his eight-volume history of the Civil War, found time also to write a spirited defense of the Rockefellers and the other wealthy entrepreneurs of the Gilded Age. His work could be seen as a rejoinder to the critical studies of the "Progressive" era and the 1930s: Matthew Josephson's *The Robber Barons* and Gustavus Myers' 1907 classic *A History of the Great American Fortunes*.

Josephson, in a reissue of his book in 1962, referred to historians like Nevins as "revisionists" who "have proposed rewriting parts of America's history so that the image of the old-school capitalists should be retouched and restored, like rare pieces of antique furniture." (Later, the term "revisionist" would be applied to writers who carried on in the Josephson tradition of historical muckraking.)

To follow my interests in history, I found that I had to go outside the reading lists of my courses, outside the traditional curriculum. So I read Matthew Josephson and Gustavus Myers. And I began to read extensively in the history of the labor movement in the United States. As an undergraduate at NYU in 1951, I could not find any course in labor history, but managed to do an independent course of study, which led me to Foner's work and other books on working-class history.

I was especially attracted to a book by Samuel Yellen (not a historian but an English teacher), *American Labor Struggles*, which told of events, dramatic and violent, that I had not encountered (except, occasionally, in the briefest of mentions) in any of my

American history classes. I read for the first time of the great railroad uprisings of 1877, of the Haymarket affair of 1886, the Lawrence textile strike of 1912. I was fascinated especially by the story of the Colorado Coal Strike of 1913–14.

That event was absent from the courses in American history at Columbia, and I decided to make it the subject of my master's thesis. The excitement of the 1930s' labor struggles was now gone, and the labor movement was in decline. With the Taft-Hartley law in effect, trade unions themselves began hunting down Communists in their leadership, adapting themselves to the Cold War atmosphere of the time. But I found sympathetic mentors in one of the grand old men of the Columbia faculty, Harry Carman, and his teaching assistant, James Shenton.

To dig into the details of the Colorado Coal Strike was to affirm and strengthen whatever radical criticism I had of American society. It was class struggle, American-style, as intense and violent as anything depicted in Emile Zola's novel of French miners— *Germinal*. It showed the ties between the Rockefeller corporate interests and the political leaders of Colorado, the use of the courts and soldiers to burn and kill (culminating in the Ludlow Massacre of April 1914), the role of the presumably "objective" press in serving the interests of the wealthy, and the role of a liberal federal government (the Wilson administration) in cooperating with the mine owners. It was also inspiring, in showing how miners and their families, apparently without resources, could resist the most powerful corporation in America.

For my doctoral thesis, I once more had to look outside the liberal-conservative consensus for a subject. I found it in Fiorello LaGuardia, who, before he joined the consensus as mayor of New York, was a radical congressman from East Harlem in the 1920s. This was presumed to be the "Jazz Age," an age of prosperity (a description never challenged in my courses in American history). But LaGuardia angrily denied this. He spoke up in Congress for the poor people of his district, as well as for striking miners in Pennsylvania and debt-ridden farmers of the Midwest. He declared:

I am not at all shocked by being called a radical. Something is radically wrong when a condition exists that permits the manipulation of prices, the creation of monopolies on food to the extent of driving the farmer off his farm by foreclosures and having thousands of underfed and ill-nourished children in the public schools of our cities.[21]

Virtually alone, LaGuardia challenged the dispatch of U.S. Marines to Nicaragua in 1927, which Secretary of State Frank Kellogg said was necessary to prevent a communist takeover of Nicaragua and to save American lives. LaGuardia said there was no proof of communist activity in Nicaragua and added: "The protection of American life and property in Nicaragua does not require the formidable naval and marine forces operating there now. Give me fifty New York cops and I can guarantee full protection."[22]

I was reading these words of LaGuardia just after the United States, in 1954, charging that the government in Guatemala, elected in one of the few free elections in the history of that country, was Communist controlled (it had taken over the lands of the United Fruit Corporation), set in motion an invasion to overthrow that government.

In the 1950s, there was no organized activity by historians (or by other scholars) and extremely few individual protests took place against the military actions of the United States. These interventions were against Third World countries, always on the grounds of "stopping Communism." The United States intervention in Korea had cost over a million Korean lives. In 1953, the same year the Korean War ended, the U.S. government organized the overthrow of the nationalist leader Mossadegh in Iran. The French were trying to reconquer their old colony in Indochina, and the United States was supplying most of the military supplies for that war. In 1958, President Eisenhower sent 14,000 marines into Lebanon to protect the government there against a rebellion.

The silence of the academy in regard to Cold War foreign policy in the 1950s was matched by its passive acceptance of the Cold War's equivalent on the domestic scene: the firings, the blacklistings, the attacks on unions, the FBI harassments—all justified as part of the fight against Communism. As Ellen Schrecker concludes, after her careful study of McCarthyism in the universities:

> Professors and administrators overrode the civil liberties
> of their colleagues and employees in the service of such
> supposedly higher values as institutional loyalty and national
> security....The extraordinary facility with which the academic
> establishment accommodated itself to the demands of the state
> may well be the most significant aspect of the academy's
> response to McCarthyism.[23]

For some historians, subservience to the state, as it pursued foreign military interventions and domestic Communist-hunting, went beyond silence to complicity. The election of John F. Kennedy to the presidency in 1960 brought into the White House as advisors a number of important scholars: political scientist-historian McGeorge Bundy of Harvard, economist Eugene Rostow of MIT, and historian Arthur Schlesinger, Jr., of Harvard.

In the presence of cold war policies he thought unwise, Schlesinger would remain silent, as when President Kennedy made the decision to go ahead with the covert invasion of the Bay of Pigs in Cuba. In his book *A Thousand Days*, Schlesinger tells how he did write a private memo to the president expressing his opposition to the invasion. However: "In the months after the Bay of Pigs I bitterly reproached myself for having kept so silent during those crucial discussions in the Cabinet Room." He attributed his silence to "the circumstances of the discussion." As he put it:

> It is one thing for a Special Assistant to talk frankly in private to
> a President at his request and another for a college professor,
> fresh to the government, to interpose his unassisted judgment
> in open meeting against that of such august figures as the
> Secretaries of State and Defense and the Joint Chiefs of Staff,
> each speaking with the full weight of his institution behind him.[24]

Schlesinger's opposition to the Cuban invasion was not based on a moral objection to a military intervention aimed at overthrowing a popular revolutionary government. The popularity of the Castro revolution was important to Schlesinger only because it meant that the invasion would be protracted. "If we could achieve it by a swift surgical stroke I would be for it." Further, "a course of bullying intervention would destroy the new image of the United States" and "might recklessly expend one of our greatest national assets—John F. Kennedy himself."[25]

Schlesinger's reasoning was well within the traditional bipartisan consensus on foreign policy, where objections to a particular tactic might be made, not on fundamental issues of right and wrong, not on something as basic as the principle of self-determination, but on grounds of "will it work?" and "what effect will it have on our image?"

In his book, Schlesinger did not reveal all the contents of his memo to Kennedy. But in an article in *The Nation* in 1977, another historian, Ronald Radosh, disclosed more information about Schlesinger's role in the Bay of Pigs invasion. It seems that in order to protect "one of our greatest national assets—John F. Kennedy himself," Schlesinger suggested that: "When lies must be told they should be told by subordinate officials."[26] (In the Reagan-era scandals of Iran-Contragate, this tactic of "plausible denial" became notorious.)

Deception would be necessary, Schlesinger said, because "a great many people simply do not at this moment see that Cuba presents so grave and compelling a threat to our national security as to justify a course of action which much of the world will interpret as calculated aggression against a small nation."[27]

He went on to include in his memo sample questions and lying answers, if the issue of invasion should come up in a press conference:

Q. Mr. President, is CIA involved in this effort?

A. I can assure you that the United States has no intention of using force to overthrow the Castro regime.[28]

Four days before the invasion, President Kennedy told a press conference: "There will not be, under any conditions, any intervention in Cuba by U.S. armed forces."[29]

Schlesinger and the other scholars who played roles as servants to national power were following the prescription of the nineteenth-century historian Leopold von Ranke, who is considered the apostle of "objective" history because of statements such as "The strict presentation of the facts...is undoubtedly the supreme law." But, at another time, von Ranke wrote: "For history is not simply an academic subject: the knowledge of the history of mankind...should above all benefit our own nation, without which our work could not have been accomplished."[30]

Few historians, of course, were in the position of a Schlesinger or a Bundy, who could possibly exert some influence on national policy. Most of us could expect, at the most, to have some influence on our students, both by what we did and by how we played our roles as citizens in the world outside the classroom.

Granted that the circumstances were difficult, as they always are, in a situation where one's job is within someone else's power to grant or to withhold, still, there is the possibility of choice. And the choice is between teaching and acting according to our most deeply felt values, whether or not it meets approval from those with power over us—or being dishonest with ourselves, censoring ourselves, in order to be safe.

For me, from the start of my teaching career, I resisted self-censorship. I do not attribute this to any special bravery but to the circumstances of my life. The fact that I entered the academic world late—after three years in a shipyard, my experience as a wartime bombardier, my various jobs—gave a strength and confidence to my political views. I knew that, unless it were simply defined as *honesty*, "objectivity" was neither possible nor desirable.

I thought that history might play some role in bringing about a better world, but not as a buttress to any particular party, nation, or ideology. I decided that, in the inevitable selection of material that goes with teaching and writing history, I would choose issues and present information designed to raise questions about war and peace, racial discrimination, and economic inequality. And I could not imagine that I would confine my life to the classroom and the library, that I would stand aside during the important conflicts of our time.

For teachers and scholars in any time, this is a prescription for

trouble. And in the atmosphere of the Cold War, college administrators were more nervous than usual about the possibility that
some faculty member would come under public political scrutiny.

The fact that my first teaching job was in a southern black college for women probably diminished the risk. I did not deliberately
seek out a position in a Negro college, but when the job was
offered to me, I was happy to accept. It did not occur to me that
Negro colleges, being out of the main line of vision in American
education, could be a kind of refuge for unorthodox teachers, but
this was often the case.

As I became involved in the developing civil rights movement
in Atlanta—the sit-ins, the demonstrations, the picketing, the boycotts—I was asked to join the executive committee of the newly
formed Student Nonviolent Coordinating Committee (SNCC),
which was born out of the sit-in movement. Along with Ella Baker,
a black woman who had been on the staff of Martin Luther King
and the Southern Christian Leadership Conference, I was considered an "adult adviser" to SNCC.

I became a kind of historian-participant in the movement,
writing articles for *Harper's Magazine, The Nation, The New
Republic*, and other publications, in the midst of teaching and
working with SNCC. I did not know that the FBI was monitoring
my activities at Spelman. But in the mid-1970s I succeeded,
through the Freedom of Information Act, in getting at least part of
my FBI file—hundreds of pages of FBI memos, news clippings,
and assorted documents.

In a memo from FBI agent M.A. Jones to "Mr. DeLoach" (a top
official of the FBI), Jones wrote: "In connection with an article entitled 'Don't Call Students Communists' by captioned individual
which appeared in the 10-24-65 issue of the 'Boston Globe', the
Director has inquired as to what do we have in files on Zinn."
Jones then went through my military and educational record. And:
"While with Spelman College he was quite active in racial matters
and information we have received indicates that he continues to
be involved in various civil rights matters. He is currently on the
Security Index of our Boston Office."

In 1961 and 1962, I was asked by the Southern Regional Council, an Atlanta research group, to make a report on the demonstrations and mass arrests in Albany, Georgia, a small city 150 miles south of Atlanta. I interviewed black people just out of jail, as well as leaders of the Albany movement, and SNCC people who had set up a "Freedom House" in Albany at the start of the demonstrations there. I also talked with the police chief of the city and the sheriff of Daugherty County, of which Albany was the seat.

My report, "Albany, Georgia: A Study in Federal Responsibility," declared very bluntly that the U.S. government was failing to enforce the Constitution in Albany. The constitutional rights of black people and civil rights statutes dating back to the Civil War were being violated again and again by local law enforcement officials while the president, the Department of Justice, and the FBI looked the other way. My report was a front-page story in the *New York Times*, and was also quoted in *I.F. Stone's Weekly*.

When the press asked Martin Luther King, Jr., if he agreed with my criticism of the FBI, he made a strong statement about racism in the FBI. This clearly infuriated J. Edgar Hoover. The FBI had opened a file on King in New York in September 1958 when King was approached outside a New York church by the black Communist leader Benjamin Davis.[31] In the report on me requested by Hoover, agent M.A. Jones said: "Zinn has written many articles criticizing the Director and the FBI in the past, some of which have appeared in 'The Nation.'"

As I observed and participated in civil rights activity in the Deep South—in Atlanta; in Selma, Alabama; in Hattiesburg, Mississippi—I continued to criticize the federal government for its failure to protect black people from violations of their civil rights by local officials. I also spoke out on other issues, including U.S. foreign policy. The FBI memo commented on my actions while teaching at Spelman College:

Zinn's continued demonstration of procommunist and anti-U.S. sympathies appears to stem from his activities at Spelman College...which involved such activities as: organizing a seminar in Atlanta, Georgia, on 'American Policy Toward Cuba' at which one of the speakers denounced U.S. policy toward Cuba; calling for a demonstration in front of the White House in February, 1962 by students from all over the United States demanding the end of the nuclear testing.

The report on me concluded:

Subject's activities make this a close case as to whether he belongs on the Reserve Index or the Security Index. [People on the Security Index were to be arrested and placed in camps whenever the president decided that national security required invoking the Emergency Detention Program passed by Congress in 1950.] He can, however, be included on the Security Index under the criterion [that] facts have been developed which clearly and unmistakably depict the subject as a dangerous individual who might commit acts inimical to the national defense and public safety of the United States in time of emergency.... Security Index cards are being forwarded to the Boston Office.

Clearly, a historian who decided to participate in history was even more dangerous to the government and its agencies of surveillance than one who wrote about it, however unorthodox that writing might be.

In 1963, after seven years at Spelman College, during which the president became more and more nervous about my political activity, he finally fired me for "insubordination." Was the problem my support of Spelman students in their rebellion against the authoritarianism of the administration? Or was it my activities in the Atlanta community in the civil rights movement, and in protests against U.S. foreign policy? I knew I was being insubordinate, both to the college administration and to the government. And I thought that there might have been outside influences at work—perhaps the conservative white business people on the board of trustees, perhaps the FBI, or both.

My closest colleague at Spelman College was a friend and fellow historian, Staughton Lynd. He also participated in various activities of the civil rights movement (he was director of the Freedom Schools in the Mississippi Summer Project in 1964). We walked the same picket line in Atlanta to protest U.S. policy toward Cuba, participated in the same forum against the House

Committee on Un-American Activities, and watched with concern the growth of nuclear arsenals on both sides, in a race which we believed was initiated by the United States, the dramatic symbol being the bombings of Hiroshima and Nagasaki.

The trajectory of Staughton Lynd, from brilliant student at Harvard and Columbia, prize-winning historian, teacher at Spelman, professor at Yale, to disappearance from the historical profession, tells much about the effect of the Cold War on the academy.

After I was fired from Spelman, and about the time I was offered a post at Boston University, Staughton resigned his job at Spelman and was immediately hired by Yale University. In 1965, as the U.S. war in Vietnam sharply escalated, he joined Tom Hayden of Students for a Democratic Society (SDS) and Herbert Aptheker, a historian and communist, in a trip to enemy territory—North Vietnam. Shortly after that, he was dropped from the Yale faculty.

One would think that Lynd, on the basis of his academic record, would be sought after by colleges and universities. But when he applied for a position at Chicago State College, he was turned down because of his "public activities." Seeking a job at the University of Chicago, he was rejected because he showed "bad judgment" in commenting on the experience of radical historian Jesse Lemisch. Lemisch had been fired after one term by the University of Chicago, told by his department chair: "Your convictions interfered with your scholarship."[32]

Staughton Lynd was unable to get a teaching job in the Chicago area. Convinced now that he was being blacklisted, he left the historical profession, enrolled at the University of Chicago Law School, and subsequently became a labor lawyer.

It was not surprising that Lynd's trip to North Vietnam made him persona non grata to the academy. The war in Vietnam epitomized the anticommunism of the Cold War years. But it was also a turning point.

In the civil rights struggles of the early 1960s, the attempts of J. Edgar Hoover and others to paint the various movements as influenced by communism (former President Harry Truman said he was sure the sit-in movement was inspired by communists) had to confront the growing acceptance of these movements by mainstream America. Martin Luther King, Jr., and sncc had such overwhelming support in the black community, and more and more in the white community, that the Communist accusations did not work. Indeed, Hoover was reduced to lascivious spying in a desperate effort to find a basis for discrediting King.

The very fact that the war in Vietnam was justified as a war to "stop Communism," that the Cold War against Communism became inextricably tied to the conflict in Vietnam, meant that as the war itself became discredited, the American public became more and more skeptical when the government invoked "a communist threat" to justify military action.

But that was a ten-year process, from 1965, when the public accepted the government's rationale for the large-scale dispatch of U.S. troops to Vietnam, to 1975, when all the surveys showed an enormous public disillusionment with the nation's political leaders. During that period, historians, like the rest of the country, struggled with their consciences and with one another over the issue of U.S. involvement in the war. But also, they battled about the proper role of historians, in the classroom, in their writing, and in the society at large.

My antiwar activity, which began in the spring of 1965 when I spoke at an early protest meeting on the Boston Common along with Herbert Marcuse, took me in the summer of 1966 to Japan. An organization of Japanese intellectuals called Beheiren, which opposed the American war in Vietnam, invited me and a fellow veteran of sncc, an African American named Ralph Featherstone, to do a whirlwind speaking tour of thirteen Japanese cities in fourteen days.

When we returned to Tokyo after our tour, I arranged a meeting with the American ambassador to Japan, Edwin Reischauer. I had known Reischauer when I was a Fellow in East Asian Studies at Harvard and he was teaching Japanese history there. I had attended a celebratory dinner for him at Joyce Chen's famous Chinese restaurant in Cambridge when he was appointed ambassador by President Kennedy.

Our meeting in Tokyo, however, was a clash of historians with opposing views on the Vietnam War. I recalled to Reischauer his 1954 book, *Wanted: An Asian Policy*, in which he wrote that a policy based largely on stopping communism was "a dangerous over-simplification of our Asian problem."[33] But now, he was defending U.S. policy in Vietnam in the traditional manner of ambassadors, who, whatever their personal views, think it their obligation to go along with their administration. Perhaps, also, those personal views change in the awesome atmosphere of an embassy.

At the very time that Featherstone and I were in Japan, Noam Chomsky was giving a talk at Harvard, which later became reprinted in *The New York Review of Books* as "The Responsibility of Intellectuals." "It is the responsibility of intellectuals," Chomsky wrote, "to speak truth and to expose lies."[34]

But, he said, there were intellectuals who had a different view. He quoted the German philosopher and supporter of the Nazis, Martin Heidiegger, who said in 1933 that "truth is the revelation of that which makes a people certain, clear, and strong in its action and knowledge." And he pointed to Arthur Schlesinger's admitted lies at the time of the Bay of Pigs invasion, and to his compli-menting the *New York Times* for suppressing information on the planned invasion of Cuba.

Chomsky wrote: "it is significant that such events provoke so little response in the intellectual community—no feeling, for example, that there is something strange in the offer of a major chair in humanities to a historian who feels it to be his duty to per-suade the world that an American-sponsored invasion of a nearby country is nothing of the sort."[35]

Schlesinger had characterized U.S. policies in Vietnam in 1954 as "part of our general program of international goodwill." Chomsky commented: "Unless intended as irony, this remark shows either a colossal cynicism or an inability, on a scale that defies comment, to comprehend elementary phenomena of con-temporary history."[36]

Chomsky pointed to statements made by other intellectual sup-porters of the Vietnam War, advisors to President Kennedy, as examples of flagrant historical distortion: Walter Rostow had written: "Throughout the 19th century, in good conscience, Americans could devote themselves to the extension of both their principles and their power on this continent"; and McGeorge Bundy wrote that "American democracy has no enduring taste for imperialism."[37]

In 1967, Beacon Press published my book, *Vietnam: The Logic of Withdrawal*, which quickly went through eight printings. Although books had been published that were critical of the war, mine was the first to call for an immediate withdrawal from Indochina.

Around that time, the Department of Political Science at Boston University was voting on whether or not to give me tenure. They were supposed to have made the decision in 1965 and 1966, but clearly opposition existed in the department by a few senior members who criticized my very public activity against the Vietnam War. However, in the spring of 1967, it finally came to a vote. Again, there was opposition, again because of my stands on the war, but I had published more than anyone in the department and had excellent student evaluations of my classes. I was narrowly approved.

It was hard to say how many academics in the United States were denied tenure, refused appointments, or in other ways punished for speaking out against the war. Or how many remained silent in order to save their academic careers. I was lucky to have barely made it. But my involvement in the antiwar movement continued to put my job in jeopardy.

When, in 1968, I traveled to North Vietnam with the poet-priest Daniel Berrigan to receive three American pilots freed by the Vietnamese, there was grumbling at the administrative level. In 1972, when I made another trip to North Vietnam, the Dean of the College of Liberal Arts suggested that I was in violation of my contract for missing classes, although I had arranged for all of my classes to be covered by colleagues for the ten days that I was gone.

And when, in 1972, I denounced the new president of Boston University, John Silber, for inviting the U.S. Marines to campus to recruit for the war, and then calling the police to arrest protesters,

I became a target for punishment for the rest of my teaching years at Boston University. My salary was kept low; I was denied teaching assistants (though 400 students signed up for my course each semester); I was turned down for a leave when I was invited to teach for a semester at the University of Paris. And when I refused to cross the university secretaries' picket line during a strike, I and a few other faculty were threatened with dismissal, then saved by an outpouring of protest.

None of this was life-threatening, and I was not willing to trade my freedom of speech and action for the tiny emoluments of the profession. But it made me wonder how many other faculty, around the country, were enduring some kind of pressure because of their stands against the war.

The risk of speaking out is always present in the academy, where jobs and prestige depend on the approval of administrators, businessmen-trustees, and politicians. But there are times when faculty are more impelled to take the risks. The Vietnam era was one of those times, because the war struck powerfully at the consciences of many scholars. And as the whole country turned, year by year, against the war, faculty felt more secure about criticizing government policy.

That security had not existed in the 1950s, when there was no domestic movement able to mount a critique of American military policy abroad, whether the intervention in Korea, the subversion of governments in Iran and Guatemala, or the enormous buildup of nuclear weapons. The resurgence of militarism after 1950 created a convenient atmosphere for weakening the labor movement in the way that foreign "threats" have been historically used to preempt challenges to corporate power.

However, the movement for civil rights of the early 1960s encouraged protest and grassroots organization, and paved the way for the antiwar movement. The struggle against racial segregation emboldened some historians, as well as other academics, to break from the stifling atmosphere of the 1950s, in their actions as citizens, in their professional organizations, and in their scholarship. Martin Duberman of Princeton, who had written some distinguished works in American history, turned his talents to the stage, and wrote a documentary drama, *In White America*, which was both troubling and inspiring as it traced the history of racism in the United States from early slavery up to the 1950s.

After the escalation of the war in Vietnam, historians, as did scholars in other fields (notably Noam Chomsky, who had made his reputation in linguistic philosophy), spoke at teach-ins, walked picket lines, joined demonstrations against the war. I became one of a crew of academics who traveled the country speaking against the war wherever we were invited.

In October of 1967, along with Noam Chomsky and others, I spoke at a meeting of thousands on the Boston Common—duly noted by the FBI in the file that I received from them. After that meeting, there was a long procession to the Arlington Street Church, where the historic church candelabra was lit and young men filed up to hold their draft cards in the flames. Harvard graduate student Michael Ferber spoke eloquently about the war. Soon he and four others (Dr. Benjamin Spock, Rev. William Sloane Coffin, writers Mitchell Goodman and Marcus Raskin) would be indicted for conspiring to induce young men to defy conscription.

Early in 1968, I traveled to Hanoi with Daniel Berrigan to bring back to Laos three American fliers who had been shot down over Vietnam, imprisoned, and were now being released by the North Vietnamese. Later that year, I made a trip to Paris with several other academics—historians Marilyn Young, George Kahin, Jonathan Mirsky, and economist Douglas Dowd—to meet with the North Vietnamese peace delegation in Paris.

The fall of 1969 saw the antiwar movement at its height, as several million people around the country gathered in towns and cities, many of them places that had never had an antiwar gathering, to protest the war. That was Moratorium Day. On the Boston Common, 100,000 people gathered. I was among many speakers that day, with the main speaker Senator George McGovern.

It is impossible to say how many of the tens of thousands of people arrested for protesting the war were historians. I was arrested five times, and I suppose my record is suggestive of the kinds of actions that took place in that time.

1970: About a hundred of us arrested for blocking buses carrying inductees at the Boston Army Base.

1971: I was one of thousands arrested in Washington in early May during several days of blocking streets and protesting the war. A few days later, I was arrested again, this time in Boston, picked out of a crowd of thousands who were encircling the Federal building.

1972: The "B.U. 62" were faculty and students arrested in the Student Union Lounge after we had occupied a dean's office to protest campus police brutality against antiwar demonstrators. Two teachers of English and one visiting writer were there. I was the lone historian.
   Several hundred of us—academics, writers, people in the arts—in an action organized by psychologist Robert J. Lifton, were arrested for sitting in the corridor of the Capitol in Washington to protest President Nixon's continuation of the war.

A number of times in the 1960s and 1970s I was called upon to testify in the trials of antiwar protesters. Here I found a way of practicing my trade as a historian in an unusual way, to "teach" juries about American history in practical situations where more than a step up the academic ladder was at stake. I often testified as an "expert witness" on the history of civil disobedience in the United States. In 1973, in the trial of Daniel Ellsberg and Anthony Russo for distributing the "top secret" documents, which came to be known as the Pentagon Papers, I spoke to the jury for hours about the history of the Vietnam War.

A few historians threw the weight of their training on the other side. They became "court historians": Arthur Schlesinger, Jr., for President Kennedy; John Roche for Lyndon Johnson. But historians by the thousands around the country participated in one way or another in the antiwar movement. And for the first time, the war became an issue at an annual meeting of the AHA in December of 1969. At that meeting, a group of historians formed a radical history caucus and decided to introduce an antiwar resolution at the business meeting of the association.

No such turnout for a business meeting of the AHA had ever taken place. A large auditorium was packed to the rafters because word had gotten out about the Radical Caucus and about the determination of the old guard of the AHA to block the caucus's plans. The resolution was introduced—it was I who was chosen to present it—calling for the withdrawal of the United States from the war. A heated debate took place and the old guard pulled a trump card: two historians associated with the left—Stuart Hughes and Eugene Genovese—spoke against the resolution on the ground that it would "politicize" the AHA, which was established for professional advancement, not political controversy.

A brief and almost comical jockeying for the microphone between me and historian John Fairbank, the dean of China scholars in the United States, with whom I had always had a friendly relationship. Fairbank wrote to me later: "They voted you down because they did not believe the Vietnam War had affected their rights, opportunities, and procedures as historians....The AHA exists for professional purposes only."

My rejoinder (we had an exchange of "open letters" printed in the AHA Newsletter, June 1970) was as follows:

> Let us assume the war does not affect us 'as historians';
> ...It only affects us 'as citizens'. Well, when *do* you assemble
> with other citizens to speak out on the crucial issues of our
> time?...What can democracy possibly mean if not that people
> assembled whenever and wherever they can, for whatever
> reason, may express their preferences on the important issues
> of the day? If they may not, democracy is a fraud, because it
> means that the political leaders have effectively isolated the
> citizenry by taking up their time in various jobs, while the
> leaders make the policies, and the citizens, in 99% of their life,
> remain silent.

C. Vann Woodward, a widely respected historian of the South, was in the chair as president of the AHA. Although he had done important pioneering scholarly work in moving away from the old racist histories, he was clearly troubled by the introduction of the Vietnam issue into the proceedings of the association.

The resolution that did get the approval of the organization shows both the broad antiwar sentiment among historians and the limits they saw to involvement in the issue. It was presented immediately after the defeat of the radical caucus resolution, and called also for the withdrawal of the United States from the war, but based this on the fact that the historical profession was being hurt by so much of the national wealth going into the war.

This belief that historians should not be concerned with what was happening in the world, except as it affected their professional lives, was even stronger in the early stages of the American war in Vietnam. At an International Congress of Historical Sciences (ICHS) held in Vienna, Austria, in the fall of 1965, with 140 historians from the United States among the 2,400 delegates, the editor of the *American Historical Review*, Boyd Shafer, reported to the AHA:

> One attempt...to introduce current political views (on Vietnam) failed. The Bureau...firmly opposed the introduction of any current political question and...the secretary-general, Michel Francois, delivered a strong admonition against such attempts, saying that ICHS had been and could only be devoted to scientific historical studies.[38]

Nevertheless, in the 1960s, affected undoubtedly by the powerful currents of the civil rights and antiwar movements, historians began to write a new kind of American history, which came to be known as "revisionist history." It repudiated the idea of "scientific historical studies" (one must recall that it was Stalinism in the Soviet Union that insisted on the Marxist interpretation of history as a "science"), called into question traditional interpretations, and explored areas of the American past that had been largely ignored in the orthodox accounts.

Forerunners of this new history, went back to the early part of century, and Charles Beard's *An Economic Interpretation of the Constitution of the United States*, when dared to depart from the traditional deification of the founding fathers. James Harvey Robinson, around the same time in *The New History*, prefigured the 1960s' call for "relevance" when he wrote: "The present has hitherto been the willing victim of the past; the time has now come when it should turn on the past and exploit it in the interest of advance."[39]

These were lone voices, not part of a larger movement in the profession. This was true also of a few historians in the 1950s such as Carl Becker, who wrote:

> Our libraries are filled with this stored-up knowledge of the past; and never before has there been at the disposal of society so much reliable knowledge of human experience. What influence has all this expert research had upon the social life of our time?...Very little surely, if anything.[40]

Philosophers who were interested in history were also divided on this issue. Alfred North Whitehead wrote: "The understanding which we want is an understanding of an insistent present. The only use of a knowledge of the past is to equip us for the present." Arthur O. Lovejoy, representing the more dominant view, wrote that the aims of the historian must not be confused with those of the "social reformer." The job of the historian, he declared is "to know whether...certain events or sequence of events, happened at certain past times, and what...the characters of those events were."[41]

The 1960s saw a movement away from the orthodoxy of "objectivity," indeed saw it as a cover for acceptance of the injustices that existed in the nation. As the status quo was being challenged in many different areas of American life, similar challenges began to appear in the realm of ideas.

The seminal work breaking from the traditional benign interpretations of American foreign policy was William Appleman Williams's *The Tragedy of American Diplomacy*, which he published in 1959, where he declared boldly that American relations with other countries "denies and subverts American ideas and ideals." He saw American policy as one of expansionism, which came out of the needs of capitalism. The worldview of the United States was that "freedom and prosperity depend upon the continued expansion of its economic and ideological system through the policy of the open door."[42]

As the foreign policies of the Cold War came more and more under criticism—the subversion of governments undesirable to the United States, the support of right-wing dictatorships around the globe, the frightening growth of nuclear weapons and the arms race with the Soviet Union—Williams's view became the basis for a new school of "revisionist" historians. A new publication of the 1960s, *Studies on the Left*, became an outlet for them.

The ranks of the new radical scholars in diplomatic history grew through the 1960s and in the decades that followed. Between Marilyn Young's 1968 book *The Rhetoric of Empire*, and her 1991 book *The Vietnam Wars*, dozens of historians began to look critically at the record of American diplomacy. Indeed, it was a tribute to their influence that Princeton University Press in 1973 published a strong critique of the W.A. Williams school (Robert Maddox, *The New Left and the Origins of the Cold War*).

As the various movements of the 1960s and 1970s influenced millions of Americans, new histories challenged orthodox treatments of every aspect of the American past. Alfred Young fathered a new school of historical interpretations of the American Revolution, emphasizing the role of farmers, working people, women, black people. Traditional accounts of slavery had been superficial and even apologetic. Now the "political economy of slavery" was analyzed by Eugene Genovese in *Roll Jordan Roll,* and the remarkable culture kept alive in the slave communities was chronicled by Lawrence Levine in *Black Culture and Black Consciousness*.

DuBois's classic, *Black Reconstruction*, was now joined by new accounts. C. Vann Woodward's *Reunion and Reaction* traced the economic motives of the northern republican establishment in bringing black Reconstruction to a halt in 1977. Black and white historians (John Hope Franklin, Eric Foner) now replaced the old racist accounts of the Reconstruction period with powerful and comprehensive histories. Vincent Harding, a historian who had been in the civil rights movement in the South, began a multivolume history of the black experience.

Whole shelves of books on the history of women began to appear in the bookstores, written by a new generation of women historians. Eleanor Flexner's *A Century of Struggle* showed how women, throughout American history, resisted their treatment as inferiors and demanded equal rights. Gerda Lerner put together the writings and speeches of black women and white women in her anthologies *Black Women in White America* and *The Female Experience*. Roslyn Baxandall, Linda Gordon, and Susan Reverby edited two editions of *America's Working Women*.

A respectful new attention began to be paid to the history of the indigenous peoples of North America, both by white historians and Indian scholars. Gary Nash's *Red, White, and Black* was an important account of the relations between the races in early America. In *The Invasion of America*, Franklin Jameson unhesitatingly described the ruthlessness with which American settlers took over Indian land and went about the destruction of Indian tribal life. In the 1980s and 1990s, Indian scholars (Donald Grinde, Ward Churchill) began more and more to reclaim the cultural history of their people.

When, in the late 1970s, I set out to write *A People's History of the United States*, I had the work of the new histories to draw upon. In the next fifteen years, the book went through at least twenty-five printings, and sold over 400,000 copies. What was clear was that the movements of the 1960s and 1970s had created a whole new generation of people—teachers, students, others in the general population—who were hungry for a history less celebratory, more critical, more conscious of the victimization as well as the resistance of ordinary people.

How powerfully the new history had gained ground in the profession could be ascertained by noting that some of its practitioners, far being marginalized, now had a certain prominence, and even became presidents of the Organization of American Historians in the 1980s and 1990s, starting with William Appleman Williams himself, and then Eric Foner and Blanche Wiesen Cook. The AHA had moved from its conservatism enough to ask Foner to edit a volume of essays, *The New American History*. The Association had come some distance since 1968, when Barton Bernstein's anthology, *Towards a New Past*, was clearly at the margin of the profession.

Published in 1990, Foner's volume began by saying: "In the course of the past twenty years, American history has been remade."[43] It devoted much of its space to "Major Themes," the choice of which reflected the new sensibility. Essays appeared by Alice Kessler-Harris and Linda Gordon, who had done distinguished work in social history and women's history. Essays in African American history and labor history also appeared, as well as one by Walter LaFeber, a diplomatic historian in the tradition of William Appleman Williams.

The new history was arousing heated reactions from defenders of both the old order in foreign and domestic policy and the old order in historiography. Conservative politicians joined conservative historians in denouncing "the revisionists." Senate Republican leader Robert Dole told a cheering audience of American Legionnaires that the purpose of the new approaches to history was "to denigrate America."

One conservative historian, Gertrude Himmelfarb, writing in the *Times Literary Supplement*, associated the new history with "post-modernism," and accused it of denying "any objective truth about the past," and of promoting "history at the pleasure of the historian." She invoked the traditional aim of historical writing as reconstructing the past as it "actually was."

This was a theme echoed again and again in the criticism of the new history. But Peter Novick, in *That Noble Dream*, had demonstrated the hypocrisy of historians who called for "objectivity," and then revealed their own strong point of view. Does not the very selection of subject matter, the decision about what is important in history, make objectivity a myth?

Himmelfarb, in that same essay, shows what she thinks is important when she expresses delight at a student's excitement in discovering that Andrew Jackson's first message to Congress was written by the historian George Bancroft. And then declares her annoyance at the emphasis in the new history on "race-class-gender."

Lynn Cheney, former head of the National Endowment for the Humanities during a Republican administration, said: "The new history is disdainful of facts, as if there are no such things as facts, only interpretation."[46] But in the same statement, she said that too much emphasis was placed on criticism of the established power structure. Would she have complained about "interpretation" if that interpretation defended the power structure?

In Dickens's *Hard Times*, his caricature of a pedant, Mr. Gradgrind, admonishes a young teacher: "Now what I want is Facts. Teach these boys and girls nothing but facts. Facts alone are wanted in life.... Stick to facts, sir." But behind every fact presented to a reader or a listener is a judgment—the judgment that *this* fact is important. And so to Himmelfarb the discovery of George Bancroft's authorship is important, but the new historians see importance in information about blacks, women, working people, whom they (we) see as neglected in the orthodox histories.

The shattering of the Soviet Union, the disappearance of "the Soviet threat," did not bring an end to the Cold War as waged by the United States, both in the world and within American society. Expansionist policies in the world, and the marginalization of opposition at home, antedated the existence of the Soviet Union and continued after its demise. However, with the social movements of recent decades, that opposition became less marginal, and the writing of history, while not replacing traditional history, became a force to be recognized.

This was evident in a number of ways. For instance, the traditional story of Columbus as hero, presented for generation after generation to schoolchildren, as well as in higher education, and reproduced in the national culture, was challenged for the first time in the 1980s and 1990s. The opening chapter of my *People's History*, drawing on the ancient accounts by the Spanish priest Bartolome de las Casas, saw Columbus, driven by a ruthless quest for gold, and bringing about the annihilation of the Indian population of Hispaniola, as a forerunner of modern imperialism.

By the time of the quincentennial celebrations of 1992, because of the pioneering work of middle-school teacher Bill Bigelow and others, teachers all over the country were beginning to teach the Columbus story in a different, and undoubtedly troubling, way.

Demonstrations took place in various parts of the country against celebrations of Columbus. A parade in Denver had to be called off because of the protests. Children's books now appeared with a new version of the Columbus story.

In the early 1990s, a group of historians drew up a set of "National Standards" for the teaching of history, with the emphases of the new history. These were distributed to 20,000 school districts around the country, and drew the ire of conservative historians and politicians. The U.S. Senate passed 99–1 a resolution denouncing it, calling for a more patriotic treatment of history and a greater admiration for "western civilization."

The year 1995, with celebrations everywhere commemorating the end of World War II, saw the controversy over the bombing of Hiroshima, which had begun right after the war, reach its height. The trajectory of that controversy through the postwar period is indicative of what was happening during that time in the field of history.

In 1962, while a fellow in East Asian Studies at Harvard (the fellowships were part of an energetic effort by American foundations, after the victory of the Communists in China, to pay more scholarly attention to Asia), I became interested in the Hiroshima-Nagasaki bombings. Part of my interest came from my own experience as a bombardier in the European theater in World War II, when I had participated in the totally senseless napalm bombing of a French village(Is there such a thing as a bombing that is only partially senseless?) just before the end of the war.

I wrote an essay for the *Columbia University Forum* called "A Mess of Death and Documents," in which I concluded that there was no justification, moral or military, for dropping the atomic bombs on Hiroshima and Nagasaki. I based my argument on the official report of the U.S. Strategic Bombing Survey, the interviews with Japanese leaders conducted by Robert Butow in his book, *Japan's Decision to Surrender*, the narrative of the Swiss writer Robert Jungk, *Brighter Than a Thousand Suns*, and Herbert Feis (who had access to State Department documents), *Japan Subdued*.

A few years later (1965), Gar Alperovitz published his ground-breaking book *Atomic Diplomacy*, which was based on extensive research into the diaries of important political leaders involved in the decision to drop the bombs (Henry Stimson, James Byrnes, James Forrestal). Alperovitz argued that the decision, certainly not necessary to win the war, was a political move, aimed at the Soviet Union.

In the decades that followed, more of the new historians did research that corroborated Alperovitz's conclusions. Barton Bernstein collected documents and wrote for the *Bulletin of Atomic Scientists*, using new data from the papers of government officials. Martin Sherwin's *A World Destroyed*, based on extensive research into government archives and presidential papers, underlined Alperovitz's thesis: "Believing that the bomb should be used if it was ready before the Japanese surrendered, Truman, Stimson, and Byrnes reasoned that such a clear demonstration of its extraordinary power would induce the Soviets to exchange territorial objectives for the neutralization of this devastating weapon."[45]

In 1995, I wrote an essay, which became part of the *Open Magazine Pamphlet Series*, called "Hiroshima: Breaking the Silence," in which I made use of much of the scholarly work that had been done on the subject, in which I raised, more sharply than I had in my earlier essay, the moral issue. I urged that we "reject the belief that the lives of others are worth less than the lives of Americans."[46]

The same year, Gar Alperovitz, having struggled for years and finally succeeding in getting thousands of classified government documents released to him under the Freedom of Information Act, published his massive work, *The Decision to Use the Atomic Bomb*. It was a powerful argument against deception and silence, and received much more attention than the book he had written thirty years before.

What was important was that now the argument against the use of the atomic bombs was no longer on the margin of the culture. It was in the forefront. There was still great resistance among the American public to accepting that the United States was wrong

in that decision. The memory of Pearl Harbor, the continued ignorance about the readiness of the Japanese to surrender whether
or not the bomb was used, contributed to that resistance. But, as
Alperovitz pointed out: "A poll taken in 1991 [New York Times,
December 8, 1991] at the time of the fiftieth anniversary of Pearl
Harbor reported that roughly half of those surveyed felt that both
sides should apologize for the respective acts which marked the
beginning and the end of World War."[47]

The intensity of the antagonism toward the new history was
itself a measure of how much had changed over the long course of
the Cold War. Back in 1961, in his presidential address to the AHA,
Samuel Flagg Bemis had declared that "Too much...self-criticism
is weakening to a people."[48] But thirty-odd years later, there was a
new generation of historians, many of whom agreed with John
Dower, who said: "We accuse the Japanese of sanitizing their history, but we're doing the same thing....anyone who's critical is
called an America-hater. Is that what America stands for—unques-
tioning, blind, patriotic nationalism?"[49]

In 1995, the U.S. Congress was dominated by Republican and
Democratic conservatives. The president was a centrist Democrat
who seemed inclined to compromise again and again with the
conservative agenda. And yet, out of the movements of the 1960s
and 1970s, even in the midst of military interventions, there had
developed in the nation something that conservatives spoke of
with apprehension as "a permanent adversarial culture."[50]

In that adversarial culture, the new history had come to play an
important part.

Notes

1. *Sawdust Caesar* (New York:
   Harper, 1935).
2. George T. Blakey, *Historians on the
   Homefront: American Propagandists
   for the Great War* (Univ. Press of
   Kentucky, 1970).
3. Peter Novick, *That Noble Dream*
   (Cambridge, U.K.: Cambridge
   Univ. Press, 1988).
4. Novick, *Dream* "Faith of a Historian."
5. "History as an Act of Faith," *American Historical Review* (1934).
6. Novick, *Dream.*
7. Ibid.
8. New York: Appleton-Century-
   Crofts, 1950).
9. Novick, *Dream.*

10. Ibid.
11. Ibid.
12. Ellen Schrecker, *No Ivory Tower: McCarthyism and the Universities* (New York: Oxford Univ. Press, 1986).
13. David Caute, *The Great Fear* (New York: Simon & Schuster, 1978).
14. Novick, *Dream.*
15. Ibid.
16. Schrecker, *Tower*
17. Ibid.
18. (New York: Knopf, 1948).
19. James Loewen, *Lies My Teacher Told Me* (New York: The New Press, 1995).
20. See Hartz, *The Liberal Tradition in America* (New York: Harcourt Brace, 1955).
21. Congressional Record, May 23, 1924.
22. La Guardia Papers, Municipal Archives, New York, January 13, 1927.
23. Schrecker, *Tower.*
24. Arthur Schlesinger, Jr., *A Thousand Days* (Boston: Houghton Mifflin, 1965).
25. Ibid.
26. Ronald Radosh, Historian in the Service of Power, *Nation*, 6 August 1977.
27. Ibid.
28. Ibid.
29. Victor Bernstein and Jesse Gordon, "The Press and the Bay of Pigs," Columbia University Forum, Fall 1967.
30. Fritz Stern, *The Varieties of History* (New York: Meridian, 1956).
31. See David J. Garrow, *The F.B.I. and Martin Luther King, Jr.* (New York: Penguin, 1983).
32. Jess Lemisch, *On Active Service in War and Peace* (Chicago: New Hogtown Press, 1975).
33. Edwin Reischauer, *Wanted: An Asian Policy* (New York: Alfred Knopf, 1955).
34. Reprinted in Noam Chomsky, *American Power and the New Mandarins* (New York: Pantheon, 1969).
35. Ibid.
36. Ibid.
37. Ibid.
38. Newsletter of the American Historical Association, 1966.
39. (New York: Macmillan, 1912).
40. Carl Becher, "What Are the Historical Facts?" *The Western Political Quarterly*, September 1955.
41. Alfred North Whitehead, *The Aims of Education* (New York: Mentor, 1956), .
42. Williams, *Tragedy* (New York: Dell, 1962).
43. Eric Foner, The New American History (Philadelphia Temple Univ. Press, 1990).
44.
45. (New York: Vintage, 1977).
46. (Westfield, N.J.: Open Magazine Pamphlets, 1995).
47. Gar Alperovitz et al., *The Decision to Use the Atomic Bomb* (New York: Knopf, 1995).
48. Novick, *Dream.*
49. John Dower, Quoted in *Boston Globe*, 25 July 1995,
50. Adam Garfinkle, *Telltale Hearts,* (New York: St. Martin's Press, 1995).

(**Richard Ohmann**)

English and the Cold War

When the lines of the Cold War firmed up, English was a pastoral retreat within the university.[1] Its practitioners celebrated verbal art and Anglo-American high culture. Little disturbed their tranquility beyond a dispute as to whether textual analysis or historical and philological scholarship was to ground their claims to disciplinarity. Few outside the field and almost none outside the university cared, so long as English took care of the familiar classics and taught freshmen to write passable themes.

When the lines of the Cold War crumbled, many outside the university cared a good deal about what English was up to. The political Right was noisily attacking it and the rest of the humanities for abdicating curatorship of the great books, abandoning traditional values, and subverting the social order. Mainstream media transmitted and amplified the exposé of multiculturalism and political correctness. Unsettling as was this hostile publicity, it could not be written off as gratuitous. English had indeed charged out of its quiet retreat, turned a critical eye on the social order, challenged many core beliefs and values, and sharply revised its cultural mission. No such defection is ever unanimous; the culture wars go on intramurally, too. Yet, in the forty years of the Cold

War, the field's center shifted (for want of a better word) left. Its leaders are guilty as charged of multiculturalism—of what the Right sees as cultural treason. Its new recruits are inducted into practices and perspectives that would have seemed scandalous to the generation that shaped it in the postwar period. Almost no one saw English as "political" then. Now, the politics of literary culture are inescapable, and to many, welcome.

How did such a change come about? The obvious explanations —Vietnam, civil rights, feminism, other movements, the subsequent conservative restoration—are right but incomplete, because they do not explain why other fields have not taken a parallel course to that of English and its neighbors. So let us consider how English was specially located in the postwar university and the consensus of the early Cold War.

I note with some bemusement that an argument can be made —*has* been ingeniously made, by William H. Epstein—that the Yale English Department in particular was there before the outset, laying foundations of Cold War intelligence work and Cold War ideology.[2] Epstein's argument places Yale criticism and scholarship at the origins and near the 1950s center of Cold War thought and method. He does not suggest that people in the field, other perhaps than a very few knowing ones, pursued their academic work in full awareness of these relations or in service to a Central Intelligence Agency (CIA) formulation of the national interest. Rather, the milieu of English at Yale was one in which tropes of textual analysis and ways of organizing knowledge that had funded cold war intelligence at the outset retained their allure and urgency.

But if English helped launch the Cold War, it reaped few tangible rewards. To think of basic and applied science in U.S. universities, powerfully shaped throughout the period by lavish government and especially military funding is instantly and obviously to see literary studies as a poor relation, an indirect beneficiary, at most, of scraps of "overhead" redistributed by administrations to the shabbier precincts (see R.C. Lewontin, in this volume). Or think of area studies, wrestled into existence and prosperity by the State Department, the CIA, Office of Strategic

Services (OSS) alums, the Ford Foundation, and so on; nourished by Cold War contracts, prestigious consultancies, the traffic back and forth to Washington; profoundly changing the shape of graduate education and research in the postwar university.

These two interventions alone substantially remade universities along the lines of a Cold War blueprint. There are many lesser instances: anthropology mobilized for knowledge and control of subaltern peoples, and sometimes recruited into secret counterinsurgency efforts; linguistics backed in its years of major development by the military and various arms of the foreign service (not always with the intended results); political science funded in some places (including the American Political Science Association itself) by the CIA and other cold war sources; free-market and "developmental" economics the same; and in these last two fields the seductions of prestige and influence, of direct and indirect participation in the making of national policy. The list could go on through less vital symbioses between the Cold War state and psychology, foreign-language instruction, even history, with its abundance of prominent OSS alums,[3] and doubtless other fields.

Whatever ties existed between English and the OSS during the war, whatever reinforcement English offered to Cold War thought and feeling afterward, whatever fields of force brought English into conformity with national purpose, meager indeed were the tangible inducements to serve it, in comparison to those visibly and persuasively offered to many other disciplines. Were there *secret* inducements of weight and consequence? Imprudent to dismiss the idea, given later revelations about CIA cultural politics: its funding of the Congress for Cultural Freedom, the money channeled to journals and publishers, the dummy foundations, secret funding of and intervention in the National Student Association, and so on—all this activity directed, incidentally, by agent Thomas W. Braden, formerly of the English Department at Dartmouth. The established foundations supported the Cold War rhetoric—in the case of the Guggenheim Foundation, its president, Henry Allen Moe, thundered in his biennial reports on behalf of freedom and against those who would restrain it, proclaimed loyalty to the nation our highest duty, held that scholarship led to a strong United States, and promised that no member of the Communist Party would receive Guggenheim funding.[4] But when one thinks, again, of patronage in other fields, and of the fact that far and away the largest amount of support for literary research in the 1950s came from the sabbatical programs of individual colleges and universities, all these suppositions and hunches about funding seem a distraction.

Literary practitioners did not live close to the corridors of power, as did people in many other fields. I never wondered why my own teachers and other important people in literary studies stayed home, why they did not serve on blue ribbon commissions, why no one sought their advice on the Cuban missile crisis. English was not producing action intellectuals; as a body of knowledge it had nothing to offer (in post-oss days) to the managers of global affairs.

By the 1950s, too, secrecy seemed an inevitable condition of world politics, of "intelligence," of special knowledges in science and beyond. Others were in charge of those matters; we lacked not only their expertise but also the right to know how they were deploying it and the right to voice encouragement or criticism, except for an occasional scandal such as the U-2 incident that lifted the veil of secrecy. Real history was someone else's business. Literary studies went along on history's margin, with little cold war money and excluded from policy circles.

No one invited us to play the great game. We[5] also *chose* our comfortable distance, with who knows what mixture of sour grapes and righteousness. Not for us the battle against international Communism. Our spokesmen (Modern Languages Association (MLA) presidents and the like) might put on the rhetoric of freedom and democracy at ceremonial moments, but, dwelling in our house of Culture, we disdained crass patriotism, reviled McCarthy and lesser anticommunists as know-nothings, looked down our noses at the bland pragmatism of the Eisenhower administration. At the core of our ethos was an antagonism toward business, commerce, and commodity culture.

Eagerly though we acquired stereos, books, eventually cars and houses, we managed to define ourselves as dropouts from the acquisitive society. A hundred years after Matthew Arnold, we adhered with just a bit of uneasiness to his critique of the philistines, often seen in 1950s America as all but indistinguishable from the aspiring populace. We lived the ideology—well analyzed by Raymond Williams in *Culture and Society*—of Culture as somehow apart from society and offering to redeem it, however deaf the ears into which we whispered the offer.

In short, English and its neighbors struck an ambivalent posture of disengagement from and antagonism toward the postwar project of untrammeled capitalist development and U.S. dominance in the world. Literary theory and its attendant practices underwrote the disengagement. The New Criticism, in this time of its hegemony, took on the task through its insistence on the autonomy of the literary work. Leading theorists such as I. A. Richards, Cleanth Brooks, W. K. Wimsatt, John Crowe Ransom, Alan Tate, and their gray eminence, T. S. Eliot, differed on some points, but their ideas fused into a catechism of denials. The "intentional fallacy": to equate a work's meaning with its author's intention, and so connect it with his or her actual life. The "affective fallacy": to locate the work in its impact on readers. The "heresy of paraphrase": to associate it with any propositional content. By such maneuvers the New Critics severed poetry from historical process, distinguished it from other practical uses of language, and defined the experience of it as a peculiarly intransitive state of consciousness. Less explicit but crucial was their separation of that experience from action: "Poetry makes nothing happen," wrote Auden, and the New Critics seconded the motion.

Instead, poetry achieves a reordering and unification of experience, as is clear in the reasons given by New Critics for setting such extraordinary value as they do on irony, ambiguity, tension, and paradox, in critical practice: these devices are important for their "resolution of apparently antithetical attitudes," which both daily life and science leave in dissonance. This idea has its origin, for the New Criticism, in Richard's *Principles of Literary Criticism*, where a "balanced poise" of the

attitudes plays a central and almost therapeutic role. Richards
supposes that our cultural sickness is an imbalance of attitudes
and impulses and that poetry can set us right by helping us
achieve a state of equilibrium. The more discordant elements
drawn into this unity, the more effective the poetry—for this
reason Richards praises tragedy as "perhaps the most general,
all accepting, all ordering experience known." And Brooks says
that the good poems manage a "unification of attitudes into a
hierarchy subordinated to a total and governing attitude. In a
unified poem the poet has 'come to terms' with his experience."
Now, putting together these suggestions with Eliot's famous
diagnosis of a "dissociation of sensibility" in the modern world,
I see a sequence of this sort: The world is complex, discordant,
dazzling. We want desperately to know it as unified and meaningful, but action out in the world fails to reveal or bring about a
satisfying order. The order we need is available in literature.[6]

Thus,

The value of poetry transcends the values of individual poems
and poets, and lies not in urging one or another moral view
but in embracing ("coming to terms with") ethical complexities.
A proper reading of poetry neutralizes and flattens out not only
impulses toward action but perhaps even those toward moral
judgment. Poetry, capital P, can prefer no one value system or
course of action, but accepts and comprehends all values,
all actions, and in fact everything that makes up reality.

We can "come to terms" with dissonance in social life by "containing it, by striking balanced attitudes, as a successful poet does."
Through this set of ideas, New Criticism made its own small contribution to the "end of ideology," much celebrated in the postwar
period, and to the eclipse of history and politics. Needless to say,
literary theory in this vein also answered well to the need for vali-
dation of our claims to professional standing by setting off the
object of our knowledge from the subjects of other disciplines, and
authorizing an equally distinct method of study and teaching.

New Criticism was not of course the only contender for dominance in literary studies, but other schools produced similar ideologies. Chicago critics called for a "pluralistic" criticism that
would take systems of thought as premises for inquiry rather than

as competing doctrines, and reduce values to methodological preferences. Northrop Frye's influential *Anatomy of Criticism* allied literature and our work with the vision of a society "free, classless, and urbane," very different, surely, from the society we actually inhabited. Many in literary studies embraced an existentialism stripped away from the politics of its European origins and taken to valorize the lone individual in company with his acts and his death.[7] Americanists began to theorize our history around hero myths, and invited us to split off the United States from Europe, class conflict, empire. Race, when not simply ignored, became a trope or a matter of original sin. In general, we reached for time-less universals in our understanding of texts: love, death, art, suf-fering, apart from the squalid mess of history.

Though rather smugly aloof from the trials and triumphs of U. S. capital, we were of course also beneficiaries of both, as uni-versities expanded rapidly to meet its needs, including (especially in the post-Sputnik period) the perceived need to compete eco-nomically, as well as militarily, with the Soviet Union. The rising tide lifted English along with engineering, math, and science, largely because composition and introductory literature courses were embedded in the structure of university requirements, but also because in those flush times many undergraduates felt at eco-nomic liberty to concentrate in the impractical humanities. Departments grew and jobs proliferated even beyond the ability of old and new Ph.D. programs to meet the demand. Salaries rose from their rather austere postwar levels to levels that almost matched our sense of professional dignity. (Friends marketing themselves at the end of my first year, 1953, took salaries of around $3,000; when I took an assistant professorship in 1961, it paid $6,400, if memory serves—more than my father had made in his last year as full professor and department head at the downtown college of Western Reserve University in 1946, before leaving for industry in despair of raising a family on an academic salary.)

In materially improving circumstances we bought into the ide-ology of the professional-managerial class, even as we abstained from the more public and explicit ideology of the Cold War system that supported it. We were for the advancement of knowledge, trust in expertise, professional autonomy, cultivation of the individual, advancement through merit, and so on; these attitudes put us at ease in the liberal universities that employed us, grumble though we might about the ascendancy of science, law, and business. More, we held that our work for Culture was in the *real* interest of American society. If only it would pay attention, we could help raise it out of the commercial crassness and jingoist anti-intellectualism that somehow kept diverting it from a nobler historical mission.

So I propose locating English, through the 1950s and early 1960s, in a safe eddy of postwar development, and also in a latent contradiction with respect to the main current. With close to 9 percent of gross national product going into military production on average, and about 25 percent to total government spending, the Cold War "solved" U.S. capitalism's problem of lagging demand and stimulated the economy to hectic expansion. It carried higher education and the professional-managerial class along with it. Literary studies were an integral if minor part of the military-industrial-government-university complex, and claimed a residual share in its spoils. But unlike many other fields, English was not recruited to fight the Cold War, not given special inducements, not directly shaped by Cold War imperatives. Sidelined thus, people in the humanities were relatively free to cultivate their own interests, in both senses, and to regard the Cold War from the standpoint of outsiders. On the whole, we went along unthinkingly with the ideology of the free world, though with no racing of the blood—after all, the Soviets were no threat to our freedom. We condemned, when we did not simply ignore, their harsh regime and those contiguous with it from Berlin to North Korea. But we dissented from the militarization of U.S. society, abhorred the bomb and "brinksmanship," disavowed alliances with dictatorships, had little use for "intelligence," and dissociated ourselves from much of what others thought an incomparable, American way of life, as well as from the project of American business that produced our comfort.

We also (to repeat) were repelled by official anti-Communism, not to mention the McCarthy version. A memory: afternoons watching the Army-McCarthy hearings over a beer, at Cronin's in Harvard Square; transcendent vulgarity, the senator's main offense to our cultural amour propre; Harold Ickes, I think, referred to his work as a "scabious putrescence," and that pretty well summed it up for us. Danger? Hardly, for what did we humanists have to do with the Communist Party, and besides, had the Harvard Corporation not made our university safe for anticommunism by (ambivalently) defending Wendell Furry's Fifth Amendment stand against the House Committee on Un-American Activities (HUAC)? The witch-hunters carried on their shameful crusade at a vast distance from "us," posing no threat to the civilizing mission or the professional aggrandizement of academic humanists—so, many of us thought.

We matched up narrow self-interest to ideological dreams, and felt pretty safe. But of course the witch-hunts did *not* bypass some of "us." Among people fined for refusing to testify or for taking the Fifth Amendment, usually for the honorable purpose of protecting former comrades, were a number of mainly tenured, academic humanists: Edwin Berry Burgum (English, New York University (NYU)), Lyman Bradley (German, NYU; for many years treasurer of the MLA), Joseph Butterworth (English, University of Washington), Herbert Phillips (Philosophy, Reed), Harry Slochower (German, Brooklyn), M.I. Finley (Classics, Rutgers), Barrows Dunham (Philosophy, Temple). Others left before they could be fired (Margaret Schlauch (English, NYU), Saul Maloff (English, Indiana)). Many were in effect blacklisted, including Kenneth Burke, turned away from a temporary job at the University of Washington in its time of purges and paranoia.

This roster, carefully assembled by Ellen Schrecker in *No Ivory Tower*,[8] bespeaks no protected enclave for humanists. How did those of us entering the profession in the McCarthy moment register the news? I began graduate study in 1952, and can recall nothing: no bulletins of the latest atrocities, no huddles of fearful or angry teaching assistants, no warnings from our elders, no

petitions or meetings in support of persecuted scholars, nothing
—except that generalized contempt for McCarthyism and assurance that it had no bearing on the conditions of our own study
and employment.

Did we think these firings had no lesson or warning for us,
because the purged were a different species, weird enough actually to have been Communists? By intention or not, the repression
encouraged such a distancing, along with the latent idea that it was
one thing to derogate business and consumer society from the airy
vantage point of Culture but quite another—and less savory—
thing to join an organization dedicated to their overthrow.

The purged were not the only ones caught up in these events,
some prominent humanists enlisted, reluctantly or righteously, *in*
the anti-Communist crusade. Those who preached its gospel or
named names or both included the prominent critic Robert
Gorham Davis, historian (later librarian of Congress), Daniel
Boorstin, historian of ideas Arthur O. Lovejoy (his *The Great Chain
of Being* a required text for aspirants in English), and philosophers
Sidney Hook and James Burnham. Lesser complicity was
common, as with Lionel Trilling, who helped draft Columbia's
instructions for faculty testimony before HUAC, and Robert
Heilman, head of English at the University of Washington, who
conceded in a memo to its president that his department had in
the past harbored too many leftists, and promised to avoid that
error in the future.[9] Such interventions, like the firings, are more
striking when retrospectively lumped together than at the time
when they occurred sporadically and when some were unknown or
only locally noted. Still, there were messages for those of us on
the sidelines, in our leaders' acts and failures to act.

The disdain toward witch-hunting achieved little organizational
form or activist power. Major academic institutions evaded issues,
sought compromises, remained silent. Universities let HUAC and
anti-Communist trustees set the agenda: they advised faculty
members to come clean; they accepted and used FBI information;
they set up their own inquisitions. Few indeed were those, such
as the University of Buffalo, that flat out refused the hysteria.

(Harvard, for all its self-commendation over the Furry case, was not of that honorable company.) Few were willing to hire the purged—even those, such as M.I. Finley, with superb credentials. Their guild organization, the American Association of Universities, publicly stated that administrations and faculty members had a duty to cooperate with investigators, and that one of the latter who declined was probably not fit to teach.[10]

The American Association of University Professors ducked appeals for help from faculty fired or under fire, and, through a combination of ineptness and fear, remained silent on the witch hunts until 1956, when they were over. Even the American Civil Liberties Union, internally divided on these questions, held back comment until that time."[11] As noted, the Guggenheim Foundation announced the blanket exclusion of Communists from its beneficence. The MLA championed foreign-language instruction as serving the national interest,[12] and held its tongue about purged members. Nor did our professional leadership find other ways to fight specific repressions, as opposed to lamenting the general phenomenon.

What, then, did we learn from the Cold War battles actually fought on our turf, especially those of us apprenticing in the early 1950s? We learned that the state could pry into and severely punish our affiliations and politics, with the cooperation of our employers, dedicated as they supposedly were to freedom of thought; that, in fact, we were *less* free than other workers to challenge power, because of the special obligations we took on with our special privilege;[13] that the stigmatized could expect little if any help from our professional and scholarly organizations, and not much from ad hoc groups of colleagues. All this was plain enough.

Slightly more oblique instruction was available on some other points of conduct. We could freely teach and do research within reasonably broad limits, but activism was risky, and membership in at least one political organization—perhaps, then, others—was suicidal. By extension, to be a professional was to be nonpartisan, to abstain from historical agency. Practitioners of literary studies, like those in all fields, should stay within their own areas of expertise.

Not only professional interests but also safety argued for an investment in the autonomy of each field. (The chair of my department strongly discouraged me in 1954 from taking a course on the philosophy of literature: what would he have said to one on the political economy of culture had such a course—unimaginably—existed?) At the same time, each field of inquiry must somehow align itself with all the rest, in the national interest. At an abstract level, truth must be the handmaiden of loyalty. And of course one emphasis, in teaching and scholarship, did lie outside those broad limits of the thinkable: historical materialism.

Marxism disappeared from the academy; the tradition dried up. The handful of its adherents in the humanities—Gaylord Leroy, Robert Cohen, Norman Rudich, Paul Siegel, perhaps a dozen in all?—were isolated from each other, from interested students, from scholars in other fields (Paul Baran, at Stanford, was reputedly the only Marxist economist in any American university), from political allies and projects. Right across the humanities and social sciences, this exclusion shut down certain kinds of inquiry, posted "no trespassing" signs around some topics (notably class struggle), and sanitized others, such as exploitation and power. In English and neighboring fields, the loss was, if not more damaging, at least more peculiar in its consequences: it left us with our moral critique of bourgeois society from the standpoint of culture, while excising culture *from* bourgeois society, severing it from its real historical and social relations, and exempting it from historical critique, as history declined into "background," biography, influence studies, history of ideas, and the other maneuvers of sealed-off "literary" history. The exile of historical materialism, along with the confidence inspired by expansion and prosperity, also turned attention away from the conditions of our own cultural work and professional consolidation—away from our embeddedness in relations of class and power, not to mention race, gender, sexuality, and those other matters that had to be discovered or rediscovered from the late 1960s on.

The provincial flavor of this account is intended. Needless to say, historical materialism remained a working tradition in Europe and elsewhere through the 1950s, but literary studies in the United States paid little attention to Lukacs, Brecht, Goldmann, Adorno, the Marxian Sartre, even Left cultural critique from Britain— though we appropriated Richards, Eliot, and what was usable from Empson for the New Criticism, and Leavis had a small, embattled following. As Noam Chomsky notes (in this volume), American military and economic dominance fostered academic insularity and arrogance as well. The only continental European work I remember as "must" reading for us was Auerbach's *Mimesis*, mined for the brilliance of its formalism, with its history muted.

In the intellectual and institutional space demarcated by those cold war intimidations, by U.S. world domination, by the rewards proffered for disciplinarity and socialization, and by the benign neglect of literary studies in centers of power, an elaboration of structures and practices went forward that has by now been the subject of extensive analysis. I wrote about it at length myself, in the central chapters of *English in America* and will not reprise the discussion here, beyond saying that its main theme still seems apt, whatever amendments and corrections I would now make (see my 1995 introduction). That theme was the concealment and mystification of conflict, power, and privilege: literary theory and criticism, in the curriculum, in departments and professional organizations, in writing instruction, in pedagogy. Practitioners of English sang the beneficence of Culture in the abstract without taking account of the relations and institutions through which Culture circulates—without taking account of Culture's role in social reproduction and the hegemonic process, as I might have put it later. Literary studies played a small part in the Cold War, not by selling our unwanted expertise, not by perfecting the ideology of free world and evil empire, but by doing our best to take politics out of culture and by naturalizing the routines of social sorting.

Nonetheless, I want to reemphasize here, as I did not in *English in America*, the ways English defined itself in *opposition* to the social arrangements on the American side of the Cold War—though not of course in support of those on the Soviet side. I have mentioned the mild critique of commercial culture and the business ethos that we brought with us to graduate study or took in as a corollary of our dedication to high culture, and have suggested that New Criticism, with its defense of poetry over and against the language of science, encouraged or at least accommodated such a critique. So did the theories of Russian formalism, when, at first mainly through the presence and work of Roman Jakobson, they came into our ken and were grafted onto the New Criticism: literature as a special language or special use of language, one that lifted it from dull routine, estranged it, renewed its materiality, freshened consciousness. Those who embraced existentialism found another way to demote the categories of bourgeois morality, as did partisans of the modernist writers: ill-assorted and politically discrepant as they were, Eliot, Joyce, Woolf, Lawrence, Hemingway, Faulkner, Dos Passos, and so on all ranged themselves against industrial capitalism and counterposed something finer in the realm of avant-garde culture. Traditionalists in literary studies, who promoted the Great Books conception of the humanities and were often hostile to modernism, also deplored capitalist reality, though from the vantage point of the classical or Catholic or monarchist past.

Many but not all of these groups abstained, also, from nationalist fervor, and from U.S. triumphalism in particular. America was raw and philistine; Europe cared about culture. Anglophilia colored the outlook of many—unsurprisingly, when one recalls that "English" did chiefly mean English, for people in our field in the 1950s. American literature had barely gained academic recognition. (Graduate students at Harvard could "specialize" in American literature only by substituting it for the medieval period, as one of the five fields on which to be quizzed in our Ph.D. examinations.) To the extent that American culture *had* become a legitimate field of study, in English and in the few American studies programs of the time, the judgment of scholars was mixed: alongside preservationist and triumphalist efforts, influential studies by left liberals such as Leo Marx, Henry Nash Smith, and the less-easily classified Leslie Fiedler refused to whitewash American history, and allowed some non-elite voices to be heard, thus quietly heralding the "anti-American studies" of the 1960s and after. Of course, few of those

86

non-elite voices were female and virtually none were black, but oppositional undertones resonated; some younger people in English began listening to the Beats, and, by the end of the 1950s, to Norman Mailer on the "White Negro."

Hardly the making of a counterculture in English, and the skepticism among us toward the Cold War and the American project of development was entangled with complacencies of class, whiteness, and a still-unquestioned male supremacy. Furthermore, the spirit of vague alienation that permeated much of our training and work almost never spilled out into political activity, beyond voting Democratic. The exception, and an interesting one, was antinuclear work (I and a few in my cohort went on marches with the Committee for a Sane Nuclear Policy; a few were Quaker activists). It is worth remembering that for many of my age, graduate school was an alternative to the draft, and that those who chose the profession after Korean War service had gained little enthusiasm for cold war police actions. "Brinkmanship" scared us; the Cuban missile crisis was worse. An informal pacifism accorded with our allegiance to Culture. We were not a promising constituency for war on Vietnam.

This take on literary studies from the late 1940s to the early 1960s prepares the way for a particular story of what happened next. I have postulated a group of educational workers organized as a profession with a core ideology of redemptive Culture, beneficiary of vast expansion in the Cold War university, yet not specifically favored or assigned Cold War tasks as many other disciplines were, and pretty much left to work out its own practices, shape its own ethos. Though there was of course no possibility of its doing so independently of or in opposition to the hegemonic process, in a number of ways English and its neighbors imagined themselves as an alternative within the dominant. Yet, this dissent, which in any case rose more from residual than from emergent values, found no political expression outside the timid and self-promoting learned societies and professional organizations. How would such a group respond to provocations and shifts that fueled its dissent and invited political response?

Even before 1960, it became clearer that the national leadership viewed education not only as building human capital for economic growth, but also as a weapon in the Cold War. The challenge of Soviet technical and scientific development to U.S. domination after Sputnik (1957) turned anxious eyes toward the American public school system, found wanting in service to the national interest by influentials such as James Bryant Conant, in a 1959 Carnegie-sponsored study, *The American High School Today.* Congress passed a frankly named National Defense Education Act (NDEA) in 1958. Such pragmatic attentiveness caused no more than mild concern among humanists who had quite different goals for education, in part because the NDEA and other efforts of the State contributed to the growth and prosperity of higher education as well. But the NDEA also required recipients of scholarships to sign loyalty oaths and noncommunist affidavits. Faculties gagged on this intrusion, which stirred memories of loyalty oaths imposed on University of California faculty members in 1949 and of the McCarthy moment in general. Many faculties (including Wesleyan's) voted noncompliance, and the issue reawakened the possibility of contesting our relationship to the Cold War state.

The nascent civil rights movement also began to have a bracing effect. Little Rock, Montgomery, Greensboro, and other landmark confrontations brought the virulence of white supremacy and the courage of protesters inescapably to liberal consciousness. A handful of northern faculty members joined in the Freedom Rides; more joined in the Mississippi Freedom Summer, and marched in Selma. Through this period, as confidence in the supposedly widening inclusiveness of U.S. democracy grew less and less tenable, so did complacency about fairness and meritocracy in the university itself, enclave of urbane culture. Were not our students and faculty members virtually all white? Were we not practicing segregation by methods less subtle but no less invidious than those displayed on national television? Agitation for the recruitment and admission of black students arose in different quarters on many white campuses. At Wesleyan, mainly younger faculty members quarreled with a director of admissions who repeatedly assured us that no qualified black students were out there. Our critique, augmented by a convenient scandal, led to his dismissal, the appointment of a new admissions man, and the arrival of a visible and soon militant cohort of black students in the fall of 1965, only a year or two before parallel events forever changed most elite campuses.

Even most of those who had favored desegregation of our colleges expected black students to assimilate happily; but their admission turned out to be just the first stage of conflict and transformation. Civil rights, like the loyalty oath controversy, broke the membrane between national and university politics, and involved even the most reclusive faculty members in both. Battles over racism in the academy are too familiar to call for narration here. What bears commentary, in the frame of this analysis, is that pressure soon built on people in history and various fields in the humanities and arts, but especially in English, to examine critically and wholesale the very subject of our knowledge and instruction: literary culture. Most black and many white students wanted curricular acknowledgment that more than one black American (Ellison) had actually made literature worth reading and studying. In response, and out of progressive commitments deepened by the civil rights movement, Americanist faculty members and graduate students began an intense project of recovery and revaluation, the first stage of the canon wars. The PMLA bibliography for 1969 listed twenty articles by Americans on Richard Wright, more than the total for all the years from 1950 to 1968; production of scholarship on Wright continued thereafter at the 1969 rate. Even to speak of "the canon," as we soon came to do, was to grant its historical contingency and admit into our conversation questions of power and authority that had been muted or absent since the 1930s. New professional terrain, new rules of engagement: no such perturbations shook the foundations of other fields, not even American history.

To disrupt chronology for a moment, the women's movement, when it erupted first in oppositional political groups and then in the university, intensified the revisionist imperative in many fields.

Feminism was perhaps less easily contained in women's studies programs than African American insurgency was in black studies, and again, the challenge in English was more immediate and direct than elsewhere. Our students were disproportionately female; a fair number of women already held faculty positions, and many more were working on Ph.D.s—a critical mass for consciousness raising and academic strategizing; the canon included a few women writers, and hundreds of others, much read at one time or another, had been excluded; many women were prominent writers *in* the 1960s. The ingredients of a feminist literary and political culture were quickly catalyzed.

Professional consequences abounded. Courses on women writers proliferated; women's studies programs sprang up, along with a ferment of insurgent meetings, new discoveries and recoveries, curricular revisions, feminist journals, feminist book-publishing ventures. This movement deeply subverted the institution and ideology of literary studies. As feminists laid out the male bias of canonical works, recovered women's writing for study and criticism, and then placed gender high on the theoretical agenda, they made evident the "unmarked" male position from which the supposed universals of literature had been elaborated. Who could believe now in the autonomy of the artwork, the disinterestedness of the critic, all those denials that had underwritten our professional charter and our claim of exemption from the oppressions and injuries of bourgeois society? There was no ignoring feminism.

Energy flowed into English from 1960s movements, calling into question both the grounds of professional legitimacy and the terms of our pact with the larger society—understood to be philistine but roughly just, within the framework of liberal political belief. Other minority movements, gay liberation, environmentalism, the "counterculture," and especially the student power movement had similar consequences, but resistance to white and male supremacy most profoundly troubled our dogmatic slumbers. Vietnam linked up these disturbances in two ways that are critical for my argument.

First, it brought large numbers of us, including white males, into sharp criticism of, then protest against, then open conflict with the government of the United States. From grousing to writing letters to signing and then circulating petitions to joining teach-ins to turning in draft cards to refusing to pay taxes to supporting draft resistance to helping actual resisters and deserters: enough academics followed such trajectories to constitute a lively culture of activism. It brought many into organizations and organizing. I worked in campus and town antiwar groups, helped found RESIST and the Radical Caucus of MLA, joined the Students for a Democratic Society for a while, then the short-lived New University Conference, and endless ad hoc groups. To see oneself as an organizer, not to mention a criminal, was a far cry from defining oneself as a detached professional and bearer of cultural wisdom and solace. The antiwar movement also put thousands of academics in an adversarial relation to their own employers and to the leaders of their professional guilds.

Second, as opposition intensified, the accompanying analysis proceeded from picturing the war as a tragic error to understanding it as the natural extension of American anti-Communist policy—imperialism, as we soon called it. This change placed the rapidly growing New Left in direct opposition to the Cold War: not, to be sure, into alignment with the Soviet Union (only a tiny handful of New Left sectarians joined old left remnants there), but in sympathy with various other colonial and socialist revolutions and in strident opposition to the industrial-military complex. Furthermore, radical analysis from various quarters sought to unite critique of the war and militarism with critique of racism and patriarchy, of ecological depredations, of the bourgeois family, of the educational system in which we worked and studied. So, by the early 1970s, an encompassing oppositional analysis of capitalist social order itself circulated widely in and out of universities.

Opposition to the Vietnam War spread across liberal arts faculties and student bodies (by contrast with those in engineering, agriculture, business, and so on), but was not, I believe, concentrated especially in English and the humanities. However, as the analysis broadened to take on bourgeois society as a whole, it did find especially fertile ground in English. That was true in part because the analysis tried to embrace insights of the antiracist and women's movements, which had a powerful and enduring impact in English. And it was also true, I suggest, because, as argued earlier, English in the 1950s had already distanced itself— quietly and inactively—from the ethos of growth and consumption, as well as from the stupidities of official anticommunism. That disaffection metamorphosed rapidly into a more articulate and principled antagonism under pressure of 1960s movements and of deepening skepticism about the dependability of the liberal state whose benign embrace had seemed to promise laissez faire for us and civil liberties for all—a skepticism fueled by attack dogs, water hoses, billy clubs, wire taps, CIA domestic spying, police riots, dirty tricks, assassinations (Fred Hampton and so on), infiltrations, and other indecencies, not to mention fragmentation bombs, napalm, carpet bombing, "pacification," My Lai, and other manifestations of liberalism abroad.

Thus, many of the challenges posed by 1960s movements to the postwar consensus were taken up and developed in English and neighboring fields. No one there could any longer take for granted—that is, without encountering dissident views among close colleagues—that American society was relatively just and marching toward equality under the banner of its corporate leadership; that policy elites were trustworthy guides in international affairs; that the war machine was an instrument of democracy abroad; that the state security apparatus was promoting democracy at home; that capitalism itself was the handmaiden of democracy; or even that any regrettable shortcomings in these areas could be justified by Cold War urgencies—the implacable enmity of the evil empire and the peril of domestic communism. What held together pretty well as hegemony in the 1950s now took on the aspect of domination. Furthermore, as I have noted, English took 1960s challenges into its own internal discourse, putting in question such givens as the autonomy of literary works, the universality of the values attributed to them, and the permanent value of canonical works outside historical process. These debates translated over a few years into curricular initiatives perhaps more disruptive than any that had occurred since the discipline took shape around the beginning of the century.

Of course many opposed these changes, and no more than a tenth of people in literary studies, I imagine, subscribed to anything like the full critique of U.S. and international capitalism that accompanied them. But neither was this fraction isolated, or on all campuses embattled against conservatives. Bear in mind, as a measure of sentiment against the war, that MLA members at the 1968 convention elected Louis Kampf second vice president (i.e., president-to-be), and that a sizable majority of the members affirmed by mail-in ballot the resolutions passed at that turbulent meeting condemning the war as immoral and illegal and urging colleges and universities not to cooperate with the Selective Service system. Certainly a majority also endorsed the movement for racial justice (if not in its "black power" form), and came around eventually to support of women's rights and feminist academic projects. And certainly these sentiments were still more widespread among graduate students, who, in spite of the job market crash of 1969 and some clearly political denials of tenure, were working their way up in English departments. By the end of the 1970s, radicals and sympathetic liberals constituted a solid bloc of people in literature whose thinking, teaching, and institutional practice were informed by 1960s movements, and the effort to preserve and unify the insights of those movements.

I hope to have offered a plausible account of where English was located, institutionally and ideologically, in the first decade and a half of the Cold War; of how 1960s events shifted those bearings, provoked a harsh reassessment of disciplinary assumptions, and thus led to many changes in disciplinary practice; and of why the changes were more thoroughgoing and less reversible in English than in most other fields. If the account *is* plausible, it goes some way toward answering the question with which I began: How was the quiet enclave of 1950s English transformed into the site of 1990s culture wars? But not quite the whole way, because in the period traversed so far no concerted assault on English and cultural studies had yet been marshalled. To explore that development, I will turn to the aftermath of the 1960s convulsions, conceptualizing the whole cold war period for a while in terms of hegemony and resistance.[14]

In a working hegemony, power filters through innumerable laws, institutions, customs, daily routines, attitudes, and historically shaped desires, so that except to those directly under the heel of the police it feels less like domination than like what Gramsci called common sense. Power saturates experience, consciousness, and habitual relations with other people to the extent that inequality seems natural or entirely escapes notice. Within an hegemonic social process, education plays an important role. It helps reproduce inequality but does so in ways widely accepted as fair and inevitable. The ideals of equal opportunity and of merit rewarded have served well toward that end through long stretches of U.S. history. Though always over some dissent, these ideals have obscured the decisive advantages of family position and wealth, the differential access of young people to cultural capital and networks of privilege, the politics of tracking, and the operation of the hidden curriculum to discourage and demote those not adapted by birth and rearing to the culture of school.

The academic professions enter this process in obvious ways, benefiting from and advancing ideologies of merit, claiming privileges accordingly, helping sort out those who will and will not succeed, administering systems of knowledge and expertise in service to (though often critical of) ruling groups, and singing anthems of culture. Within a discipline, rituals and assumptions reproduce hierarchies and proclaim the legitimacy—the objectivity—of the ranking and sifting. When the hegemonic process is working smoothly, not only its main beneficiaries but also its victims see their life chances and trajectories as resulting from differences in individual ability, effort, choice, and luck.

But of course no hegemony stays automatically in place or unproblematically retains its semblance of common sense. As Raymond Williams put it:

> a lived hegemony...has continually to be renewed, recreated, defended, and modified. It is also continually resisted, limited,

altered, challenged by pressures not at all its own.... At any time, forms of alternative or directly oppositional politics and culture exist as significant elements in the society.[15]

Plainly, through the period covered here, the American hegemony, and beyond that the hegemonic order of world capitalism, lost its plausibility as common sense, as it was vigorously "resisted, limited, altered, challenged" by 1960s movements. And we have lived since in a time both of challenge and of a strenuous effort to renew, recreate, defend, and modify that hegemony.

Higher education is not the most critical terrain of contestation. Still, both left and right have thought it moderately consequential over these three decades. Sixties movements took root especially in universities, noisily disturbing the smugness of meritocratic ideology and bringing in previously excluded groups of students, with different needs and earnest demands. Comprehensive schemes of oppositional thought—ecological, feminist, Marxist—took root especially there. Challenges to the authority of high culture, to bourgeois political economy, to the exclusions of traditional history, to Eurocentrism, to male and heterosexist assumptions in many disciplines, and to power relations embedded in the whole educational institution and its pedagogies, amounted to a running battle over cultural capital.

As the university system expanded and took on new tasks through the postwar period, it became more vital than before to social reproduction, and a central locus, too, for the vastly expanded professional-managerial class, whose activities mediate and sustain the late capitalist social order in innumerable ways. Sixties eruptions showed that the loyalty of this class, particularly of its youth, is far from secure. So the questions of who might act as organic intellectuals of the professional managerial class and of what forms its cultural capital might assume have taken on a good deal of political significance—the more so in a time when the place one may hope to attain in the social hierarchy depends increasingly on access to education. Such considerations amply explain why those seeking to defend and recreate domestic hegemony have chosen to engage in combat over the practices and content of higher education, and concentrated their attack on English and the humanities, so distant from the practical work of capitalist accumulation and social control.

A number of skirmishes built toward the "PC" spasm that coincided with the end of the cold war. Although the efforts at conservative restoration itemized here emphasized school more than college, that very fact demonstrates the integrity of the Right's project, even as its leadership and tactics have changed.[16]

—Vocational education

Beginning about 1970, the Nixon administration and some allies began a campaign to promote "career" education, as they dishonestly if more palatably called it; Nixon's Commissioner of Education, Sidney P. Marland, put it at the center of his program. With backing from a Carnegie report and others, he advocated and supported tracking through secondary schools and community colleges to prepare students for the work they were likely to find, not the work toward which they might aspire. Vocationalism aimed also to forestall discontent by lowering expectations and by cutting back on liberal-arts work in schools and community colleges.

—Literacy crisis

In 1975, articles appeared in *Newsweek, Time,* the *New York Times,* the *Chicago Tribune,* the *Saturday Review, Reader's Digest,* and many other mainstream periodicals exploring—as the *Newsweek* cover story put it—"Why Johnny Can't Write." Academic authorities such as Jacques Barzun and A. Bartlett Giamatti, the head of the National Endowment for the Humanities (Ronald Berman), and a slew of pundits taught us that we were in the midst of a literacy crisis, instanced by falling SAT scores and even or especially by the inability of college students to write standard English and put forth simple arguments in coherent prose. Since there was no unambiguous evidence suggesting that anything so dramatic as a decline in literacy had in fact taken place, the outcry was remarkable. I am unaware of a conservative design to scare the public in this way, but some familiar conservative bogeys figured prominently among the many causes assigned to the purported decline: open admissions programs, 1960s indulgences such as

the free speech movement, popular culture, drugs, permissive-
ness, and so on.[17]

—Back to basics

In any case, the literacy "crisis" was accompanied and followed
by the usual spate of commissions and studies, and by concerted efforts to promote hard-line educational strategies
that would curtail liberal and critical tendencies and oblige
instructors to intensify drills in fundamentals of language.

—Excellence

In 1983, several highly publicized reports came out from the
National Commission on Excellence in Education, the
Education Commission of the States, the Twentieth Century
Fund, the National Science Board, and the College Board.
Two of their titles, A Nation at Risk and Action for Excellence,
defined the range of their concerns: our educational system was
sinking into mediocrity, and so endangering the future of our
society, a familiar cold war theme by now. The remedy this time
was not basic education but the boosting of higher-order skills,
especially scientific and technical, for those who would be competitive, and for the national interest. George Bush, the
"education president," gave a blunt justification for the
"Educational Excellence Act of 1989": "I believe that greater
educational achievement promotes sustained economic
growth, enhances the Nation's competitive position in world
markets, increases productivity, and leads to higher incomes
for everyone." The insistence on an economic rationale for
education flatly ignored not only the liberatory ideals of the
1960s and 1970s but also humanistic ideals that dominated
1950s thought on the subject.

—Cultural conservatism

By then, these efforts of the conservative restoration to make
schooling basic and economically functional had joined
uneasily with another project, one more centrally coordinated,
more openly ideological, and more combative. The New Right
identified its enemy from the start as people who had come out
of 1960s movements, gained (in the Right's view) dominance in
colleges and universities, and there orchestrated an assault on
core values of the free-enterprise system, the family,
Christianity, and Western civilization. The Heritage Foundation,

Free Congress Foundation, and other institutions founded and handsomely funded in the 1970s (by Coors, Olin, Bradley, and so on), attempted to advance a right-wing agenda in politics and the media, as well as in universities. The scandalized attention accorded to political correctness and multiculturalism from 1990 on has been a direct, intended, and largely successful outcome of this right-wing organizing.[18] Another was the elevation of William Bennett, Lynne Cheney, and other New Right leaders to key positions in cultural policy.

So in its New Right phase, hegemony was conceived in very different terms from those of the postwar consensus that the 1960s had undermined, and the Right took aim not only at higher education but also with surprising accuracy at English and cultural studies. Much that has changed in those areas since 1965 has indeed carried forward the momentum of 1960s movements and affronted those who identify the well-being of our society with the alliance of Western high culture, Christian values, and free-enterprise economics.

Just to mention Afro American studies, women's studies, cultural studies, Chicano studies, Native American studies, Asian American studies, and lesbian and gay studies is to name some outposts of those movements and demarcate a new understanding of what culture might deserve academic study and appreciation. As noted earlier, these enlargements of interest affected English more quickly than other fields, inaugurating a debate over the canon and cultural value that has occupied us for twenty-five years, convicting us in the Right's eyes of relativism or, worse, of sullen enmity toward Culture itself.

The genesis and role of "theory" in all this is a vexed question, but clearly the poststructuralisms that came forward in the 1960s and after answered to strategic and theoretical needs of some critical groups in universities, including feminist and gay and lesbian activists as well as scholars. Although conservative critics have often seemed to dismiss theory as foolish preening, a kind of academic speaking in tongues, many (e.g., Lynne Cheney) have also taken it on as a serious antagonist. And no wonder; though some in our profession have deployed the thought of Foucault, Barthes,

Derrida, Lacan, Cixous, and so on mainly to build reputations and harmlessly decenter meaning, poststructuralist theory has served others in the demystification of patriarchal and expert authority, and in the project of social constructionism, which has won academic ground well outside the precincts of literary study. All this is reasonably seen by the Right as a strong intellectual challenge to traditional hierarchies and cultural verities.

Equally vexed is the role of Marxism(s) in this redrafting of the academic agenda. Relatively few people in the humanities define themselves primarily as Marxists. These few have almost no allies in economics and political science, where a vigorous Marxism might connect to nonacademic political thought and to public policy. Still, it is more than an irritant to the Right that Marxism has regained influence and legitimacy even in a limited sphere, and that some terms of Marxist analysis—commodification, class, ideology, for instance—have lodged in the commonsense vocabulary of historical and cultural study.

In higher education as a whole, by contrast to English, the socialist and feminist Left amounts to a tiny minority (only five percent of faculty members place themselves on the "far Left"), and a weak counterhegemony. Yet, the Right accurately perceives that the academic wing of 1960s movements has over time redrawn the intellectual landscape. Look at English then and now: feminists, Marxists, and Foucauldians hold major professorships. Journals put out endless issues, and book publishers run series, on a range of concerns from postcoloniality to the politics of knowledge to popular music to the construction of sexualities that were hardly on the horizon in 1970. The annual program of the MLA gives space and legitimacy to similar inquiries, providing an array of sessions that each year provokes the risibility but also the rage of New Right commentators and their media followers. (An obscure special session on "Teaching the Political Conflicts," in which I spoke at the 1994 meeting, attracted the dour presences of both Hilton Kramer and Roger Kamball.) I conjecture that many students choosing graduate work do so in part because in English they have found an ethos hospitable to the ideal of social justice, and quite different from what they expect to find in law or business.

Nor has the teaching of writing eluded politicization. Composition may be the most conservative venue in English because its work must respond to perceived economic needs. But even in composition, progressive ideas and methods contend seriously for professional space in journals, at the meetings of the Conference on College Composition and Communication, and in many a writing program—as witness the repression brought smartly down on the founders of a composition course at Texas grounded in issues of social justice. When you look around at the English curriculum in the most generous sense—not only courses and requirements and majors, but also the questions embedded in the course of study, the ideas and perspectives that students are likely to encounter in and out of class, the things we tell them are worth their intellectual work, the very academic agenda—the curriculum has been deeply altered, and indeed politicized since 1965. That is why the Right pays English the courtesy of its bellicose attention.

It has been clear for quite a while that long before the Soviet empire began to quake, American capitalism too had run into a difficult patch. The trouble began to show—it had of course been brewing for longer—about 1970, the year the academic job market collapsed. National unemployment has never again dropped to anywhere near the level of 1969 (below 4 percent). Real wages, which had risen steadily since 1940, stalled for a few years after 1970 and then declined about 10 percent. The balance of trade went negative in 1975 and has gotten much worse. The dollar faded against stronger currencies from the early 1970s on. The federal debt began its notorious rise in the late 1970s; so did personal debt, with corporate debt following a few years later. Profits as a portion of national income sagged after 1968.

Capital was responding to these challenges in ways far-reaching enough to justify seeing the period since 1970 as one of transition to a different phase of capitalist development. A variety of labels have gained currency to name parts of it: globalization, finance capital, deindustrialization, the knowledge society, the "regime of flexible accumulation."[19] We have experienced a painful disloca- tion of the old industrial base; the torrent of financial and indus- trial bankruptcies; a merger frenzy of the 1980s; the 1987 crash and subsequent boom; the internationalization of production, so that even when one wants to "buy American" it is hard to know how; the evolution of a world financial system so intricate that almost nobody can understand it. Employers of all sorts have long been responding to these conditions by breaking up the rigidity of Fordist work regimes: flex-time, part-time, and temporary labor; subcontracting and out-sourcing; job sharing, etc.

Part of this is no news to those of us teaching English in the United States. More than people in other academic fields, we know firsthand the use of flexible labor: adjuncts, part-timers, moon- lighters, and an army of graduate students, paid at a national average of around $2,000 per course, usually with no benefits. In the mid-1960s over 90 percent of new humanities Ph.D.s had full- time, tenure-track appointments; in recent years the figure has hov- ered around 40 percent. The full-time job market has never regained its capacity to absorb new aspirants, and at this writing it is disastrous. In short, the conservative restoration has combined with a global economic shift to put extreme pressure on English as reconstituted after the insurgent 1960s. Furthermore, the old Sputnik rationale for strengthening American education and for deficit spending lost its force as the Cold War wound down.

The easiest way of responding to the "downsizing" imperative in English and in other fields that train Ph.D.s mainly for academic employment has been to continue overproducing them and ABDs by admitting more graduate students than the core labor market can possibly employ, and turning the unfortunate ones out into the peripheral market, thus haplessly following the script of flexible accumulation. The profession, however radicalized, is not well equipped to resist such developments. Organized as it is to regu- late careers and maintain hierarchies of status among practi- tioners and institutions, the profession is all but unable to act in solidarity with its most weakly positioned members. Throughout the years of job famine, top departments have gone right on competing for "stars," not only at entry level but also at the top.

Economies made possible by the reserve army outside our professional gates have not escaped the notice of administrations. One department I visited put each of its new M.A. students to work teaching two sections of composition per semester, and had a number of postdoctoral "fellows" teaching three courses per semester at meager salaries. Another, when I first visited, staffed its comp courses largely with experienced, full-time, decently paid, benefitted, but nontenure-track lecturers. By my second visit, two years later, these people had been fired and replaced with the usual cadre of part-timers, by order of the provost who said this campus had lagged behind the state system's "benchmark" for part-time employment. At my own relatively posh but financially straightened college, the English department used to hire a few part-timers to cover specific needs; now in any given year almost as many of them are on the roster as full-timers. The two-class system thus created—our own local version of peripheral and core labor—works to perpetuate the invidious opposition between literature and composition.

As the framework of global politics collapsed with the decline and disappearance of the Soviet Union, so did a durable structure of domestic ideology. Of what use now in galvanizing political emotion was the anti-Communism that had been the air we breathed for forty years and more? With domestic dissidence pried loose from any illusion of links to the evil empire, the task of restoring hegemony in the United States requires a new basis, a new organizing principle. With internal challenges to domination and privilege no longer graspable as tentacles of communist subversion, the Right and many not on the Right turn to an assault on social movements that have in fact grown more and more separate since 1970, when *the* movement began to lose what coherence it had, and many of its constituent groups veered toward identity politics or, worse, a politics of lifestyle. The Right has picked up on that change in the forms of dissidence, and has mounted one assault after another on entitlements won in the

1960s and 1970s: on affirmative action, women's rights, lesbian and gay rights, children's rights, workers' rights, welfare rights. We have seen a coordinated attack on multiculturalism and political correctness, specifically targeting colleges and universities, and with the crosshairs right on English.

"Universities have become saturated with politics," said Benno Schmidt. Lynne Cheney picked up the assertion on the first page of her final National Endowment for the Humanities report, *Telling the Truth*, and made it her theme. Meanwhile, the fundamentalist Right subsumes an older, class-based politics in the crusade for "family values," attacking much the same groups as Cheney, but from another flank. Yet, despite the forces arrayed against identity politics, with entitlements and affirmative action put under fire by the Right, and with the stakes raised by the pressure on schooling to track the young toward increasingly separate slots in core and peripheral labor, our existing social categories of difference remain explosive.

Black Americans and other groups seen as *racially* different continue to face repression, discrimination, and the hard choice whether to resist in separatist or integrationist terms; Afrocentrism and black Islam are insistent tendencies. Gay and lesbian people are finding more of a voice and forming more of a movement: queer politics, Queer Nation, and queer studies gain strength. Asian American studies appears alongside Afro American studies, Chicano studies, women's studies, postcolonial studies. All these movements overlap with and infiltrate English. Multiculturalism is still with us, and will be for some time. And I suppose that English, along with some of its academic neighbors, will continue in a gritty relation with strong political forces on the national scene.

Although I have concentrated on a chain of events that set English somewhat apart from other fields, the post–Cold War university as a whole has been under ideological pressure from the Right and severe economic constraint brought about by changes in global capitalism and cutbacks in public funding. More and more tasks of higher education are shifting to other sectors, while the university itself turns more to private sources of funding and so bends its efforts to the bidding of corporations. These developments are beyond the scope of this essay, but it seems plain that English has a lot of other company in this engagement, including those who will fight for public education at all levels.

Finally, I have suggested an obvious periodization of the cold war into three stages: postwar consensus from the beginning through the early 1960s; strong and open opposition through the rest of that decade and into the 1970s; a conservative restoration thereafter. That restoration, however, has not restored hegemony, or anything close to it, in or outside the university. In the turbulence ahead, English will not become once again a pastoral enclave.

Notes

1. I say "English" for simplicity. The range of my discussion will sometimes widen to include other literary studies, foreign- language instruction, American Studies, occasionally the humanities in general. I hope these expansions and contractions of scope will not confuse.

2. William H. Epstein, "Counter-Intelligence: Cold-War Criticism and Eighteenth-Century Studies," *English Literary History* 57 (1990).

3. See Robin W. Winks, *Cloak and Gown, 1939–1961; Scholars in the Secret War* (New York: William Morrow, 1987) 495–97.

4. If scholars belong to "any movement, organization, group which does their thinking for them… they get no help from us. Without qualification, we know that this condition of un-freedom of mind includes all those who have membership in the Communist Party…." (*1951 and 1952 Reports of the Secretary and the Treasurer*, 15). Thanks to G. Thomas Tanselle of the John Simon Guggenheim

Memorial Foundation for sending me these reports.

5. Who were "we"? I am drawing on memories of my graduate school cohort and teachers at Harvard through most of the 1950s and my colleagues at Wesleyan in the early 1960s, as well as of scholarly and professional talk at meetings and in journals. My contemporaries who apprenticed in other venues will have to judge how well my memories match theirs.

6. I quote my *English in America: A Radical View of the Profession* (New York: Oxford Univ. Press, 1976; republished, with a new introduction, by Wesleyan University Press, 1995), 75; the quoted phrases not from Richards are from Brooks's *The Well Wrought Urn*. Throughout this section on the New Criticism, I paraphrase my argument of twenty years ago.

7. Women didn't figure much in the making or propagation of these ideas, but it may be worth noting that actual women were beginning to enter the profession: only about

one-fifth of each new graduate class at Harvard/Radcliffe, but then there were virtually *no* women coming into science, the harder social sciences, law, medicine, business. Their presence in English, along with that of gay men (of whom there was a lively subculture at Harvard, some all but "out") and indeed that of many Jews, may have contributed subliminally to our sense of apartness from business and government elites.

8. Ellen Schrecker, *No Ivory Tower: McCarthyism and the Universities* (New York: Oxford Univ. Press, 1986).
9. Ibid., 267–68
10. Ibid., 188–89
11. Ibid., 189–90
12. See *English in America*, 45–47
13. Schrecker, *Ivory Tower*, 189.
14. Here I condense an argument made in my "Introduction to the 1995 Edition" of *English in America*, and in my "English After the USSR," Christopher Newfield and Ronald Strickland, eds., *After Political Correctness: The Humanities and Society in the 1990s* (Boulder, Col: Westview Press, 1995).
15. Raymond Williams, *Marxism and Literature* (Oxford: Oxford Univ. Press, 1977), 112–13.
16. I take the phrase "conservative restoration" from the subtitle of Ira Shor's *Culture Wars: School and Society in the Conservative Restoration, 1969–1984* (Boston: Routledge and Kegan Paul, 1986), an excellent account that has helped me organize my thoughts on this subject.
17. See my essay, "The Strange Case of Our Vanishing Literacy," in Richard Ohmann, *Politics of Letters* (Middletown, Conn.: Wesleyan Univ. Press, 1987), 230–35.

18. This story is told in splendid if revolting detail by Ellen Messer-Davidow, "Manufacturing the Attack on Liberalized Higher Education," *Social Text* 36 (fall 1993), 40–80.
19. David Harvey so names it in *The Condition of Postmodernity: An Enquiry Into the Origins of Cultural Change* (Oxford, U.K.: Basil Blackwell, 1989), which has influenced my analysis here.

(**Laura Nader**[1])

The Phantom Factor: Impact of the Cold War on Anthropology

Introduction

This is a story about the impact of the Cold War on anthropology. It unfolds from a collection of variegated and entangled people and stories: the House Hearings on Un-American Activities, the University of California loyalty oath, the Human Relations Area Files (HRAF), the evolution of the Office of Strategic Services (OSS) to the Central Intelligence Agency (CIA) after World War II, self-censorship and fear in the universities, resistance to the Vietnam War, counterinsurgency and the Camelot Project, the Thai affair, radar stations in Canada, nuclear power and the University of California weapons labs, and anthropologists and the people anthropologists study—Native Americans, Guatemalans, Eskimos, Pacific Islanders, Yanomani. This story is about research topics eliminated, area courses not covered, area specialists not hired, about a network of collegial relations relatively invisible to the naive or excluded, about the numerical expansion of anthropologists. It is about the outlawing of leftist discourse, the invention of a discourse of indirection, a valuation of order, the threat of democracy in action. It is about generational oppositions, positivism versus interpretivism, about archaeology, and biological and social-cultural anthropology, about Cold War technologies that revolutionized methods, and about people and professional associations torn asunder. This story is about us, one not written about in history of anthropology texts, which only rarely discuss external factors in the making of anthropology. The wider story is about Sputnik and research funding, jobs and academic freedom, ordinary people and extraordinary evil. I call it the Phantom Factor.

It is difficult to write an ethnography of anthropology. In this, my colleagues have humbled me—as they have talked about how the Cold War had an impact on *their* anthropology. It was a prismatic experience, one person noted—kaleidoscopic actually. For each of the ten colleagues that spoke in my 1994 seminar about the Cold War and anthropology, the experiences have been different and for a multitude of reasons—age, place of graduate training, area experiences, personal life history. Only varieties of experience can hope to illuminate the Phantom Factor—the missing links that have yet to be elucidated.

Personal accounts can point the way. My colleague, Elizabeth Colson, experienced the Cold War in Africa, England, and in the United States during a time when if you were pro-civil rights you were considered pro-Communist, a position that merged pro-Communist with the non-Communist Left. She spoke of colleagues who resisted self-censorship on nuclear policies, on Cuba, on Vietnam, only to be denied full academic privileges. Nelson Graburn spoke about the Cold War from Canada, in northern locales spotted with missile detection stations, well before the small band of Canadian and American anthropologists were sought out for work on the Indian and Eskimo north, a security area. He reminded us that social scientists in Canada were more activist than their U.S. counterparts, more like the Europeans. Sherwood Washburn began his story in 1936 off the coast of Thailand when the Japanese attempted to bomb his boat but missed. He spoke mainly about race and tests used to *establish* racial biases, and about military funding during the Cold War that carried with it priorities about hierarchy. Herbert Phillips spoke of Thailand and counterinsurgency accusations, ethics, scholarly independence, the interlinking of private foundations with the U.S. government, and our professional association; while Gerald Berreman, whose experiences had taken him to the Deep South as well as to India, spoke extensively about race and inequality, about the loyalty oath, about the Vietnam War, and about sabotage in response to his candidacy for president of the American Anthropology Association (AAA).[2] James Anderson raised concerns about ecology and the antimaterialist aspects of inward interpretivist ideologies, and about militarized development. After David Szanton introduced us to an intellectual history of Southeast Asian area studies at the Social Science Research Council (SSRC) over a thirty-year period, Paul Rabinow and Sherry Ortner illustrated what Vietnam and civil rights meant for them as Chicago graduate students who sought refuge in their generational opposition to positivist science, in favor of interpretive anthropology. At the end of the seminar John Gumperz brought home the manner in which area studies, originally funded for military purpose, affected how we conduct linguistic anthropology, and along with Gerald Berreman, detailed how counterinsurgency, which assumes dissent *is* insurgency implying violent insurgency, works on our own U.S. populations.

But what follows is my story, a limited story covering my experience since the 1950s, enlightened by my Berkeley colleagues, informed by my own participation. What interests me are the events that led me to discover the mechanisms whereby the Cold War had an impact on funding, dissent, academic freedom, nuclear power, weapons labs, area specialties, research tools, and more generally how we anthropologists study what we study. In the final analysis, I am led to think about the unique effects of the Cold War in light of the proposition that repressive and fear-generating events such as the cold war periodically appear in the history of American universities, thereby facilitating industrial and military regulation of academic affairs—and in the case of anthropology, the absence of autonomy over the direction, content, and style of the field.

From Harvard to Berkeley: From Invisible to Visible Power Networks

By the time I attended graduate school at Harvard University in the early 1950s, the Cold War was well underway. Soviet troops had blockaded West Berlin in 1948, which survived by supplies dropped by U.S. planes; Moscow had a stranglehold on Eastern Europe. World War III was thought to be only a matter of time. Already, U.S. nuclear weapons were believed by many to be essential to a military balance of power with the Soviet Union. Political opportunism and public fear stimulated charges of being Red, Pink, or "soft on Communism," just as it had in 1919 after World War I. As if the Soviet atomic bomb and the existence of Red China were not enough, the psychodrama of purging the "Red Menace" accelerated when North Korean troops stormed across the 38th parallel in 1950. The belief quickly spread that Moscow sought to dominate the world, and the only way to stop Soviet nuclear destruction was by means of nuclear deterrence. As we know, there were disbelievers.

At Harvard, the search for Communist infiltrators and spies was whispered about in every corridor.[3] The House Un-American Activities Committee (HUAC), encouraged by the activities of Senator Joseph McCarthy, had already targeted Alger Hiss, a Harvard Law School graduate, East Coast liberal, upper-class lawyer, and New Deal aristocrat; subversives were to be found in the top echelons. The then-presiding president of Harvard, James B. Conant, first expressed fears about the dangers of witch-hunts spreading to academia, only to move to a position he had previously resisted—the banning of Communists from the teaching profession. Debates over universal military service were ongoing with the complete takeover of China by the Communists in 1949 and China's intervention in Korea. It was a time of deep pessimism and concern in the university. The "military-industrial complex" was real, but it did not mobilize graduate student resistance.

The issues for Harvard were those of President Conant: the Red Scare and academic freedom, the military and classified research, fantasies of nuclear war and nuclear peace, and, in particular, what was happening to science as scientists were lured into military- and government-funded projects. He also worried about what was happening to social reformers suspected by reactionary red baiters who easily equated Communist and leftist New Dealers. Fear spread throughout the university system. The Senate Subcommittee to investigate the administration of the Internal Security Act held hearings in 1952 on communist influence in New York City schools and colleges. Gene Weltfish, a Columbia University anthropologist, was called as a former member of the Communist Party. In 1956, a congressional committee holding hearings on arms control, nuclear weapons, and civil defense called on another anthropologist, E.A. Hoebel.

In 1950, the Regents of the University of California added the loyalty oath to the employment contract. The university was ripped apart: faculty were fired, while others simply left. The heart of the loyalty oath document brings to our attention that there are enemies of the United States, that they are *here and abroad*—foreign and domestic enemies are equated. In this context dissident voices were branded as seditious, thereby encouraging a culture of false patriotism and conformity, a society where independence of thought and action are frowned upon.

But the McCarthyites, a small part of a wider antileftist movement, ostensibly had it in for Harvard—where America's youth were vulnerable to indoctrination and use of the Fifth Amendment.[4] At Harvard and elsewhere faculty were called before the HUAC. Harvard waffled on a number of issues, but held the line on banning classified research, while insisting publicly that regardless of its views, faculty were to be judged on the quality of scholarly work. The effect of the Cold War as a state of permanent emergency and Constant readiness of a national security state to defend civilization from "naked aggression" by powerful Communist forces left students marked. We students of the 1950s were dubbed "the silent generation"—conformist, cautious, passive, paralyzed. President Conant summarized the situation at Harvard when he noted that "student morale is pretty well gone to pot."[5]

The same decade also militarized more of American science, and anthropology was part of that science. After Sputnik, defense research was at the top of the national science agenda. The National Science Foundation (NSF) emerged along with the debate over whether it should have a national defense label so as to get more appropriations and personnel. Academics were rightly worried about the domination of scholarship by federal monies, and also about being tainted.

Stories concerning the erosion of the academy came out bit by bit in anthropology. The linguist anthropologist Maurice Swadesh could not find a job and eventually relocated to Mexico. According to Elizabeth Colson, Kathleen Gough was considered an embarrassment to Brandeis and not promoted because, according to university officials, she was a bad teacher. Knowing Gough to be an excellent teacher, Elizabeth Colson resigned from Brandeis. Gough and her husband, David Aberle, moved west from Brandeis and later to Canada.[6] Paul Radin, Marc Borofsky, and Jack Harris were other target cases. McCarthyism was not confined to the United States. In England, following years of army service and employment on the Tanganyika Groundnut Scheme in Africa, Peter Worsley was banned from British colonies by intelligence services and later was refused entry to New Guinea by the Australian colonial authorities. Worsley was forced out of anthropology.

Although Conant discouraged classified research at Harvard, he encouraged his faculty to participate in the cold war research effort. The Russian Research Center was founded in 1947 with an initial grant from the Carnegie Corporation and the blessings of the U.S. State Department, the military, and the newly created CIA —a fruitful collaboration between the intelligence agencies and Harvard.[7] The center had as its director, veteran OSS anthropologist Clyde Kluckhohn, whose World War II experience involved analyzing Japanese cultures at a distance. The center was to satisfy the requirements of open scholarship and covert government needs by exploring Soviet culture and its military. But the center, which symbolized the growing web connecting government and the university, was a test to peacetime academic freedom that failed, and final proof that the university was not autonomous but indentured.[8] Political interests interpenetrated scientific research. Involved social scientists included Talcott Parsons, Sam Stouffer, Jerome Bruner, and Kluckhohn. Nearby, Project Troy, a secret study headquartered at Massachusetts Institute of Technology (MIT)explored how the U.S. government could use communications technology to penetrate the Iron Curtain, then expanded to research on political and psychological warfare.

For a young graduate student such as myself, *the structures of power were invisible.* Clyde Kluckhohn was my advisor. I knew that Kluckhohn had close ties to the State Department; his oss work was less known, yet all of us had read Kluckhohn's 1949 book, *Mirror for Man*,[9] hardly a reactionary document. His chapter, "An Anthropologist Looks at the United States," was a critique of the nature of our social and political system, and his dedication to the rights of native peoples was openly discussed. World War II activities had involved "patriotic" anthropologists working in the war effort; however, wartime networks merged into a Cold War period that was something of another character. An ideology of freedom versus totalitarianism created Cold Warrior academics, such as Kluckhohn, academics who acquiesced to external funding authorities. Kluckhohn agreed to political firing and to censorship of his own scientific work, while providing cover for clandestine activities. He was startled when I quoted my father—"Those who fund can determine what you study, and what you find, tax free." Kluckhohn resigned from the Russian Research Center in 1954. I never heard why he resigned and he never spoke of his resignation. No other anthropologist subsequently joined the center.

Earlier, anthropologists had done "good"—writing the document for MacArthur's entrance into Japan, sharing ethnographic knowledge about the Pacific Islands of the war zone (Ward Goodenough), producing studies of national character.[10] Anthropologists had worked in Japanese war relocation camps. This much I knew. After the war, many continued to serve the national security state such as in the work of the Harvard Russian Research Center or in new projects devoted to another purpose:

the containment of Communism, work sometimes described as development, sometimes as counterinsurgency. We were not assigned readings on such subjects, and as a profession we barely spoke openly about ethics in the way that Franz Boas at Columbia University had in the period prior to World War II.

At Harvard, a group of anthropology students (all older than I)—Alice Dewey, Clifford Geertz, Hildred Geertz, and Bob Jay-joined a group of new nation builder economists at MIT to work on an ambitious Ford Foundation project in Indonesia, a country that was considered vulnerable to takeover by Communism. All of this I recall was in the background, not in class, not at student meetings, not at parties—maybe on the Peabody Museum steps. The foreground was to come later, but the issues for anthropology were all there in the 1950s: academic freedom and academic fear, temptation, the funding carrot, red baiting and the McCarthy repression, nuclear power uses for war or peace, and concern for those we study. It was as if we lived in a fog; we saw such happenings as extraneous to the study of anthropology. We had bought into the notion of an uncontaminated sample. Suddenly, the picture changed.

In the 1960s, when the U.S.–Soviet Cold War turned into a "hot" war in Indochina, when civil rights unrest and protests against the military draft erupted in the United States, university students and faculty publically mobilized against the specific ways in which anthropology was being used. Those were the years of emerging introspection, and although self-assessment had already begun in the colonialist period, earlier than the Cold War in most parts of the world, most of us were politically naive or ideologically "caught." The 1960s were years of betrayal and outrage, soul searching about the persecution of innocent family members, vociferous university meetings, the gassings at Berkeley, and the omnipresence of the police. How could we respond as anthropologists and as citizens. Is there any difference? Should we take money from the government for our research? With Vietnam, what was in the background came to the fore—the brutality of ideological infection by the national security state. As Marshall Sahlins said in 1965: "Advanced anti-communism trades places with the enemy."[11]

The disturbing question repeatedly asked by younger anthropology professors like Jack Stauder at Harvard was: "To whom has anthropological work been relevant?"[12] Critics returned to classic monographs such as Evans Pritchard's *The Nuer*, whose research was financed by the colonial government of the Anglo-Egyptian Sudan.[13] Evans Pritchard did not describe the British war against the Nuer, less the nature of British colonial policy. His work was relevant to a peaceful domination, which relied on knowledge about native peoples. Social anthropology was the handmaiden of colonialism, a role documented by Lucy Mair in her survey of the practical contributions British anthropologists made to colonial administration and economic "development" from 1943 to 1960.[14] Slowly I became aware that most social anthropology research in the colonies was not only financed by the British government, but also by the Carnegie Corporation, the Rockefeller Foundation, the Rhodes Trust, and others who had financial and mineral interests in Africa.

Controversy over firing was fierce. Jack Stauder, an anthropologist who had degrees from Harvard, and from Cambridge University, and who had completed original work in Ethiopia on subsistence and environment, was fired, then rehired by Harvard, then finally his contract was not renewed. He was banned from teaching the fall semester after the student strike in spring 1969, and suffered the loss of salary in these transitions. The fact that his contract was not renewed was undoubtedly related to difficulties in finding employment during a time when the university had become the object of CIA activity. Stauder became an activist lost to scholarship because he analyzed the meaning of anthropology under imperialism, a contribution later generations of anthropologists too easily forgot.

It should be said that many anthropologists whose work we were reading probably thought of themselves as doing work that was scholarly rather than aiding practical problems of administration or economic development. Although harmony of interest between ruler and ruled was assumed by some, the exceptions were white liberal reformers who were—as with British-trained

Max Gluckman, Ian Cunnison, and A.L. Epstein—thought to be enough of a threat to be denied visas to sensitive areas in Africa such as the Copperbelt, the Sudan, or New Guinea. Actually Gluckman's troubles started when he was in his late twenties. Historian Hugh Macmillan reconstructed the tales of Gluckman, the Zulu Nation, and anthropological theory, and what it will take to understand the way in which colonialism, racism, Communism, Marxism, structural functionalism, and the Cold War form a whole picture.[15] Gluckman's landmark *Analysis of a Social Situation in Modern Zululand* was a contribution to ethnic theory and political practice.[16] According to Macmillan, "Gluckman noted the tendency of the South African government to attribute occasional outbreaks of violent African resistance to 'communist' influence." But Gluckman himself was criticized for his methods of dealing with natives, for his sympathies for them, for his Communist affiliations, and for his analysis of the intersection of Zulu and European social systems as they fit into the world capitalist system. Macmillan continues: "There can be no doubt that it was the fear of such accusations which inhibited the academic pursuit in South Africa of many of Gluckman's themes."[17]

Race and resources were volatile issues. Some anthropologists of the colonial era were writing about their native informants in progressive terms—by stressing common rational humanity and social coherence. Much the same was true elsewhere. Anthropology in the New World was also funded to help facilitate the administration of Native Americans, most recently peoples who worked the uranium mines that fueled nuclear technologies, and who, currently are targets for nuclear waste burial sites. My teaching and research on alternative dispute resolution is necessarily interwoven with new instances of persuasion by U.S. government officials.

The effect on aboriginal peoples of the exploitation of uranium reserves and the destruction of Indian lands is found in 1960s headlines on Brazil or Venezuela: "Uranium Discovery Threatens Yanomani Tribe"; or in Saskatchewan, Canada: "Save Wollaston Lake—Leave Uranium in the Ground." People were forced off the land and into dangerous work in the mines. The high capital cost of jobs at uranium mines generated little income for native peoples. For the white man's corporations it was a lucrative business. The Canadian north was almost entirely dependent upon foreign-owned uranium developments for the nuclear industry. The discipline's problems were inseparable from what was happening to "our informants." Our access to these cultures was closing. By 1995, hardly an Indian reservation existed in the more than 1,000 reservations in the United States and Canada where an anthropologist could do fieldwork without formal application to native authorities.[18]

Neocolonialism replaced older varieties of colonialism, with the United States as leading power—in Vietnam, Guatemala, Chile, Dominican Republic, Bay of Pigs, and at home. In 1954, the CIA toppled an elected leftist government in Guatemala, leading to decades of turmoil and the genocide of tens of thousands of native peoples and the displacement of thousands more. Academic research began to focus on colonialism, but concepts of neocolonialism or U.S. imperialism were aggregated and presented as communist propaganda. Appeals to anti-Communist propaganda obfuscated the reality of U.S. imperialism in Latin America and Southeast Asia. In Ralph L. Beals's *Politics of Social Research*, the phrasing is smooth:

> The growth in U.S. power and wealth and its global
> foreign policies have led, not without some justification,
> to identi-fication of this country with imperialism and
> neo-colonialism. That these terms are the creation of doctri-
> naire communist propagandists...should not lead us to
> ignore their partial basis in fact or the extent to which they
> influence opinion abroad.[19]

The realities of American interests abroad had yet to be faced by anthropologists, when our policies adumbrated the end of the uninvited ethnographer, or even when anthropologists were killed while doing their work in Guatemala or earlier in Indonesia. There is little room for disgust and outrage in the American university. The university buries emotions, and faculty look for "balanced" opinions. Critical anthropologists documented numbers of anthropologists who joined with other social scientists in employment and projects funded by governmental and nongovernmental bodies. Anthropologists worked for the Agency for International Development (AID), the CIA, the Defense Department's Advanced Research Projects Agency (ARPA), the Center for Research in Social System (CRESS) (formerly the Special Operation Research Organization or SORO), and other government research agencies. In addition, private research corporations such as Arthur D. Little and the Atlantic Research Corporation specialized in classified government research. Classified projects were sometimes found in the *Congressional Record* under project titles such as Rural Village Systems, Republic of Vietnam, Thai-Mal Village Study (Project Agile), and more specifically research interest in minority group areas of Thailand. Sometimes such research followed anti-American rioting, as in Panama or the Sudan. What I call the Phantom Factor, Jack Stauder referred to as "hidden anthropology," an anthropology that, to this day, is *still* virtually undocumented and unstudied except for a spate of writings on anthropology and ethics during the Cold War period and reevaluation afterwards.[20] From what we do know, it is clear that anthropology was considered useful in the construction of major world events. Otherwise, critics asked, why would the U.S. government and U.S. corporations pay for such knowledge?

The Ford Foundation set out "to provide assistance...in designing research so as to be useful to government and business," and to this end gave $138 million from 1952 to 1964.[21] Tom Fallers was the consulting anthropologist. The joint MIT-Harvard project, The Cambridge Project (CAM), was financed by the Defense Department's ARPA to develop a sophisticated set of computer programming techniques to enable the use of masses of social-science data on the peoples of the world. The HRAF was a similar information retrieval system used during World War II by a navy unit working in Micronesia. Questions such as under what conditions do peasants revolt, or information on conditions of stability were used in managing people as if they were isolated and autonomous actors independent of foreign government interference and international business interests.

Project Camelot, one of the more blatant counterinsurgency research efforts in the 1960s, was a baptismal experience. The letter of recruitment read: "The U.S. Army has an important mission in the positive and constructive aspects of nation-building in less developed countries as well as responsibility to assist friendly governments in dealing with active insurgency problems."[22] For the U.S. Army the purpose of counterinsurgency movements was to eliminate the means used by people to resist oppression, in this case totalitarian oppression.

Project Camelot never got off the ground, but less visible counterinsurgency projects moved ahead, and some anthropologists cooperated. They did so for a variety of reasons, which included "doing good," patriotism, desire for money and power, awe, and the desire to prove the "worth" of social science. Others summarized the participation as due to "naiveté, carelessness, callousness, stupidity, or some culpable defect."[23] Many participated wittingly, although the majority of anthropologists maintained an arm's-length relationship with the Department of Defense, the CIA, and like groups. On the other hand, the National Institutes of Mental Health (NIMH), the National Institutes of Health (NIH), the NSF, the Ford Foundation, the SSRC, the American Council of Learned Societies (ACLS), and other funding agencies were regarded as less compromising or at least not classified—an illusion of free and open funding based on the presence of anthropologists on panels that decide grants and fellowships. As evidence that having an anthropologist on board need not ensure free and unfiltered funding, earlier unself-conscious statements were publicized, such as the following from the Ford Foundation's African Research Group: "In an age of complex organization and multinational operations, no empire can contain conflicts or manage change without collecting, analyzing, and acting upon detailed information about states and people."[24]

Stauder was articulate in arguing against the illusion:

anthropology, as an institutional activity, is not autonomous and not unrelated to other institutions of our social system....
[It is] dependent for its support on the dominant institutions of

> our society (the federal government, the large corporations and the large private foundations); anthropology is expected to serve the interests that control these and the universities. As these interests extend to foreign countries, anthropological research on foreign people can provide...knowledge.[25]

Stander continues that insofar as anthropologists see the U.S. government, corporations, and foundations as "promoting genuine and beneficial social change, democracy, freedom, economic development, etc.," they will not hesitate to serve. Therein lies the rub. Many Americans deny the history of U.S. imperialism or corporate politics; other anthropologists are aware of the contradictions of our work, and we are troubled knowing that our work has been used for harmful purposes.

Government-funded projects for counterinsurgency were only part of the picture. Domestically, the relationship between power and discourse in the American academy also took the form of state intervention in the classroom.[26] As indicated earlier, there were "subversive" organizations and "subversive" persons ineligible for federal and state employment. There was direct questioning of individuals about the content of classroom lectures. Ex-Communists named names; anthropologist Karl August Wittfogel testified before the House in the 1950s that members of a student study group at Columbia were Communist. Hundreds of teachers lost their jobs, many left the country; some committed suicide.

Not surprisingly, in the *Selected Papers from the American Anthropologist* from 1946 through 1970, there is not a single citation of Karl Marx. Ashraf Ghani quotes the late Morton Fried as saying: "Very definitely there were many anthropologists, many scholars at that time, who wouldn't write what they really thought, because they were horrified by the thought of what might be made of what they said."[27] Karl Polanyi had to work under conditions of censorship, for his wife, once a Communist, was not allowed to enter America. Ghani noted that Polanyi's claim that the validity of economic theory is limited to the analysis of the society that has produced it was part of an investigation to which Marx's analysis of money would have been central. He concludes:

Had the times been suitable, Polanyi could have channeled
the interests of anthropologists into...a fruitful anthropological
confrontation with Marx. Censorship not only forces the
suppression of connections. It suppresses the very asking
of some questions.[28]

On the other hand repression also stimulates the asking of
questions. Eric Wolf's book, *Peasant Wars of the Twentieth Century*,
originated from a paper on Vietnam, which Wolf presented in the
1960s during one of the "teach-ins" on the University of Michigan
campus.[29] Ironically, *Peasant Wars* was not only read by anthropologists but also used as a handbook by Americans involved in developing strategies for counterinsurgency, and later even turned into
a comic strip by a guerrilla press in Peru. *Peasant Wars* was about
peasants in six major upheavals in the twentieth century: Mexico,
Russia, China, Vietnam, Algeria, and Cuba. Wolf concluded that
peasants are more likely to rebel when they both have something
to lose and have the means to mobilize. "Tactical power" was key
to understanding the revolutionary orientation—the most conservative segment of rural populations can develop effective resistance to the old order. These conclusions, which proved useful to
counterinsurgency development, were hardly Wolf's intent, as can
be documented by the battles over counterinsurgency fought out in
anthropology's professional association.

Crossfire at the American
Anthropological Association

What happened at the AAA now seems very remote for colleagues
who have no scars. But such was not true for everybody. A reading
of the AAA *Newsletter* from 1961 would capture the debates and
agonizing realities of what Dutch anthropologist Anton Blok refers
to as the "naive involvement of American anthropologists in the
war in Southeast Asia.[30] But one would have to be an anthropologist to read between the lines of the discussions of ethics and
morality, or to talk to those deeply scarred to hit a raw nerve in
1995. The innocence of anthropology was lost even before the
crossfire began, and so was the unity of professional anthropology.

Ten years after the *New York Review of Books,* publication of "Anthropology on the War Path in Thailand," Wolf had this to say:

> Yes, they had a lasting effect, because they scared the day-
> lights out of people. It was like raising Genii. Only it dest-
> royed, I am sorry to say, a sense of belonging to the same
> church. All of these co-religionists used to come to the
> meetings and get drunk happily. Suddenly they had to cope
> with these things. I suspect it's in part responsible for driving
> a lot of anthropologists back to trivia, because one can feel
> comfortable with trivia.[31]

Trivia was not what captured the AAA in the decade of the 1960s and early 1970s. It was a struggle with realities—the threat of nuclear war or nuclear holocaust. The 1960s began with a call by Margaret Mead (herself fraught with contradiction in relation to the military goals of her country) for the discipline to involve itself in the alleviation of world crisis by a science of human survival.[32] The resolutions on war and race came together. There was wide-spread interest in a fuller use of anthropology in the pursuit of peace (the Peace Corps had recently started) and civil rights. Some argued about the ethical problems involved in participation as a scientist in political-action groups. Yet, I thought the ethical prob-lems were about silence among scientists.

In 1964–65, the issue of anthropologists being recruited for work in counterinsurgency exploded. Some of us participated in the public unveiling of Project Camelot; I wrote an early warning letter to a member of the executive board outlining consequences of such activity. The unveiling of Project Camelot was followed by a move to develop guidelines on research and ethics for anthropologists, cul-minating with the Thai affair, the multipurposes of modernization and development projects, the role of the AAA for studying the use of defoliants in Vietnam, and the move by the executive board in 1972 to establish a committee on harmful research. Finally, there came the dissolution of the AAA as we had known it—an associa-tion for the whole of anthropology rather than its subdivided spe-cialties. Holism was what distinguished anthropology as a discipline, but integrated perspectives (as the Gluckman example illustrated) are rarely befriended by repressive forces. Some high-lights are relevant to my story.

The containment of communism was to be handled through multipronged projects of which modernization/development was only one tool of U.S. military power. Containment was based on a notion of linear evolution, the parts of which included intervention and stability following periods of destabilizing efforts, efforts which were only one of many strategies that involved the United States in Southeast Asia. Anthropologists such as Clifford Geertz accepted the basic assumption of stability and development; there was no cri-tique in his work. The disastrous view of a "balance of instabilities" also recognized that repressive governments in the area could con-tain Communist expansion; the United States was making sure by backing authoritarian regimes and leaving democratic development for the future when we had rid ourselves of the Communist threat.

U.S. government interest in academic social science research did not begin with American involvement in the Vietnam War; it had increased since World War II. At Yale, the Institute of Human Relations and its Cross Cultural Survey collected anthropological data on Pacific Islanders for use by the army and navy. These files became the HRAF. The Office of Naval Research (ONR) also sup-ported social science research before the NSF came into being. But it was the Kennedy administration that pushed the effort to use social science know-how in an effort to contain the Communist threat by countering insurgency, which included behavior ranging from violent and organized rebellion to lesser resistance. Presidents Johnson and Nixon followed suit. For social sciences this meant a lot of money. One estimate observed that the amount allocated for behavioral and social-science research between 1966 and 1970 was between $34 and $48 million under the Department of Defence (DOD). It is difficult to estimate how much of this was spent on counterinsurgency.

When Project Camelot came to the attention of the AAA, mat-ters became specific. Project Camelot was the result of a govern-ment directive: the U.S. Army should play out its mission to contribute to nation-building projects, which included actively assisting governments in their dealing with insurgency problems. Gossip moves quickly; word got around that anthropologists were consulting on the project—Hugo Nutini of the University of Pittsburgh was widely believed to be involved. Project Simpatico in Columbia and Project Colony in Peru involved work relating to the state integration of peasants, and later of indigenous peoples, all part of a coordinated program of social-science research in support of counterinsurgency. American anthropologists could no longer ignore involvement of anthropologists in counterinsurgency work. Fieldworkers unfairly accused of being CIA agents were in danger of losing their lives. In 1965, the AAA appointed a committee to examine ethics and responsibilities associated with anthropological research for the government.

Ralph Beals of University of California at Los Angeles (UCLA), appointed to head the Committee on Research Problems and Ethics, testified before a congressional subcommittee on government in 1966. His language was ambiguous. On the one hand, he argued, anthropologists should not be involved in intelligence gathering. On the other, Beals did not rule out government use of social-science research to improve decision making. The Beals report, issued in 1967, warned of projects being planned in other agencies. In 1968, the AAA created an ad hoc committee on ethics. The pages of the newsletter indicate the beginning of a divide. Some AAA members were enraged at the "political" direction the AAA was taking; others argued for political resolutions; still others were outraged at professional society regulation. The question of anthropology as a value-free science was disputed, and so was the dual role of the anthropologist as scholar and as citizen. For me, the idea of the anthropologist as scholar and citizen made the case for the collective well-being of anthropologists and their informants.

The committee on ethics invited anthropologists to help build a file of anonymous cases. At this point, the Student Mobilization Committee (on the war in Vietnam) sent an ethics committee member, Eric Wolf, who purloined documents from the files of Michael Moerman at UCLA—documents dealing with what seemed to be plans for counterinsurgency activities in Thailand, in the event of a future struggle for Thailand. Private organizations were involved; the most well-known was the Institute for Defense Analyses (IDA), which subcontracted through the Pentagon and ARPA, which contracted out to the American Institutes for Research (AIR) in Pittsburgh, a network of agencies and institutes. At the University of California, USAID signed a contract with a group of scholars also dealing with development and counterinsurgency problems in Thailand. Anthropologists working with such missions were named (though not by the ethics committee), primarily Lauriston Sharp, Michael Moerman, Charles Keyes, and my colleague Herbert Phillips among others. The controversy that erupted over the Thailand issue aroused a level of controversy rarely present in professional societies.[33] Concern ranged from the observation that documents were purloined, to statements about the paramount responsibility of anthropologists to those they study. The late Kathleen Gough Aberle was clear: "We must dissociate ourselves from the acts of governments that seek to destroy the people about whom we have gathered knowledge."[34] She was right.

Those who did not agree thought the study of Thai Communists interesting, or thought it to be our patriotic duty to help the government formulate better policies, even though it was apparent that independent advice was not what was wanted. But the controversy, the subject of a recent publication—*Anthropology Goes to War*[35]—involved not only the AAA, but also my Berkeley department in particular because our faculty were key players. David Mandelbaum had been chief of the Southeast Asian office at the OSS during World War II. Herb Phillips, who had cut his teeth at the Harvard Russian Research Center, was a Cold War government consultant on the Thai people; George Foster was president of the AAA; Eugene Hammel was a member of the executive board; and Gerald Berreman, a vociferous antiwar activist, and William Shack were members of the ethics committee. The Thai issues were serious and we learned later of horrible government repression of people labeled Communists in order to liquidate all government opponents. Planning for insurgency in Thailand became a growth industry, and part of it included rural development to meet the Communist challenge. ARPA itself had an annual budget of $5 to $12 million.

The tragedy, however, was that the AAA investigation was not about the Thai people or Thailand. It was about "one's own moral business" rather than "something to be established by some external moral authority"; it was about whether Eric Wolf and Joe Jorgenson had exceeded their mandate using the tactics of McCarthyism, sources of research support, purloined documents, responsibilities to colleagues; about U.S. government tactics of neutralizing individual or collective protest. The investigation was also about the perceived threat of democracy in the AAA when the membership added Gerald Berreman as their nominee for president to that of the nomination committee. The Third World was no longer the central issue. We were sidetracked and we turned inward, or maybe homeward.

Thomas Gladwin urged colleagues "to forget such trivia as who released which documents and think now about what they are doing in the Third World. As it gets later we only compound our faults."[36] Paul Bohannan proposed that the concern with ethics is misplaced: "The real issues lie not in the procedures and practices currently being argued, but rather in the larger goal of anthropology, the morality of what anthropology should or should not be about."[37] Meanwhile the consequences of the counterinsurgency efforts of the U.S. and Thai governments laid heavily on the "hill tribes" of the north. Local situations of political resistance were overreacted to and interpreted in terms of the international struggle with Communism. In Thailand, the Hmong, one of these groups, were bombed and napalmed in early 1969. We *knew* this was happening.

The Mead Ad Hoc Committee to Evaluate the Controversy Concerning Anthropological Activities in Thailand wrote its report in 1971 exonerating all nonmilitary members of the AAA from the charges that they had acted unethically, an outcome that fits with Margaret Mead's ambivalence in seriously confronting powerful institutions within U.S. society.[38] The committee lost its credibility and the report was rejected by the membership. It was rumored that the committee destroyed the data. Some said the vote represented an organized body of younger anthropologists rejecting the values of its elders; however, age alone did not predict how people voted. The trust in the AAA establishment was lost.

Looking back, the long-term impact on the AAA's code of ethics was to water down the 1971 AAA Principles of Professional Responsibility. National backlash had already set in. By 1982, the draft code had made several fundamental changes, including downplaying anthropologists' paramount responsibility to those they study, eliminating accountability and the possibility of sanction, and eliminating the responsibility of anthropologists to contribute to an adequate definition of reality—all changes that reflect the Reagan years and moves to protect academic careers.[39] Although the proposed 1990s version is improved, questions of professional responsibility raised in the 1960s remain largely unresolved, and I have not been involved with AAA business since it in practice stopped being an association of the whole of anthropology.

Early on, many of us were pulled in on ethical issues by special missions or committee work. In 1994, just three years from my Ph.D., I was involved with a committee to work out ethics of government interest in social-science work for the Latin American Studies Association. More traumatic was the request by AAA President George Foster for South African anthropologist Peter Carsten and me to travel to Simon Fraser University in British Columbia to investigate the firing of Kathleen Gough. We found that her firing was in no way based on the quality of her research as was claimed by the university. Our investigation indicated a political firing that permanently damaged a distinguished anthropologist and for which Simon Fraser, censor or no, never claimed responsibility. In 1993, Kathleen Gough's contribution to analyzing the forces of imperialism and resistance was published posthumously in a special issue of *Anthropologica*. Her work was a first-class model of a responsible researcher. It still makes me angry to think about how easily a reputation can be damaged by utterly irresponsible parties, and how easily we were all pulled in at the microlevel.

Throughout this period I was appalled by U.S. policies and anthropological involvement in Southeast Asia, but not surprised. I grew up with talk of colonialism and imperialism as part of our family dinner conversation, but this was the present. In the Pacific, anthropology and nuclear sciences came together. The effects of nuclear weapons testing in the Pacific since the 1940s silenced a whole panoply of knowledgeable and distinguished anthropologists. In the wake of radiation poisoning and the contamination of whole islands, there was perhaps an expected outcome of referring to other places as "laboratories," indicating that human experimentation was acceptable. What were we afraid of? Objection to such policies was responded to by silence. In 1959, Edward Teller was in Alaska promoting the nuclear excavation of a harbor in the Arctic. The use of wilderness areas and small human populations to test atomic technology is a frightening illustration of the danger of secret and unaccountable science; the Inupiat Eskimo were dispensable for some Livermore scientists.[40] Such ideas are part of the deep structure of the modern science of which anthropology was part. I came to recognize this incrementally as a result of the 1960s ferment and the growing nuclear question.

What really changed my level of activism was the knowledge that in the mid- to late 1960s, the counterinsurgency or mind-set was being applied to domestic issues. I had three young children and they were growing up in this country. Atomic science seemed to be running amok and moving beyond nuclear weaponry; national security now included urban problems previously outside the conventional definition of national security. The organizing forces against poverty became a national security problem, and the evaluation of antipoverty programs took its start from defense work. Gone was the naive idea of conducting objective, sanitary science free of politics. The fog began to lift and the sunshine revealed an ugliness. Berkeley was an experimental station. We were gassed from the air ("chicken shit" they called it, as distinct from tear gas); so were the children of Berkeley. When I complained to the medical doctor in charge of student health he responded: "It serves the students right." Bay Area health departments did not know how to treat the innocent bystander who happened to be in the wrong place, because they did not know what the gas was. Later, Governor Ronald Reagan announced on television that he did not know who was responsible for the gas air attacks. This was the United States!

Domestic and international insurgency were conceptually merged, just as in the loyalty oath. Civil rights leaders were shadowed as were leaders in the American Indian movement. Racial protests, as earlier in Africa, were merged with Communist provocateurs. So, too, as indicated by my colleagues Berreman and Gumperz, race was intermixed with strategies of counterinsurgency that thwarted indigenous leadership possibilities. A decade later, Gumperz discovered that teenage Native Americans were being tracked to adulthood and sometimes entrapped in criminal behavior, which then became new subject matter for the linguistic anthropologist interested in courtroom behavior. More new subject matter resulted when Charles Murray, who in the 1960s was in Thailand working in counterinsurgency, published (with Richard J. Herrstein) *The Bell Curve*, and anthropologists came face to face with the new eugenics.[41]

Area Research: Who Decides Which Areas?

Bruce Trigger wrote a thought-provoking paper in 1984, arguing that the nature of archaeological research is shaped to a significant degree by the roles that particular nation states play, economically, politically, and culturally, as interdependent parts of the modern world system.[42] David Szanton, in his article "Southeast Asian Studies in the United States," addresses how anthropology connects with current affairs:

> Any review of American academic interests in Southeast Asia must begin with a recognition that scholars do not work in isolation. American businessmen, missionaries, diplomats, intelligence analysts, military planners, development specialists, and journalists, all have their own interests in Southeast Asia, interests which play a major role in shaping general American perspectives on the region...the research agendas of many academics are inevitably affected by the nature and direction of the interests of their counterparts in those other fields.[43]

He was in a good place to know as staff to the Committee on Southeast Asia, jointly sponsored by the ACLS and the SSRC. His analysis of doctoral dissertation research proposals submitted to the Foreign Area Fellows Program from 1951 to 1984 indicated that intellectual and national concerns within our country had indeed affected the interests of American scholars in the region:

> In the decade immediately following World War II, the dominant concern with a communist menace to the American Way of Life deeply influenced the kinds of questions Americans asked about the rest of the world....Then followed an overriding interest in economic development or modernization, coupled with a strong sense that America held the answers, the techniques, the models, to rapidly advance the welfare of all people everywhere. Deeply rooted in an old American missionary tradition, aid programmes of various sorts were mounted, often intruding...into the internal affairs of the host countries, with a complex mix of motives.[44]

American ignorance of Southeast Asia was not limited to Southest Asia, an observation recognized by the U.S. government with increased availability of funds for area study. David Schneider and Jack Fisher, and before them William Bascom, received such monies for Pacific studies. John Gumperz records how the area trust funded people like himself, a linguist headed for a career in Germanic languages, by providing fellowships to learn and then teach Hindi to American scholars funded for work in India, a subcontinent also perceived as capable of sliding toward communism. African countries were hard hit by the Cold War and became of academic interest in the West as the Soviet Union began to invest in selected African countries. So, too, was the interest in Cuba; the threat of Soviet influence through Cuba opened research in Central America, not Cuba. The Canadian north had become a northern hemisphere security area by virtue of its proximity to the Soviet Union; research funds flowed and area studies in the United States expanded, as did anthropology, as more native peoples and lands were destroyed.

Certain areas, however, were not funded. The Soviet Union was closed to area study, as if it were somehow unpatriotic to know the enemy. Eastern Europe, with the exception of Yugoslavia, was difficult both to enter and to receive funding. China, until the Nixon administration's renewal of diplomatic relations, was not funded. The Middle East was variably funded: North Africa, with the exception of Algeria, was relatively open, the parts under Soviet influence—Syria and South Yemen, and at some points Nasser's Egypt and Gadhafi's Libya—were neither easily funded or entered. Needless to say, the fact that the United States was utilizing Israeli intelligence networks for Cold War purposes meant that money to the area was carefully channeled away from areas in conflict with Israel. There are side effects as certainly any quick survey of major anthropology departments would indicate. Anthropologists working in the core Middle East area (Syria, Lebanon, Jordan, Iraq, and Egypt) have not been hired in the top universities.

In short, anthropology—the study of humankind—had uneven access to the peoples and cultures of the world through area monies, and as well to indigenous scholarship, some of which came to us via Canada. Notions of world systems were incomplete. Yet, several generations and many young anthropologists were funded for area fieldwork. Generous funding allowed for an enormous expansion in numbers of anthropologists and of departments of anthropology. The expansion of the field also meant that the number of years of graduate preparation was often determined by availability of funding: shorter years of graduate work meant a different kind of education. In terms of research area, regional training meant a broadening of focus from village or tribe to region, a setting that often encompassed wide varieties of languages and cultures. Regional comparative studies entered the landscape, often of an interdisciplinary sort that was archetypally anthropological. The growth of interest in linguistics and other humanistic fields indicated a need to examine the basic conceptual and aesthetic units from which… societies are constructed." David Szanton continued:

> as political events in the [Southeast Asian] region continue to defy predictions, and the problems of development seem to remain intractable, American scholars have grown increasingly

disenchanted with models and analyses, essentially based on
Western experience, as useful means of understanding....
[S]cholars with strong universalizing or prescriptive tendencies...
are backing away.... On the other hand, scholars...who tend to
explore the internal logic of systems of ideas or actions, how
they operate on the ground and in the particular, and also the
processes by which they seem to be changing, are becoming
increasingly prominent.[45]

In a 1994 issue of the ssrc newsletter, *Items*, an article entitled
"Rethinking International Scholarship" points to the shift in focus
from country and area to theme and context—namely, sensitivity.
As an indicator of what that might mean—university-based
research funded by the dod has risen 22 percent in the past four
years, while the western megacorporate model is sweeping
through Asian economies.[46]

The Legacy of a Forked Road

When we look at the impact of the Cold War period on what kind
of anthropology we do, or indeed on how we see the role of
anthropology, intellectual or other, the picture is not easily sorted
out. With distance and availability of period documents, it may
become easier. In order to start somewhere, I will focus on *generation* breaks and *writing*, and what this might mean for the people
to whom we are indebted—our "informants."

No doubt, there was deep disillusionment among 1960s graduate students that could not be ameliorated by the kind of hopeful
experience those of us had had growing up prior to the nuclear
era, and who now are in our sixties. The future looked bleak for
many of the counterculture. The call, as Norman Klein and others
have put it, was for mass participation: "Do it—there's no such
thing as a bad tactic"; or Abbie Hoffman's words: "Revolution is
the highest trip of them all," "revolution for the hell of it," and
"don't trust anyone over thirty" were slogans of the period.[47] The
graduate students of this counterculture period are now in their
fifties. The meaning of such slogans in counterculture anthropology was poignantly put by Marcus and Fischer in 1986:

Their work addresses less a new generation of graduate students than each other, who are survivors of a period of cutbacks [a relative concept]...aware...of the marginality of their discipline...in terms of how little it is valued or how suspiciously it is held...younger anthropologists are not concerned with superficial piety toward their mentors, and not burdened with preserving an authoritative pose for large bodies of eager graduate students.[48]

Marcus and Fischer meant it. History *was* bunk. Out of 225 references in their book only nine were of pre-1960 vintage. Interpretive perspectives were positioned against older and, from their point of view, exhausted approaches—a *transition* that was not only a new paradigm juxtaposed against another "to avoid a rhetoric of a clash of paradigms." It was paradigm busting. For them, power had a distinctly subterranean component.

Before commenting on the implications of this break, I contrast it to *Reinventing Anthropology*, a book for people concerned and critical about the way things are, "who think that if an official 'study of man' does not answer to the needs of men, it might be changed; who ask of anthropology what they ask of themselves— responsiveness, critical awareness, ethical concern, human relevance."[49] Hymes spoke of reinventing anthropology, not of abandoning it, of having a critical anthropology that takes its ethics and political responsibilities and its trained incapacities seriously. The book about the anthropology of anthropology was summarized in *Science* by Walter Goldschmidt as "disaffection with Western civilization." Later, Goldschmidt also dismissed Marcus and Fischer's book—ironic because Goldschmidt's pioneering work on California agriculture generated accusations of leftist leaning.[50] It was in *Reinventing Anthropology* that I, then among the young guard mediating between graduate students and the older guard, published "Up the Anthropologist," a call for a more adequate anthropology, one that recognizes the concreteness of power structures.[51] (We were mostly in our thirties when we wrote these pieces.) Other articles indicated other ways in which anthropological training was "trained incapacity." Richard

Clemmer wrote about the theoretically bare cupboards of American Indian research. A decade earlier it seemed that most American Indians would be assimilated into the dominant culture. Yet, suddenly, things changed. Indians became "militant," and before most anthropologists knew what had happened, journalists were writing about "Red Power." "Objectivity," Clemmer argued, "had kept anthropologists from identifying too strongly with the subordinate society they were studying."[52] Gerald Berreman wrote about "Bringing It All Back Home—Malaise in Anthropology."

In that same volume, the late Bob Scholte, a Berkeley Ph.D., was arguing for a reflexive and critical anthropology that would subject anthropological thought itself to ethnographic description including the ideology of a value-free social science. William Willis, an impassioned black anthropologist, wrote a piece on the subjective distortion by anthropologists who have compounded the objective distortion created by colonialism and imperialism. His most piercing critique was that "[t]he closer the anthropologist comes to his own society, the more culture escapes him as a viable concept...not only Afro-American culture that is escaping our grasp but American culture."[53] Brilliant observation on our penchant for denial.

I juxtapose the Hymes and the Marcus and Fischer volumes because they indicate a fork in the transitions of that period.[54] Ostensibly, both volumes share the need to change something about anthropology. Yet, the paths are different—the difference between "ideas and life, theory and fieldwork, ethnography as writing or observation, literature or science," the difference between responsibility and commitment, or the escape of "literary fictions and criticism."[55] Discussions about Writing Culture captured a reason to reinvent armchair anthropology, and, intentionally or not, legitimated a retreat from responsibility. Although enthusiasts like Paul Rabinow often recognized the double-talk in Writing Culture on the power and authenticity of the anthropologist —a power that had been lost by Cold War experiences and the movement to destroy the notion of scientific ethnography—others saw it differently. Elizabeth Colson responded in 1974 to the double-binds alluded to earlier:

> If the anthropologist concentrates upon the formal aspects of political and social structures...[h]e provides the tools that allow the foreigner to become expert on local usages and so assume the right to arbitrate in local affairs.... If the anthropologist attempts instead to describe the dynamic processes...[t]his entails exposing the strata-gems.... It is perhaps not surprising that so many of our contemporaries have retreated from...either...and have turned instead to concentrate upon symbolic systems. These by definition are assumed to be impersonal, above the battle, and to operate by their own logic.[56]

Later Gavin Smith described fictions and criticisms as a style "by which they [the new ethnographic writers] can remain ethically pure while also staying on the political sidelines."[57] There was a retreat from standard English that was ultimately a political cop-out, a form of intellectual hubris.[58]

A path different from what Marcus and Fischer described was about integrating intellectual practice with social life—the awkward outsider crossing boundaries. The citizen-anthropologist (of all people) cannot operate with narrow professionalism. My work on nuclear energy and nuclear war technologies took me into decision-making circles—work referred to by new cultural critique anthropologists as "policy work," indicating continued cooperation with the system. It makes me wonder which generation was silent. Is arguing with nuclear scientists about objectivity or twenty different kinds of warheads any more policy oriented than arguing about the same with students?

In my case, it made a difference that I was teaching at a university in charge of managing two weapons laboratories that were responsible for designing 90 percent of the U.S. nuclear warheads arsenal. I pursued the question of academic freedom at the labs along with distinguished colleagues at Berkeley. We encountered organized power directly—the military-industrial-university complex. In 1991, University of California faculty senates voted to discontinue the contract to manage the labs, using for the first time the argument that managing weapons laboratories was bad for the academic side of the university. Significantly, participation of younger and otherwise intellectually active faculty was minimal. The younger Berkeley faculty were self-engrossed. Cynicism was rewarded; the Regents ignored the faculty vote. In 1996, the issue of weapons lab contracts is once again being examined by faculty.[59]

As a class, intellectuals have been caught by the military-industrial bureaucracy. We practice what Dorothy Lee called unfreedom. We oscillate between asserting our individualities and serving the ruling powers. Maybe Thorstein Veblen was right—the university has become a factory undermining independence and separating us from social life.[60] But the strength of anthropology is to have one foot in academia and one in the "outside" world. The department of anthropology at Berkeley has inspired ethnographers to do this kind of work, looking at development, revolution, or weapons scientists in a critical way; others have self-trained. Paul Farmer knows you have to speak about arms dealing in order to understand the "Uses of Haiti." In 1985, over $500 billion was spent worldwide on arms alone. Paul Farmer understands selective blindness: "If the social is left out of socio-cultural…good analysis is unlikely to follow…. Given history it is difficult to explain current killing by referring only to local actors and local factors."[61] Farmer is moving against the cold war generation, following Clifford Geertz who wrote about cock fighting while footnoting massacres; more than a million people were killed in Indonesia.

Selective blindness means we missed predicting the revolution in highland Peru because anthropologists largely depended on conceptual categories rather than ethnographic realities.[62] "Man meets the problems of the atomic age with the biology of hunter-gatherer" is a quote from Washburn et al. and used by Donna Haraway to discuss the way physical anthropology from 1950 to 1980 made use of the Cold War discourses, nuclear technologies, sexual politics and racism, and ecological crisis. Such were to be found in the bodies of living primates and early man. Haraway interprets the stress idiom of the biological humanism of that period as part of an anxious discourse, which she finds important but flawed in the struggle against scientific racism.[63]

Omissions or denials are due in part to the relationship between anthropology and power, a relationship that issues triggered debate in the 1960s, but not now. What has been missing in past and current anthropology is the creative impulse that connects us and the institution of academic bureaucracy to a democratic social life. Such a project requires an understanding of the American university and the impact upon it of the military-industrial complex, a story that begins long before the Cold War, and the seduction inherent in Cold War tools, especially for archaeologists.

Cold War Technologies: Whose Benefit, Whose Cost?

Cold War tools have had variable effects on the subfields in anthropology. Archaeologists are funded to investigate sunken ships, missile-launching facilities, and the Nevada test sites historic structures as part of a program to preserve the Cold War legacy.[64] Artificially subsidized technologies, such as neutron activation analysis (NAA), accelerator mass spectrometry (AMS) or trace element analysis, remote sensing, thermoluminescence (TL) dating, and other technologies, were introduced to archaeology as new tools in addition to old ones, or as new tools that should replace older techniques. Archaeologists retooled at locales not usually frequented by anthropologists—Brookhaven Laboratory, Lawrence Berkeley Laboratory, the Oxford University AMS facility, and even nuclear reactor facilities such as the University of Missouri at Columbia. The military technologies were further justified by the addition of academic use. With such developments, archaeologists now have to argue to granting agencies such as the NSF why they were *not* intending to use such technologies.

Methodological pluses and minuses exist, affecting analyses of archaeological data. Some of these technologies merge data that should not be merged and would not be with the use of the traditional, more labor-intensive methods. Remote sensing has been used to recognize ancient landscapes such as canals and profiles within sites as those deeply buried in the Amazon. Ground-penetrating radar has been used to map anomalies. The overall result has been the valorizing of one method over another irrespective of the knowledge gained and more importantly the valorizing of quantitative over qualitative data, dramatic over mundane approaches. For example, nuclear submarines are being put into the service of classical archaeology and scholars interested in studying ancient trade routes in the Mediterranean. A U.S. Navy nuclear-powered (N R-1), deep-diving submarine is being shared with researchers excited about the possibilities of going beyond the shallow water work, to explore a millennium in deeper waters.

Archaeology may have benefited. Satellite-based geographic information systems are invaluable. Remote sensing has become a commonplace tool, facilitating for archaeologists what would have taken decades to discover.[65] The same remote sensing systems, however, have quite a different impact on social-cultural anthropology. Here the story is even more double-edged, not only in terms of methodological preferences of quantitative over qualitative, but in terms of the lives of people that social-cultural anthropologists learn from and about.[66] Computer technologies developed to locate very specific geographic sites (for bombing) provide the base technology for Geographic Information Systems (G I S) being used today.

Early in the 1980s, the Bureau of Indian Affairs (B I A) established G I S for ten U.S. tribes. The technology for tribal use in the management of their lands has turned out to be a mixed blessing. The dilemma has been over the concern that G I S maps detailing archaeological and cultural sites fall into the wrong hands, and are then used to deny Indian peoples their rights under existing law, or that they might result in wrongful exploitation. Subjecting indigenous peoples to remote-based imagery and surveillance without proper guarantee of their rights to privacy and self-determination is not far-fetched. On the other hand, a G I S is being developed in Oaxaca, Mexico, as the basis for communal forestry planning among Zapotec and Chinantec communities.[67]

Elsewhere, the United States has cooperated in the use of its satellite imagery capabilities to combat the drug trade, but drug production areas often coincide with repressed indigenous groups such as the Baluchis of southwest Pakistan, or the Tarahumara of northern Mexico. The Japanese are known to have used GIS data for the deforestation of Sarawak, and GIS data may have been instrumental in locating petroleum reserves in the southern Mexican state of Chiapas in the 1970s. The Mayans probably have good reason to resent PEMEX, the Mexican state oil company, the development projects that built dams along the Grijalva River in Chiapas thereby flooding Mayan lands, and the World Bank's role in freeing access for American multinationals to land. Elsewhere, as in Iraq, expulsions of people could be mapped directly to areas containing oil reserves.

The point here is that data retrieved from the use of GIS technologies affect people's lives through deforestation and depopulation—the peoples that anthropologists live and work among. Their problems become our problems in a way that is not comparable to other social scientists who may not be directly and intimately involved with the peoples of the world who, in the case of anthropology after all, are our teachers. If places are exploited, the peoples located there will suffer exploitation, expulsion, genocide, and cultural assimilation. Space-based, remote-sensing platforms, a technology inspired by military goals, comes to ravage human diversity and human rights. The recent French accusations over CIA reports on French bribes to Brazilian officials has reminded us that the line between military and industrial activity is blurred. CIA espionage work helped Raytheon Corporation snatch a $1.4 billion project to build a high-tech radar system.[68] As we move from the Cold War to cultural and industrial wars, "hot" and "cold" are hard to separate.

Postscript: The Military-Industrial Capture

What is the reader to make of this story? The issues for the discipline seem obvious. The Cold War had an enormous effect. Our numbers were expanded for Cold War research, our subject matter was channeled and defined by funding agencies, our methodologies were revolutionized by military technology. Leading anthropologists, in the complicitous role of activist Cold Warriors, wittingly participated in or at least condoned formulation of CIA and DOD plans for secret interventions into the internal affairs of soverign states; testing in the Pacific was condoned by omission. Some anthropologists monitored the political loyalty of other anthropologists and our informants, created a climate of intellectual repression, or at least encouraged intellectual products that fit with the Cold War Syndrome, promoting the opposition between freedom (us) and totalitarian (them) and meeting the intelligence needs of the feds rather than grappling with any notion of a professionally free and unfettered social science.

There were objections to the above, but objection was minimally effective; in fact, there was a negative impact on those who objected to corporate and state pressures on academic freedom and to the political shaping of scientific research. The patronage networks linking the academic with the political and social setting produced a mindset compatible with the political interests of the national security state. This situation created a social science generally uncritical of bias and allegiance in dominant paradigms, and unhelpful to reality testing for government. Positivism and later interpretivism were flights from facts of power which expressed denial of domestic repression and U.S. imperialism abroad. Negative ripple effects from the Cold War became customary and are passed on with reward and sanctions of academia. The fiction of an autonomous university becomes transparent especially in historical context.

Historians of the American process inform us that antebellum universities taught morals and political economy, and that from the Civil War onward industrial and military powers began to shape the American university to their ends.[69] In this light, the Cold War political impact on American universities was no political aberration. There was a silencing of open intellectual debate, and there was sanitizing of concepts like materialism. For anthropology it meant political management of anthropological work.

Today, probably more anthropologists work for military and corporate forces than study those forces in the world. We anthropologists are now wittingly participating in democratic illusions.

The Phantom Factor is the sum total of all the processes and
mechanisms of indirect control, which are for most of us invisible.
Invisibility is achieved through mind colonization. Wrong seems
right or trivial. Killing people becomes patriotic, denied, or just
okay. Nuclear testing in the Pacific is viewed as something the military has to do. Unthinkable behavior becomes normalized.
Independents who object are considered contentious finger
pointers, jeopardizing funding and jobs. Incrementally, the road is
paved to meet the goals of industrial and military powers, goals not
often coincident with "patriotism." Even more anthropologists work
for, rather than on, the corporate world than ever before, and this is
not even an issue for the AAA except in the "new jobs" domain. In
the meantime, other anthropologists have been caught up in the
diversions—the stylistic or double-edged landmines—of multiculturalism, sexual orientation, feminism—issues that are used to displace attention from root problems. Academic radicals all too often
are abstract radicals; epistemological radicals I call them.

Entire books have been written on the American fear of "Reds,"
linking this fear to the destabilizing impact of industrialization in
the nineteenth century and to perceptions of global and national
security in the twentieth century, and finally to reactionary politics
and scholarship. None of this is new. But what is new for each era
is the form in which professional autonomy gets compromised.
In the modern epoch, autonomy is compromised by power and
funding, by buying into the mainstream ideology of the Cold War
syndrome and the ideology of science as well. The postmodernists
have their own version of how they think of themselves. They are
free from a single narrative, but what have they done with this
freedom? In fact, postmodernists might read this story and claim
that it is nothing more than just another narrative. Or, anthropologists can think about the meaning of the proposition that each
era has its own version of how autonomy gets compromised in
terms of what it means to be a professional. Anthropology is not

about the particular or the universal, it is about connecting the particular and the universal. The new social positioning of anthropology must be eclectic and connective and ultimately global. It requires a democratic inspiration because free and unfettered inquiry is a critical scholarship about ethnographic realities. We did not have that in the Cold War period and we do not have that in the post-Cold War period.

Talal Asad once observed "a strange reluctance on the part of most professional anthropologists to consider seriously the power structure within which their discipline has taken shape."[70] The macro-politics of anthropology require revealing the phantom to know what kind of a discipline we have. To comprehend the pernicious effects of the Cold War on anthropological understandings today, requires a renewed realization of what Aldous Huxley meant by *Brave New World*. Colonization of the mind by self-censorship is the most efficient effect of repression or censorious relationships. Once we have weapons laboratories as part of the university, then the Pentagon views the university as a national security problem. The university responds by selecting administrative heads who will protect the interests of the national security state for whom academics become not an independent force but subsidiaries, a system that requires more conformity than the factory floor. The test is to examine systems of promotion and reward, and negative sanction. The national security state demands loyalty. "I keep my mouth shut" translates into respecting taboos, and self-censorship becomes the emissary of a taboo culture. Questions close to the jugular do not get asked. The greatest number of atomic bombs were exploded *in* the United States. The madness of it all rarely occurred to anthropologists. The national security state has to have adversaries to justify its existence. The inclusive study of humankind places a special responsibility on anthropologists to recognize the forces that shape the anthropological intellect.

Notes

1. I wish to acknowledge the help of colleagues in anthropology who participated in the Cold War seminar: R. Joyce and D. Price, T. Duster in sociology; research associates R. Gonzalez, N. Milleron, N. Milleron, R. Milleron, and J. Ou; and office support staff V. Tung and N. Chaisson. Especially critical was the aid of librarian Suzanne Calpestri, without whom the finding of documents would have been a nightmare. Any flaws are my own.

2. See Gerald Berreman, "The Greening of the American Anthropological Association," *Critical Anthropology*, II, no. 1 (spring 1971): 100–4, and his "Ethics Versus 'Realism' in Anthropology," in *Ethics and the Profession of Anthropology*, ed. C. Fluehr-Lobbaw (Philadelphia: Univ. of Pennsylvania Press, 1991), 38–71.

3. See Sigmund Diamond, *Compromised Campus—The Collaboration of Universities With the Intelligence Community, 1945–1955* (New York: Oxford Univ. Press, 1992).

4. See James G. Hershberg, *James B. Conant—Harvard to Hiroshima and the Making of the Nuclear Age* (New York: Alfred A. Knopf, 1993), 636.

5. Ibid., 546.

6. See Elizabeth Colson, *Tradition and Contract: The Problem of Order* (Chicago: Aldine Pub. Co., 1974).

7. See Diamond, *Compromised Campus*.

8. See Charles T. O'Connell, "Social Structure and Science: Soviet Studies at Harvard" (Ph.D. diss., University of California at Los Angeles).

9. *Mirror for Man: The Relation of Anthropology to Modern Life*

(Tucson, Ariz.: Univ. of Ariz. Press, 1985).

10. See Ruth Benedict, *The Chrysanthemum and the Sword* (Boston: Houghton Mifflin Co., 1946); Robert Lowie, *The German People: A Social Portrait to 1914* (New York: Farrar and Rhinehart, Inc., 1945); Margaret Mead, *And Keep Your Powder Dry* (New York: William Morrow & Co., 1942).

11. Marshall Sahlins, "The Best Torture—'Once You've Broken Him Down...'," *The Nation*, 25 October 1965, 266–69.

12. See Jack Stauder, "The 'Relevance' of Anthropology Under Imperialism," in *Critical Anthropology* 1972, 2:65–87.

13. E.E. Evans-Pritchard, *The Nuer: A Description of the Modes and Livelihood of a Nilotic People* (New York: Oxford Univ. Press, 1968).

14. Lucy Mair, *Safeguards for Democracy* (London: Oxford Univ. Press, 1961).

15. Hugh Macmillan, "Return to the Malungwana Drift—Max Gluckman, the Zulu Nation and the Common Society," in *African Affairs* 94 (1995): 39–65.

16. Max Gluckman, "Analysis of a Social Situation in Modern Zululand," in *Banu/African Studies*, 1940–42 14:1–300.

17. Macmillan, "Return," 55.

18. See Thomas C. Greaves, "Cultural Rights and Ethnography," in AAA *General Anthropology Bulletin* 1, no. 2 (spring 1995): 3–6, for a full preview of the cultural rights movement.

19. Ralph Beals, *Politics of Social Research: An Inquiry Into the Ethics and Responsibilities of Social*

Scientists (Chicago: Aldine Pub. Co., 1969), 64.

20. For reevaluation, see Leonora Foerstel and Angela Gilliam, *Confronting the Margaret Mead Legacy—Scholarship, Empire, and the South Pacific* (Philadelphia: Temple Univ. Press, 1992). For writings on anthropology and ethics, see M.A. Rynkiewich and James Spradley, eds., *Ethics and Anthropological Dilemmas in Fieldwork* (New York: Wiley Press, 1976).

21. L. Gary Cowan et al., "Report of the Committee on African Studies," prepared by the Ford Foundation, 1958, 1.

22. I. Horowitz, ed., *The Rise and Fall of Project Camelot: Studies in the Relationship Between Social Science and Practical Politics* (Cambridge, Mass.: M.I.T. Press, 1967), 47–49.

23. *AAA Newsletter*, January 1972, 13, no. 1:2–4.

24. Cowan et al., "Report,"1.

25. "'Relevance,'" 80.

26. Ashraf Ghani, "Conceptualizing Money: From Polanyi to Marx," prepared for annual meetings of the American Anthropological Association, Nov. 21 and 31, 1987.

27. Ibid., 9.

28. Ibid., 21.

29. Wolf, *Peasant Wars of the Twentieth Century* (New York: Harper and Row, 1969); see J. Abbink and H. Vermeulen, *History of Culture: Essays on the Work of Eric R. Wolf* (Amsterdam: Het Spinhuis, 1992).

30. Abbink and Vermeulen, *History of Culture*, 13.

31. Cited in B. McBride, "A Sense of Proportion: Balancing Subjectivity and Objectivity in Anthropology," (M.A. thesis, Columbia University), 126.

32. *AAA Newsletter*, 1969, 2, no. 10: 1–2.

33. See John Voss and Paul L. Ward, *Confrontation, and Learned Societies* (New York: New York Univ. Press, 1970).

34. *AAA Newsletter*, June 1967, 8, no. 6: 11.

35. Eric Wakin, *Anthropology Goes to War: Professional Ethics and Counterinsurgency in Thailand* (Madison: Univ. of Wisconsin, Center of Southeast Asia Studies, 1992).

36. *AAA Newsletter*, Oct. 12, 1971, no. 8 : 10.

37. Ibid.

38. See Foerstel and Gilliam, *Confronting the Margaret Mead Legacy.*

39. See Gerald Berreman, "Ethics Versus Realism," in *Ethics and the Profession of Anthropology Dialogue for a New Era,* ed. Carolyn Fluehr-Lobban (Philadelphia: University of Pennsylvania Press, 1991), 38–71.

40. For the Eskimo versus atomic energy story, see Dan O'Neill's *The Firecracker Boys* (New York: St. Martin's Press, 1994), a riveting report. Anthropologist Glenn Alcalay has written on what atomic testing has meant for Pacific Islanders, their health and their autonomy. See "Pacific Island Responses to U.S. and French Hegemony," in *What Is 'In a Rim'? Critical Perspectives on the Pacific Region Idea,* ed. A. Dirlik (Boulder: Westview Press, 1993), 235–49. A decade earlier, the Anthropology Resource Center, under the direction of Shelton Davis, was publishing on these issues in its publication, *The Global Reporter.*

41. See Berreman, "Greening"; Ellen McDonald Gumperz, *Internationalizing American Higher Education:*

Innovation and Structural Change (Berkeley, Calif: Center for Research and Development in Higher Educations, 1970), 6.

42. "Alternative Archaeologies: Nationalist, Colonialist, Imperialist," in *Man* 19 (1984): 355–70, 356.

43. "Southeast Asian Studies in the United States: Towards an Intellectual History," in *A Colloquium on Southeast Asian Studies*, eds. S. Tunker et al. (1977), 73.

44. Ibid., 74.

45. Ibid., 81.

46. *Science*, July 1994, 22. Items SSRC 46, no. 2–3 (June–Sept.): 33–40.

47. Jeffrey Mervis, "Defense Bill Targets Universities," *Science*, vol. 265, July 1, 1994, 22.

48. George Marcus and Michael M.J. Fischer, *Anthropology as Cultural Critique—An Experimental Moment in the Human Sciences* (Chicago: Univ. of Chicago Press, 1986), xi–xiii.

49. Dell Hymes, *Reinventing Anthropology* (New York: Pantheon Press, 1972), 7.

50. Norman Klein, "Counter-Culture and Cultural Hegemony: Some Notes on the Youth Rebellion of the 1960s," in *Reinventing Anthropology*, 312–34.

51. "Disaffection," review of *Reinventing Anthropology*, by Walter Goldsschmidt, Science, 180 (11 May 1973): 612–13

52. Ibid., 243.

53. William Willis, "Skeletons in the Anthropological Closet," in *Reinventing Anthropology*, 121–51.

54. For a review of current claims over the domain of a critical anthropology, see Robert C. Ulin's "Critical Anthropology Twenty Years Later—Modernism and Postmodernism in Anthropology," in

Critique of Anthropology 11, no. 1 (1991): 63–89.

55. Gavin Smith, "Writing for Real-Capitalist Constructions and Constructions of Capitalism," in *Critique of Anthropology* (New York: SAGE, 1991).

56. Colson, *Tradition and Contract*, 81–82.

57. Smith, "Writing," 213.

58. Bourdieu of practice theory fame provides us with a sample: The structures constitutive of a particular type of environment (e.g. the material conditions of existence characteristic of a class condition) produce habitus, systems of durable, transposable dispositions, structured structures predisposed to function as structuring structures, that is as principles of the generation and structuring of practices and representations which can be objectively "regulated" and "regular" without in any way being the product of obedience to rules, objectively adapted to their goals without presupposing a conscious aiming at ends or an express mastery of the operations necessary to attain them and, being all this, collectively orchestrated without being the product of the orchestrating action of a conductor. (*Outline of a Theory of Practice* (Cambridge, Mass.: Cambridge Univ. Press, 1977))

59. Warren M. Gold et al., "Report of the University Committee on Research Policy on the University's Relations With the Department of Energy Laboratories," University of California, Academic Senate, January 1996.

60. For Dorothy Lee, see *Freedom and Culture* (Englewood, N.J.: Prentice-Hall, Inc., 1959). For Thorstein

Veblen, *The Higher Learning in America* (New York: Hill and Wang, 1957).

61. Paul Farmer, "Conflating Structural Violence and Cultural Difference," MS presented to Department of Anthropology, University of California at Berkeley, November 10, 1994.

62. See Orin Starn, "Rethinking the Politics of Anthropology," *Current Anthropology* 35, no. 1 (Feb. 1994): 13-26.

63. Donna Haraway, *Primate Visions, Gender, Race, and the Nature of the World of Modern Science* (New York: Routledge, 1991).

64. See William G. Johnson and Colleen M. Beck, "Proving Ground of the Nuclear Age," in *Archaeology* 48, no. 3 (May/June 1995): 43–47; Ricardo J. Elia, "Presenting the Cold War Legacy," in *Archeology* 48, no. 3 (May/June 1995): 48–49.

65. See Anna C. Roosevelt, *Moundbuilders of the Amazon—Geophysical Archaeology on Maraho Island, Brazil* (New York: Academic Press, Inc., 1991).

66. Wayne Madsen, *Protecting Indigenous Peoples' Privacy From "Eyes in the Sky"* (Falls Village, Va.: Computer Sciences Corporation, n.d.).

67. [Type of communication & date required] A. de Avila.

68. "CIA and Raytheon Corp.," *San Francisco Chronicle*, 28 February 1995, A9.

69. See Mary O. Furner, *Advocacy and Objectivity—A Crisis in the Professionalization of American Social Science 1865–1905* (Lexington, Ky.: Univ. Press, 1975).

70. Talal Asad, *Anthropology and the Colonial Encounters* (Ithaca, N.Y.: Humanities Press, 1973), 15.

(Raymond Siever)

Doing Earth Science Research During the Cold War

A well-known geophysicist once remarked, only half-jokingly, that the plate tectonic revolution and the contemporary view of Earth was a product of the Cold War. Supported dominantly by the Department of Defense (DOD) (especially the navy), a global network of standardized seismic stations was installed in the 1960s. The DOD wanted to detect, among other things, nuclear bomb tests. Geophysicists wanted to detect earthquakes as evidence of the dynamics of the interior of the Earth. At about the same time, the navy supported a systematic measurement of Earth's magnetic field at the oceans' surface, which also served the interests of both DOD and scientists. By 1967, when plate tectonics was first proposed, hundreds of cruises of oceanographic research vessels to undersea mountain chains and deep trenches, many of them supported by the DOD, had provided the observational basis for the new theory. This theory was only one of a great number of scientific discoveries that were made as a result of Cold War support of the sciences. The story of how the Office of Naval Research (ONR) bootlegged support of fundamental research after the wartime Office of Scientific Research and Development (OSRD) was closed down at the end of World War II has been told many times. What has not been part of those thrice-told tales is the interaction of Cold War funding and the Earth Science community in universities and related institutions. Yet this was a revolution both in the ways the government supported science and in the size of the enterprise. How did we get from a small group of researchers in universities who were supported largely by private funds to a huge agglomeration of researchers in all sorts of departments and institutions, mostly federally supported? And what is the future now that the Cold War is "over" and budget slashing is a current obsession?

The Early Days: The 1940s and Before

Let's start with my first national scientific meeting, in 1946. There I sat, a graduate student at the University of Chicago, listening to the outgoing president of the society, a tall, elderly, craggy geologist, give his valedictory. I had been with J.L. Rich at field conferences and knew him as an astute observer, a quiet, soft-spoken, reasonable man. I knew nothing of his politics but suspected that he, like many field geologists, was conservative in his beliefs. But here he was all Hell and Damnation, delivering warnings of doom with fire and passion. The Devil was ONR, seducing once-honest geologists with lavish grants, distorting the scientific goals of free, unfettered scientists, and leading us down the path that would lead to governmental control of science. We would be doing the research that "they" wanted, rather than choosing our own tangled trails of pure research. Although in his politics he may have been conservative, he was certainly not so in his scientific ideas. He saw the necessity for new lines of research and worked at the frontiers of his field. It was just that he saw neither the necessity nor the wisdom of being paid from outside the university for doing research while sacrificing complete liberty to do whatever research appealed. He was a field geologist who needed little research support and got what he needed from grants of at most a few hundred dollars from his university or a professional society. In these days of helicopter support for field geologists working in wilderness terrains, it is startling to realize that the dominant mode in that day was camping out and hiking many miles each day, with food, supplies, and gasoline coming from personal funds.

In contrast to the solitary geologist using his own money for research, in the 1920s and 1930s a small number of experimental Earth scientists built what were, for then, expensive laboratories at non-university endowed institutions such as the Geophysical Laboratory of the Carnegie Foundation of Washington. Norman L. Bowen, one of the great figures in experimental geology of the first half of the twentieth century, worked at the Geophysical Laboratory in the teens and twenties. In the 1930s, he moved to the University of Chicago, where he set up a new laboratory for the study of melting and crystallization of igneous rocks with university support. A decade later he tired of the difficulty of running a laboratory at the university with limited resources and returned to the Geophysical Laboratory. Most university science professors, like Bowen, eked out a precarious existence in small laboratories, dependent on small grants (in most cases a few hundred dollars) from the university or from professional societies to give them the help they needed to build instruments and run experiments. At many of the less prestigious colleges and universities there was no support at all.

The most handsomely rewarded university geologists and geophysicists worked for the oil industry during summers, but few companies supported any significant amount of pure research at universities. The U.S. Geological Survey and State Geological Surveys hired university professors for summer fieldwork, normally not paying salaries but supporting research expenses.

Oceanographers—there were only a few of them then—sailed on small ships run by the Woods Hole Oceanographic Institution (WHOI) on the East Coast and Scripps Institution of Oceanography (SIO) on the West. Here, too, research was supported in part by personal funds. Some of the leaders in the 1930s, like Columbus O'D. Iselin, later to become director of WHOI, and Francis Shepard, a professor at SIO, had grown up sailing their own boats along the New England coast. Iselin once snickered to me that much of early oceanography was supported by family fortunes originally accumulated by pirates—the New England china trade in his case—and robber barons such as E.W. Scripps.

World War II: The Watershed

By 1940, World War II had started and the university world had begun to change. The United States was arming itself to prepare for entering the war against Hitler and the Axis powers. The nation eased from the continuing depression of the 1930s into an economic boom as "defense" took up residence in industry, in Washington, and not long after the universities. Soon we were in the war, and the war effort overrode all other considerations. Scientists of all kinds applied their expertise to winning the war. The OSRD was formed and put under the direction of Vannevar Bush of Massachusetts Institute of Technology (MIT). Soon "radiation" laboratories devoted to various facets of armaments and detection systems, including radar, were set up at MIT and other universities. Under the strictest secrecy the Manhattan Project was assembled, including all the best nuclear physicists. Although the Los Alamos laboratory was isolated, much of the work went on in universities, such as the Metallurgy Laboratory at the University of Chicago, where the first self-sustaining chain nuclear reaction was tested. A checklist of the many Harvard University scientists engaged in war work, to take one prominent example, would include Louis Fieser, an organic chemist who invented napalm, as well as other incendiary devices; George Kistakowsky, a physical chemist working on new explosives (later to direct work on the explosives that armed the atomic bomb), and two large projects, the Radio Research Laboratory (radar and anti-radar) and the Underwater Sound laboratory (sonar and submarine detection). Fifteen years later, when I was appointed to the Committee on Oceanography at Harvard, I wondered why the members included Frederick V. Hunt, a physicist and communication engineer, and E. Bright Wilson, a physical chemist involved in microwave spectroscopy. I learned that Hunt had been head of the Underwater Sound Laboratory and Wilson led a team working on underwater explosives. Such work was carried on both at Harvard and at

WHOI and gave many scientists in various disciplines a lasting interest in oceanography.

Money and technical help seemed unlimited for war work. Large laboratories and working teams of scientists and engineers were built in a matter of a few months. It was not only new labs and abundant financial support, it was a new ethos that permeated all the research groups in the many universities cooperating with the army, navy, and air force. The overwhelming majority of research scientists previously had no connection with the federal government other than the small number of physicists working at the National Bureau of Standards, chemists in a few places in the Department of Agriculture, and a small group of geologists working at the U.S. Geological Survey. Suddenly, there were thousands of scientists employed by Washington. Scientists accepted all these arrangements pretty much without question, for we were in a war that virtually everybody supported whole heartedly. Much of the "science for the war effort" had nothing to do with weapons but was devoted to support for the war economy. I saw a little of this aspect when I joined a program at the Illinois Geological Survey to expand the search for new reserves of oil, gas, and coal so vital to the war effort. Our object was to do the background geologic research to provide an adequate data base for the private companies, large and small, that were drilling for oil and gas and opening new coal mines. This was not a totally new policy. It simply amplified to a crash basis a long tradition of geological surveys, at both state and federal levels, of serving the natural resource industry, a form of subsidy that was —and is—widespread throughout the world. Regardless of the unquestioned economic arrangements, we all felt we were making our contribution even if we weren't in uniform.

So in many ways a new system of support for science had begun. The real question was: when the war was over, would we go back to the old system? Within a few years the answer became clear.

The Early Postwar Years

Just as the Truman administration kept the Selective Service System tuned up in peacetime, it also continued to support the war establishment, and through that vehicle, scientific research, even though the Cold War was fully started. Direct weapons-related research continued at full speed, led by continuing research on atomic weapons. Some of the university groups disbanded or transferred to a non-university setting. Even with this diminution of the university's role, individual faculty members maintained strong connections to the DOD, working on research that they felt to be challenging and worthwhile. Some university laboratories built during the war continued to have an active DOD role while remaining essentially autonomous within the university. Typified by the Lincoln and Draper Laboratories at MIT, these laboratories sheltered scientists doing weapons-related research while they remained faculty or staff members at the university. Some faculty and staff who were not members of these laboratories nevertheless engaged in collaborative research with laboratory members in order to take advantage of newly developed instruments or computer technologies. The AEC sponsored the building of new laboratories under the sponsorship of the University of California at Berkeley: Lawrence Berkeley laboratory, Lawrence Livermore Laboratory, and the Los Alamos Laboratory. Elsewhere, the AEC built the Argonne (Chicago region) and Brookhaven (Long Island) laboratories, both with strong university ties. Many of the scientists who worked at these laboratories were convinced of the necessity of the Cold War to check the Soviet Union and saw nothing wrong with their presence in the university. For them, the Cold War was truly a continuation of World War II. It was not until the anti-war movements of the 1960s that students and faculty protested in a serious way the presence of these kinds of laboratories on university campuses.

The changes in direction of university research in the postwar world were remarkable. Nuclear physics and chemistry greatly expanded and sparked the emergence of new fields of application, such as nuclear, or, as it came to be called, isotopic geochemistry. Nuclear scientists played a role in the early postwar attempts to keep atomic energy under civilian control, culminating in the formation of the Atomic Energy Commission (AEC), which promptly did whatever the DOD wanted while eventually becoming a spokesman for the infant nuclear power industry.

Scientists in other areas wanted to continue the research support from the federal government that many had become familiar with during the war. For example, many of the geologists who wanted to lay a sound experimental basis for many geological ideas found sympathetic ears on the program directors at DOD. The navy and other branches of the armed forces wanted to know more about electronics, the then primitive computing machines, and synthetic and natural materials. These were just a few of the many scientific areas in which dramatic progress had been made during the war, primarily in laboratories set up at various universities. Physicists, chemists, biologists and geologists had seen how much could be accomplished with ample research support and wanted to pursue their various peacetime interests with new methods and instruments. One example, is the instrumentation for X-ray diffraction to determine crystal structures, which today occupies a central position in geology and mineralogy, structural chemistry and materials research, and molecular biology. Before World War II a few prestigious universities had a single, usually handmade, unit. At one of these, the University of Chicago, the sole unit was in the Physics Department in the laboratory of W.H. Zachariasen. When a young professor of mineralogy, D. Jerome Fisher, asked to use the unit, Zachariasen told him, "Go get your own money and build one yourself."

After the war, behavior changed markedly as grant funds became available and new young faculty members found it easy to buy modern, off-the-shelf units. Soon, every department concerned had several units freely available to staff and graduate students. Scientific administrators in the DOD and elsewhere fully sympathized with the need for new instrumentation and support for advanced research. It was their job to get the best scientific researchers the means to do their work and, incidentally, use them as consultants for the DOD. The navy especially wanted to know more about the oceans and how they could use that knowledge to operate our submarines without detection and how to detect our enemies' submarines without fail, all lumped under the appellation "anti-submarine warfare" (ASW). The scientific research funding agencies that we are so familiar with, NSF, NASA, NIH, and the Department of Energy (DOE), had yet to evolve in their present form and size. Without federal support that progress was now in danger of lapsing. Congress had a history of supporting small science in a very limited way, chiefly by federal agencies such as the Geological Survey, the Coast and Geodetic Survey, and the Bureau of Standards. The idea of funding research grants without strings to individual scientists at universities was foreign to senators and congressmen who knew little or nothing of science (they still don't). The decision was made by the Truman administration that the scientific research establishment had to be supported somehow and that there was no prospect that the Congress, particularly the Republican-dominated Congress elected in 1946, would appropriate money for such purposes. However, the DOD continued to have swollen budgets that Congress accepted without question. It was decided that the defense establishment was to be the sponsor, at least until other kinds of arrangements could be made.

So the money came. It was liberally supplied and the directions of research that were supported were broadly defined. ONR funded all sorts of pure research that at first sight seemed to have little to do with any possible mission of the navy. For example, experimental geochemists built laboratories to study the melting behavior of volcanic rocks at temperatures of over 1000°C. The presumable connection was the prediction of volcanic activity on the sea floor. The new presence of externally sponsored research on the campus immediately created two classes of university faculty—those who had grants and those who did not. Among those who didn't there was some resentment of the grantees, some of whom seemed to have entered on a new academic lavish lifestyle out of keeping with the traditional university. It was, in fact, the beginning of a shift in allegiance of scientists from exclusively the university to mostly the scientific discipline and government panels in Washington. The mechanism of getting a reputation was not by concentrating on university matters and faculty committees but achieving prestige from awards from one's peers in the same discipline at other universities.

Secrecy, Unamerican Activities, and McCarthyism

Secrecy in scientific research was an important part of the wartime system; the tight lid on the Manhattan Project became legendary. But there were a great many other developments that were as secret, such as cracking the German code. Virtually everything was classified, at least at the lowest "Confidential" level. At this time security clearances for many projects that were not top secret were fairly relaxed. But by the late 1940s the new Cold War world was shaken by the defection of Klaus Fuchs and the acquisition of atomic weapons by the USSR. Many believe that this was inevitable without any spies or defectors, but the Fuchs case was ammunition for those who saw security risks everywhere, especially among liberal academics.

By the 1950s, the Cold War had fully evolved and loyalty oaths and McCarthyism had taken center stage. That story too has been told and retold, particularly by and about Hollywood writers who were blacklisted. What is less well known is that many scientists, as well as professors in other fields, became victims of the nurtured hysteria. Non tenured faculty were let go without formality while some of those with tenure had to endure a degrading process of investigation by a faculty-administration committee. At the end of this process, if vindicated, they were told essentially, "You showed poor judgment in joining communist front organizations but we won't fire you." Few were defended or vindicated by their university. Some naturalized citizens, once happy to take part in the burgeoning scientific enterprise in the United States, had to flee again, this time back to Europe or Third World countries. Grants were suddenly canceled when scientists were investigated for "subversion." The program for Cold War science in the universities nevertheless continued full speed, tacitly supported or ignored by apolitical scientists who just wanted to get their work done in their own quiet laboratories. Yet there were some who came to the defense of scientific colleagues under attack, especially in the case of J. Robert Oppenheimer, when the accusations became front-page news. For some university scientists, being denied security clearance meant the abandonment of a research career because they could not work in a sensitive area. For many it meant the loss of a job. Some physicists left nuclear physics for areas, such as cosmology, that had no conceivable relation to atomic weapons. Others made a wholesale move to research in molecular biology. Still others left science entirely. It was a bad time, but we cannot say that advances in science suffered greatly. Had it continued for a long time our science might have ended like Soviet science, subject to extreme distortion and terrorization by the political masters.

The anti-nuclear war movement was part of the Cold War too. Though individual faculty and students were involved in antiwar campaigns, science in the universities, whether DOD-sponsored or not, was not seriously affected. The full story of the anti-nuclear war movement is beyond the scope of this paper but it was part of a pattern of resistance to the Cold War. The Bulletin of the Atomic Scientists, run largely by university physicists, was one of the leaders of the continuing resistance to the possibility of using atomic weapons. Much later, university physicists and other scientists were leaders in the 1970 campaign to stop work on the anti-ballistic missile (ABM), the precursor of Reagan's "Star Wars" program. In fact, it was remarkable how all of this was happening amid the excitement of all the new discoveries being made in all the sciences, from the structure of DNA to our deepened understanding of solid state physics and the structure and dynamics of the oceans.

The New System in Operation

By the 1950s, new sources of funds for scientific research became available. In 1950, the National Science Foundation (NSF) was established and started in a very small way to fund pure research in the natural sciences. NSF grants were given solely, it was said, to advance knowledge by support of pure science research; yet even early on the NSF was seen to have an indirect mission of making our scientific establishment strong so that we could lead the world. NIH, growing fast each year with congressional urging, became a source of research funds and training grants, not only in medicine and biology but in related fields of chemistry. The AEC was an important source of funds for physics research, and this has continued to the present under the various successors to the AEC. At the moment the DOE includes this research budget, but that agency is under threat of being eliminated by Gingrich and Company.

The funding of scientific research entrained a great deal of student scholarship and fellowship support, thus in an indirect way relieving the universities of the necessity of supporting graduate students in the sciences and allowing more support to students in the social sciences and humanities. At the same time, overhead charges on grants helped subsidize the universities in general. Although university administrators are fond of saying that overhead doesn't really help the universities much, in today's climate of retrenchment in grants they are seriously worried about the loss of overhead.

What kinds of research were being supported at the universities? The words of John Rich proved prophetic. Government panels and committees were subtly—and in some cases not so subtly—directing many lines of research in every scientific discipline. Although the granting agencies always denied this, saying that proposal pressure alone was the basis of funding, it was clear that the agendas were being set by the agencies in consultation with leading scientists on panels and committees. When I served on a panel for the NSF in the mid-1960s, it was obvious that grants in certain fields were favored while those from other fields were poorly funded or not at all. Grants in experimental geochemistry and geophysics necessarily involved more money for equipment and supplies than the modest budgets submitted by field geologists. This was not to say that there were not important field investigations that required expensive logistical support. As happens in many areas of science, it was relatively easy to reach a consensus on areas worthwhile supporting, though we never actually wrote down lists of worthwhile research areas. Scientists, however able, who worked in unpopular areas or seemed too far out were by and large left out of the system.

In some universities alternative funding could be found from small endowed funds, but these sources could not usually support projects of any size.

Funding from the DOD was continued along lines laid out by the military, who recognized that fundamental research was needed in many areas to support the applied weapons research that they were really interested in.

Solid state physics serves as a case study of force feeding by an alliance of the DOD with the young but rapidly growing electronics industry. The attractiveness of solid state physics to the DOD stemmed from its ties to new developments in weapons systems, electronic surveillance, and other detection and control systems. The attractiveness to the commercial world became obvious as television, followed by magnetic tape recorders and other inventions, became major players in the electronics industry. In this way solid state physics, together with nuclear physics, which had its own ties to atomic weaponry and nuclear power (at first for submarines only) came to dominate physics for decades. Although many of the advances in solid state physics showed it to be an important new area of research, there were numerous other areas just as deserving of support but without military applications. Those areas were not supported to any great extent until much later, when the NSF began to be better funded.

During the late 1940s and early 1950s, I was involved in neither grants nor loyalty oaths, for I was a research scientist at the Illinois State Geological Survey and had nothing to do with the federal government. The State of Illinois had its own milder version of a loyalty oath (a promise that I wouldn't overthrow the government by force). My situation as far as research support was concerned was ideal, for I had only to estimate my relatively modest needs at budget time. My fieldwork was paid for and my laboratory equipment and supplies needs easily met. If it was deemed important for me to attend a national meeting or research conference, my way was paid, in contrast to many university colleagues, who most often went at personal expense. It was only in 1956, when I made a shift in career, that I had to enter the grant system. I left Illinois for a position at Harvard University, where I set up a university-supported laboratory for experimental geochemistry (yes, Harvard had money for such things). At the same time I became an Associate of WHOI. I started to learn my way through the intricacies of research funding when it soon became apparent that university support was too limited for me to do what I wanted. I had become uninsulated from the realities.

The Cold War and Oceanography

In the mid-1950s, my research interests turned to oceanography, especially the geological and geochemical aspects, and I became acquainted with the small but active community at WHOI. It was also my first encounter with a soft-money, quasi-governmental laboratory with strong ties to the university community (in the case of WHOI, Harvard and MIT). The modest endowment of WHOI, a private institution, was much too small to support any significant number of research scientists. It was certainly not possible for small private funds to shoulder the expense of sending specially equipped ocean-going research vessels to sea in various parts of the world for ocean cruises that might last several months. The ONR had filled the gap since the end of World War II, effectively turning WHOI into a government laboratory that was privately run. At that time the only major oceanographic institutions other than WHOI was the Scripps Institution of Oceanography (SIO) at La Jolla, California, a semi-autonomous branch of the University of California at Berkeley. Although they had university funds to draw on, they were in much the same position as WHOI.

During World War II a major job of the two institutions was to provide the ocean science background for anti-submarine and other forms of marine warfare. Some physicists and chemists who had become summertime oceanographers in the 1930s were converted to design radar-based navigation systems, proximity fuses and other niceties of technological warfare. During reconversion to civilian work after the war, many oceanographers found that the spurt in technology during the war had started to change oceanography to a field that went far beyond a few hardy sailors in small ships like the ocean-going schooner *Atlantis* of WHOI. In the late 1940s, two developments took place almost at the same time. The first was a massive continuation of ONR-sponsored war work, primarily ASW, only now with a new enemy, the USSR. The second was the subsidization by ONR of pure research in all fields of oceanography: physical, chemical, biological, and geological, not to mention the new and fast-growing field of marine geophysics. The ONR sponsored the conversion of small warships, such as mine sweepers, to oceanographic research vessels and liberally supported individual scientists from universities who spent summers at Woods Hole and La Jolla. At the same time, WHOI and SIO started to build up staffs of year-round scientists and technicians with the infusion of federal funds, some now coming from the infant NSF. Other oceanographic institutions began to arrive on the scene, including Columbia University's Lamont Geological Observatory (later renamed Lamont-Doherty) and the Schools of Oceanography at the Universities of Washington, Texas A and M, and Miami (now the Rosenstiel School of Oceanography).

The expansion went on at a fast pace at WHOI as new laboratory buildings were built and new ships commissioned. Year-round staffs underwent steady enlargement, and summer scientists crowds started to tax the small facilities that had grown around the sleepy little institutions of the 1930s. Virtually all of this expansion was supported by the navy and NSF by grants and contracts. The navy, of course, was not the only arm of the DOD that supported research. For the research fields of their interest the air force and the army played a significant role.

Much of the space in the first of the new buildings at WHOI was devoted to ASW and related research. Entry required security clearance. Soon after arriving at Woods Hole, I was told by one of the WHOI administrators that as a matter of course I should get security clearance. I replied that I was not involved in any classified research and so saw no reason to be cleared. He said that it was an important security matter. I would not be able to go anywhere in the new building and would be barred from the ships, which presumably might have classified equipment and data. In sum,

I would not be able to function as an ordinary staff member should. I continued that not only was I not doing any classified work and needed no access to any, but that all of the other scientists I had to work with were in the old building. If necessary, I would forego working at WHOI.

An impasse, resolved some weeks later by the security people agreeing that if I would read the espionage act and sign a witnessed statement that I had read it, there would be no problem, except that I could go into the new building only on the main floor, where the seminar-lecture room was located. A few years later, during a research conference, I was sitting at the bar with a navy program director and after too many drinks we got into a discussion of the possibility that the Cold War would turn hot. He said that in that event we would need all our oceanographers for war work and when we did, we would know exactly where to go to find them, using a list of all the oceanographers supported by grants. I demurred, saying that I had never been cleared and so would not be eligible for war work—aside from the absurdity of discussing a post-nuclear world in rational terms. He laughed and informed me that whether I knew it or not, I had been investigated and that was already taken care of. So much for trying to stay out of the system; though I continued working with WHOI, I was able to do my work without ever taking grant money from the DOD. This didn't make me "pure," however, for I am sure that during some cruises part of the ship time was paid for by the navy. If I had insisted on having absolutely nothing to do with the DOD in any way, however indirect, I would have had to leave oceanography. During this little negotiation it became obvious that none of my scientific friends at WHOI were interested in talking about such things. There was a class of subjects that were better left alone. In this way the system was reinforced by silence.

The secret classification of some oceanographic data caused a minor fuss some time later. The New England Seamounts were discovered and mapped—and immediately classified. The nature and location of these undersea mountains not far from the New England seacoast proved to be important for then current theories of the origin of seamounts in general and the geological history of the western North Atlantic Ocean in particular. Oceanographers wanted to publish but the navy was fearful that Soviet submarines would get accurate geographic fixes from the location of the seamounts. After dickering, the Navy agreed to publish the maps if the seamounts were incorrectly plotted. We were not at all sure that the Soviet oceanographers, an active group, would not have already mapped them. So probably the only sufferers were scientists who were not in the word-of-mouth network and privy to the falsification. To this day, because of a lack of security clearances, both old and newly classified data of various kinds remain unavailable on a general basis. To be sure, there have been slow motions in the directions of the declassification. In early 1995, the CIA declassified the first photo by U.S. spy satellites covering parts of the former Soviet Union. This extensive data set (which included 800,000 individual photos) is likely to be a valuable aid to all researchers in surface geological processes, as well as extents of deforestation and glacial melting related to global warming. Since that release, other satellite data have been declassified. The most important to date is the GEOSAT altimetry information, which can be processed to provide gravity maps of the world's oceans. The GEOSAT data can then be used to map the ocean floor and past and present plate tectonics. These declassifications are promising, but there is still a hugh backlog of secret data locked away in DOD and CIA files. There is no doubt that the Cold War's imposed secrecy had a cost in the damping of the free exchange of ideas that is necessary for high quality science.

Soviet oceanographers, with whom relations were distant during the early and main phases of the Cold War, were well equipped with large research vessels, and this gave typical Cold War ammunition for American oceanographers to argue for bigger and better ships to keep up with or keep ahead of the enemy. Soviet scientists were playing the same game for they too were caught up in the same arms race and feeding of war science. In 1959, the first world oceanographic congress, held at the United Nations in New York, provided a major opportunity for American and Soviet oceanographers to freely mix and exchange ideas. It was a wonderful time for those of us who participated and signaled what a peaceful international community could be like. The free discussion at the congress was partly a product of Khrushchev's taking of power in the USSR and his rapprochement with Eisenhower. Research in oceanography was responsive to such periods of detente in the Cold War. When the Cold War heated up, communication cooled down.

Everyone knew about the existence of Cold War research and most scientists accepted the fairly well-defined boundaries between specific weapons and detection work and more or less pure research that may have had Cold War applications. On a typical cruise both kinds of activities may or may not have gone on side by side. Just as pure researches were scrutinized for Cold War applications, so the pure scientists waited with anticipation for the application to pure research of advanced detection systems invented for the Cold War. It was remarkable that in the midst of some of the most worrisome moments of the Cold War, brinkmanship style, some ocean scientists doing pure research adapted themselves to the situation by carrying on pretty much the same kind of research they would have without the Cold War if they had got funding elsewhere. At the same time, there were important groups of oceanographers devoting much if not all of their time to ASW and similar war work. Those of us not part of those groups knew nothing of the classified research. Until this material, if ever, becomes declassified, we will not know how exactly how much we could have known that would have materially advanced the science generally.

The 1960s: From Easy Money to the Vietnam War

My younger colleagues shake their heads ruefully when I tell them how easy it was to get grant money in the early 1960s. By then the NSF budget was growing fast and supporting significant amounts of research in the universities. Cold War funding was still there but played a less dominant role as funding from civilian agencies increased. And, while not lavish, research support was ample. Some grant applications were funded in excess of what was asked. A number of people were funded in omnibus grants that ran for three to five years. Money for expensive ship time was available, subject only to the scheduling of ships, still too few for the number of scientists who wanted to go to sea. Typical of the time was a telephone call I received one morning. It was an army research program director who was interested in some work I had done on beaches and inquired if I wouldn't like to submit a grant application. He was sure that I would be able to do much more research if I took the liberal funding he could assure me of.

Ph.D. students began to write grants as junior investigators (with the sponsoring professors as principal investigators) so that they would have the full experience of being young academics. The NSF not only funded individual research projects, it became a source of funds for new ideas in education in science. In addition, a strong new funding source came into being, NASA. Tied to Kennedy's promise to land a man on the moon and the Soviet space effort starting with Sputnik in 1957, NASA sponsored a wide range of research in solar system astronomy, the biology (was there any?) of the other planets, and studies of Earth's systems for comparison with what we might meet on the moon or Mars. NASA was able to fund projects with large budgets for new instruments, such as the electron microprobe. The "probe," with a $1 million price tag, was virtually impossible to get from other sources. It is an instrument for the chemical analysis of microscopic grains and crystals such as those expected to be found in moon rocks when they were brought to Earth by the Apollo Project in 1969. Of course, there was a strong tie to the military through the need for powerful rockets that had been developed at various arsenals and the opportunity for spy satellites that were better and less vulnerable than the U-2 plane that was shot down in 1960. It was clear that NASA had a mission separate from the DOD, but it was equally clear that the DOD was monitoring closely and cooperating in various ways. Even without a specific mission, the NSF-supported research in areas, for example, materials science, that were potentially useful to the military. This period was a golden age for those who believed that government should be a strong force for good in the science world. You could have found few who would subscribed to the idea that government was evil. Virtually everybody came into the system, even those engaged in relatively inexpensive fieldwork.

The research history of one professor in my department exemplified the changing nature of support. Starting out in the 1930s he and his colleagues were granted Harvard University funds to get several X-ray diffraction units to study mineral crystal structures. During the war he engaged in various war researches involving the synthesis and growth of crystals that were vital components of weapons or communication devices. After the war he embarked on a massive study of uranium minerals. This work in fundamental mineralogy, funded by the AEC, was related to the need for new reserves of uranium to support atomic weapons production and the future need for nuclear power reactors. A few years later he organized a mineral synthesis laboratory to study the behavior of minerals at high temperatures and pressures under the aegis of the air force, which was interested in new materials and methods for studying them. Later he got one of the first NASA grants, enabling him to build a good new laboratory for the study of moon rocks, which he continued to work on until retirement.

The end of this "golden age" was signaled by the growing involvement of the United States in the Vietnam War. As the war escalated, it became clear that it was not going to be guns and butter as before. Although funding remained at high levels, some contraction began—primarily in the slowing rate of increase of budgeted funds. But Cold War reasoning remained supreme and there was little change in the outlook for science, at least during Johnson's administration. But when Nixon took office, some retrenchment took place, again not much more than reducing marginal projects. But this was in the face of growing numbers of scientists wanting to board the grant wagon. From this time on until the 1980s, growth in the research budget grew moderately, held in check by the increasing call for cuts in government programs. Government funding was also responsive to the general course of the Cold War. When there was detente and decreased anxiety about nuclear war, science funding seemed to suffer a bit. When the Cold War heated up, as it did in Cuba and then Vietnam, funding improved. This was bound to be so, given the rationale for government funding of much of science. There was less real cutting of science budgets than there was worry about it among scientists.

The political movements of the early and mid-1960s seemed to have only marginal effects on the main scientific enterprise, with significant exceptions. One was the restriction of the DOD to fund only direct mission research, instead of supporting a wide variety of pure research that had only an indirect relation to weaponry or warfare. This was accomplished via the Mansfield amendment, named for the senator who sponsored the amendment to a budgetary bill; it was a real break in the continuity of DOD funding of research. Many academics doing pure research who had been well supported by the DOD were now to face a choice: either go to alternate sources of funds or move to direct contract work with the DOD. Arguments between those who took DOD grants and those who didn't headed up a good many academic discussions. The question was: If you were not doing war work, what was wrong with getting DOD money? The Mansfield amendment was an indirect result of the Vietnam War and was seen to be such. It was related to student movements of the 1960s that were hostile to the science establishment as a working party of the DOD—and indeed the entire governmental system that had made the war.

There were a good many talented undergraduate and graduate students who agonized over a career in science while so many people were being killed in the war. Many of us who took a public antiwar position through full-page ads in the *New York Times* were asked for advice by science students. They wanted to be told that science was still a worthwhile thing to do in spite of its misapplication. Others attacked science as part of a corrupt establishment. New organizations came into being, such as Science for the People, that took political stances with respect to the undesirability of DOD-sponsored research. Perhaps the biggest change came with the beginning of the environmental movement and the inauguration of Earth Day. Less political than the antiwar movement, the new emphasis on the environment drew many students and faculty into protests over pollution of water supplies, air pollution, and the like. In the 1970s, it became more important in public policy and became part of university life as courses and programs of study started to include coverage of the environment.

The End of the Cold War?

As the 1980s and the era of Gorbachev and the breakup of the USSR spelled a new dynamic in international relations, the scientific world responded in a variety of ways, not unlike the disarray of the media commentators. Some simply wanted to go on as before, hoping that whatever new rationale for science evolved, it would suffice to continue the present system. Others, more simply, denied that anything was different and thought that the cold war would continue. Some took a pessimistic view, that without the cold war, scientific research would gradually wither. Yet the first group seems to have been more nearly correct. Even though the DOD is trying to prepare for different tasks, and dedicated to keeping the United States the dominant world power, it is unsure of what those international policing responsibilities will be after the experience of the Persian Gulf, Somalia, and Haiti. And there is little doubt that the DOD continues to have its eyes on Russia and China as major enemies. Funding continues, though at an ever-decreasing rate, but there is no real program for the future.

More significant now is the rightist domination of the Congress and the ruthless budget cutting that is decimating social programs. Major scientific programs are being scuttled in every field, and the future of some of our best laboratories is in doubt, even some that are tied to the military. Yet the DOD budget remains secure and right-wing congressmen are insisting on a continuation of Star Wars, an outstanding example of cold war pork. It seems that many right-wing congressmen are so ideologically tied to destroying social programs that they extend their so-called mandate to cutting science. The universities have remained relatively passive actors in this argument.

Some right-wing members of Congress call for the privatization of science research but there is little chance that the private sector will take up any significant fraction of what has been cut. Instead, in the Earth sciences we have the example of the oil industry. The major companies, which used to support large, in-house fundamental and applied research groups as well as giving grants to university faculty, are now cutting their own research establishments to the bone and cutting most of their support of university faculty. In the past large oil corporations paid attention to education as well as research, awarding scholarships and fellowships to many departments of geology and chemistry. Many of these have been terminated, partly in response to ups and downs in oil company prosperity. I had benefited from oil company grants myself. Soon after I came to Harvard a senior representative of the Shell Oil Company visited me and offered a $5000 grant, a great deal of money in those days, to continue doing whatever research I liked. No strings—just an agreement that they would get copies of any papers I wrote. That kind of research support, common twenty-five years ago, is now practically unheard of except in small bits and pieces. Nowadays the universities are on their own, except for contract work that some departments do for companies. Increasingly, scientists orphaned by the end of the Cold War and the New Right have found funding under major research contracts that companies, such as pharmaceutical and chemical manufacturers, have negotiated with universities, typically in the health sciences.

This commercialization of faculties seems now to be most widespread in the expanding biotech industry. The enthusiasm of molecular biologists for setting up their own biotech companies while continuing to teach and hire large groups of graduate student and postdoctoral fellows is not a new phenomenon. Their behavior is reminiscent of the electronic engineers, solid state physicists, and computer scientists who in earlier times were responsible for the agglomeration of companies along Route 128 outside of Boston and the Silicon Valley in the San Francisco Bay area.

What, after all, does society expect from scientists? That answer is clear enough in the health sciences, though particular strategies for cancer research, AIDS research, and programs like the human genome are still arguable. The answer for Earth scientists seems to be concentration on the environment in all its many aspects.

Chemists and physicists too are displaying new interest in environmental problems. Yet the funding level for environmental research, twenty-five years after Earth Day, is low, and few university departments show any tendency to have departments seriously interest themselves in environmental research. The Environmental Protection Agency has never seen its main mission as research in environmental problems. It is devoted to analyzing existing data and promulgating regulations as directed by various acts of Congress.

Many "hard" scientists starting in the 1970s, and continuing still somewhat today, have little respect for environmental research. In their view the "important" problems remain basic research, and much of the subject matter of environmental concerns seems intrinsically less interesting. But there is a growing group of Earth scientists who see these concerns as basic to the survival of Earth as a working system habitable by humans. If a high-quality environmental science is to be carried on, it will have to be funded at a significant level.

In the absence of any other program to support Earth science it may prove to be the only way for many to do science. However, more than other areas, environmental science is a target for right-wing budget cutters. Industry has fought the environmental movement all the way and now sees its chance to eliminate the EPA and environmental regulations in general.

The Global Change Program, primarily focused on changes in atmospheric carbon dioxide and climate, which has strong implications for agriculture and many other segments of the world economy, has only recently grown to significant size. Yet it has come under fire from the right wing. The Republicans have picked up the words of the few scientists who doubt global warming instead of the views of the overwhelming majority of knowledgeable scientists and do not believe in the predictions of global warming and climate change. This suits their belief in a market economy and strong resistance to any move to reduce carbon dioxide emissions. This is one example of how the Right has politicized science research in ways unthinkable just a few years ago.

It is paradoxical that many right-wing congressmen and senators who enthusiastically supported the Cold War, which funded science research so well, now want a continuation of militarism, with high budgets for the DOD, yet want to cut science funding. Is this confirmation of the view of 1946, that without the navy, Congress would never have funded science in the first place?

Prospects for the Future

Cold War support of science at the universities showed how continuity of adequately funded research could build a scientific enterprise that led to immense advances in every field of science. Other countries, notably Germany, have shown how a non-military based government-funded science could also be successful. One cannot replay history to find out how U.S. science would have done without the impetus of the Cold War. It is not easy to compare with other countries, for some of them have also participated in the cold war and none has the magnitude of our economy and our dominating presence during most of the Cold War years.

What is more important is to establish some guidelines for continued research support by nonmilitary agencies such as NSF and NIH. How society will set the agenda for science in a self-maintained economics of scarcity is going to determine the future. We can see how shabbily the Endowment for the Arts and Humanities has been treated in the new rightist climate. The danger is that the sciences too will become both the victim of know-nothingism and the prisoner of the business world's priorities. We have already seen how the scientists have been able to move back and forth from the university to the business world. In the absence of any rational decision based on society's real needs, we can expect business to call the tune, either by its control of Congress or by its choice of subjects for contractual research. So far there is little indication that scientists will actively resist the downsizing of the research community in the university. And severe downsizing may end in killing the golden goose. While scholars in the humanities rely on libraries, scientists can no longer do any useful work in poorly equipped laboratories with minuscule budgets. In that respect we will become an undeveloping country.

(**Noam Chomsky**)

The Cold War
and the University[1]

Intellectual Climate During the Cold War

The history of intellectuals and dissent during the Cold War period must first be seen in light of the changes in the American psyche that the dramatic rise in international power created. During World War II, vast changes took place. For one thing, wartime spending got the United States out of the Depression. The industrial economy in the United States boomed, while much of Europe was devastated or destroyed. It was pretty clear as the early 1940s went on that the United States was going to come out of the war with an enormous degree of domination of the world on every front: industrially, diplomatically, militarily. By 1945, the United States had a level of preponderance in the international sphere which probably has no counterpart in history. It had fifty percent of the world's wealth, most of the world's industrial production, military dominance, security, control of both oceans—the opposite sides of both oceans!—and so on. Such power was simply unparalleled, and that sank in. American planners had very ambitious and sophisticated ideas about organizing the entire world, and they carried out many of those ideas.

There was a reflection of this shift in power in the cultural sphere and in the universities. It had a complicated background. Part of the reaction was against the prewar sense of inferiority, when the United States had, culturally speaking, a subordinate relationship with Europe. If you were an American artist or a writer, you would go to Paris; if you were a mathematician or a physicist, you would go to Germany; if you were a philosopher, you would go to England; and so on. The United States was thought of as a cultural backwater, somewhat like the Midwest is regarded by Easterners now. This reaction was epitomized during the war when many European scholars, scientists, and intellectuals fled the Nazis and tried to come to the United States. Many were treated pretty shabbily, partly out of fear that they would dominate if they were allowed in, and partly out of outright hostility. So when these distinguished scholars and scientists arrived, many of them could not get decent positions. For example, Roman Jakobson came to the United States in 1941 as a refugee from Sweden, where he had gone from Prague. Although he was an extremely distinguished linguist and literary scholar, one of the leading figures in these fields, a petition actually circulated by leading American linguists to universities urging that they not hire him, that it would be bad for American linguistics. He ended up, through the good offices of two linguists—Zellig Harris and Carl Voegelin—translating at Yivo Institute, and later got a position at the University of Chicago. Jakobson's case was not an anomaly; many European scholars and scientists were treated in the same manner.

By the late 1940s and early 1950s, the reaction was in full force. Throughout the world, American planners developed a kind of can-do sense. European civilization was viewed as a failure; after all, it collapsed. Planners did not want to worry about that dust anymore. Things would be done our way, the right way, the American way. There was a lot of jingoism, supported by the American victory, power, and global dominance. A recent study of the Cuban missile crisis and the attitude of the Kennedy intellectuals and planners to the Europeans at the time, as expressed in internal discussions (since declassified), is pretty dramatic: it simply never occurred to them to consult the Europeans. To do so would be to bring in, it was supposed, people who were emotional, unserious, backward, and so on. The attitude was that we will do this ourselves and then we will tell them, including the British. That is one of the reasons Charles De Gaulle became so infuriated and attempted to move toward an independent European course. Europe's fate was certainly at stake—the planners saw a war as rather likely, and in it Europe might be smashed. But the Kennedy administration did not consult with the Europeans; it was a case of total contempt.

I remember what the feeling was like in the late 1940s and early 1950s when I was a student. I was doing mainly linguistics and philosophy, first at Penn, then at Harvard. We were never expected to read anything on the history of the subjects. It was as if the history was nonexistent; everything serious was done by Americans and a few other people. In philosophy, we read Quine's response to Carnap in 1951; that is where philosophy started. And we had to know what they were talking about: Frege, early Russell. And we read some modern British philosophy. Then there were the pre-Socratics, and you had to know that there was somebody named Hume, but that was pretty much it.

This is a caricature, but not by much. In American linguistics, the tone of it is very clearly exhibited by a volume called *Readings in American Linguistics*, published in 1955 and edited by Martin Joos, a highly respected American linguist. His comments on the articles are filled with utter contempt for anything that preceded modern American linguistics. It was considered old-fashioned European metaphysical nonsense; the attitude was that we are doing stuff so important we cannot pay any attention to that. Even classics such as Otto Jespersen, in the early part of this century, I read on my own, out of personal curiosity. It was simply not part of the canon. I had the good fortune to obtain a graduate fellowship at Harvard, at the Society of Fellows, which gave me the opportunity, for the first time, to be at a university without working on the side and so to browse in the marvellous resources of Widener Library. I found plenty of important work by linguists and philosophers.

I was quite surprised to discover how much of the earlier work had been forgotten, or derided if mentioned at all.

The same was true in other disciplines. In the mid-1950s, I was teaching cram courses for Massachusetts Institute of Technology(MIT) students who had to pass doctoral exams in French and German. We read articles in their subjects, often from early in the century. Sometimes students (in engineering particularly) were shocked to discover that the "incompetent" Europeans, who had to be "rescued" by America from the consequences of their own supposed backwardness and depravity, had discovered things long ago that they were just beginning to learn about and work on in their graduate studies.

Such attitudes were stimulated by a number of factors. One was that during World War II substantial technological developments had been made; computers were coming along, and the field of electronics generally was developing significantly. There were new ways of studying things that really had not been available before. In the 1930s, a major scientific event took place when Linus Pauling analyzed the chemical bond in quantum theoretic terms, which unified chemistry and physics for the first time. Chemistry had been a separate field, which had no solid physical basis and seemed even inconsistent with physics. Through the 1940s, these developments were pursued further by Pauling and others. In the early 1950s came the unification of good parts of biology with biochemistry, which meant that you at least had a sense of the unification of science. Somehow the whole range, from the new physics (quantum physics) to theoretical chemistry through at least the foundations of biology, were all part of one unitary enterprise. The next obvious place to look was the brain sciences, the mind, the behavioral sciences, and so on.

And that time, with the Macy conferences, cybernetics, communication theory, and so on, there was a feeling that the horizons were unlimited. We had gotten to biology, the next thing would be psychology, and then we take in other aspects of human life and existence. Here, the American way entered in, through behaviorism. That was the heyday of the "behavioral sciences," and that was supposed to be an American innovation, not mystical like what the Europeans did. We are serious scientists, we study behavior, and are hard-headed and operationalist—Skinner had shown this, the behavioral sciences have shown that, and so on. That was very much the mood of the 1950s—thinking of itself as innovative, very arrogant, ahistorical—part-and-parcel of the general sense of America taking over the world.

Now, it was not entirely uniform. For example, at Harvard, where I was, virtually no interest existed in Continental philosophy, or even history of philosophy. That was virtually unknown except for Frege and early Russell, or parts of logical positivism, and they were known mainly for their influence in contemporary work. But British philosophy was still very much respected. And, in fact, something of the 1930s attitude of cultural subordination still existed, in funny ways. It was considered proper for graduate students in philosophy to adopt British manners, clothes, style—even accent. And of course everyone went to study in Oxford or Cambridge if they could, and there was a significant influence of Wittgenstein and Oxford philosophy that was intermingled with a kind of homebred, arrogant sense of "we know it all," in a very strange brew.

I believe something like this was happening across a large part of American intellectual culture in those years. This arrogance became tied up with what was called anticommunism, which also had a strong jingoistic element. This continued right to the revival of Europe; the missile crisis was a striking and dramatic example of it. And it continues right to the present. Only the other day, the U.S. ambassador to the United Nations(UN), Madeleine Albright, said something that would be considered scandalous if it came from any other country, but here it is considered perfectly normal. The UN Security Council was wavering on a U.S.-supported resolution on Iraq, and she simply said that this is a region where our interests are at stake, that we will act multilaterally if we can, unilaterally if we must. Well, that is the American way. When the World Court condemned the United States for "unlawful use of force" against Nicaragua, the general reaction here across the board— virtually with no exception, including people who write eloquently about the sanctity of international law—was contempt for the Court. The Court, it was said, had dishonored itself by daring to condemn the United States. When the UN Security Council debated a resolution, not mentioning the United States, simply calling on all states to observe international law, the United States just vetoed it. It was considered so insignificant it was barely mentioned here. When it went to the UN General Assembly and the United States voted virtually alone against it, that was not even reported. We do what we like, and in the cultural sphere that has had its analogue.

The beginnings of the Cold War increased the jingoism, the sense of self-righteousness, the narrowness of perspective, the rallying around the flag. It might well have gone on anyway, but the cold war intensified elements that were there.

Activism and the University

As an intellectual, if you were critical of the developing Cold War system in those years, you were so far out of the mainstream you did not talk to anyone except your few friends—I remember that very well. So if you felt qualms about the U.S. war in Greece in the late 1940s—I had more than qualms, I thought it was horrifying—you were marginalized. I cannot remember anyone else I knew who felt the same way. The same was true of Korea. It was not until the early 1960s that this near uniformity of subordination to domestic power combined with arrogance and self-righteousness began to erode significantly.

Of course it is not that in all of Cambridge in the 1950s no one shared my reservations about Greece or Korea. But it did not come out publicly very much. It was marginal at best; for example, the journal *Dissent*, which must have been started about 1953 or 1954. These people were Trotskyites—Irving Howe, Lewis Coser, and others—but left the Trotskyite organization around 1950. By the mid-1950s, it was pretty much as it has remained: social democratic, critical of extremes of American power. But it was at the time regarded as—and in the sense it was—a very courageous break with conformity. But that was very much the exception. Much more typical was, to mention only one case, the reaction to the Hungarian uprising and the brutal suppression of it by the Russians in 1956. I was once with a group of faculty at Harvard who were bitterly denouncing the Russian invasion of Hungary, which I agreed with; it was horrifying. But I remember saying, "Look, you're right about this but it's not the only terrible thing that's going on in the world." I mentioned what the British were doing in Kenya, at the same time, which was also horrifying. And there was a kind of silence. Then someone who knows better said, "Well, it's not comparable because there are very few people in Kenya, unlike Hungary." The idea that colonial atrocities could even be considered was remote from understanding.

Another example can be found by looking at the reaction to the overthrow of the government of Guatemala, which led to a real reign of terror, with thousands if not tens of thousands killed. Nobody batted an eyelash. I think perhaps the most dramatic example, specifically because of what came later, is what happened in Vietnam in 1961, what happened in Indochina altogether. In 1954, the United States took over and quickly undermined the Geneva accords, blocked a diplomatic settlement, and set up a typical Latin American-style terrorist state in South Vietnam, which had probably killed 60–70,000 people by the end of the decade —not a small amount. It was not unknown, but unimportant, simply standard Latin American-style terror, like Guatemala, no big deal. In 1961, Kennedy took over. By then the repression and violence had elicited resistance, and the U.S.-client government was going to collapse; that was clear. So Kennedy simply escalated the war. He moved from a war of terror to outright aggression against South Vietnam. And it was not secret. We know a lot of details we did not know then; but the main outlines were clear. I remember, in October 1962, I read in the *New York Times*—hidden in the back pages, but it was there—that American pilots were carrying out a third of the bombing missions in South Vietnam in planes disguised with Vietnamese aircraft markings. It was known that American forces were either involved in or close to combat, that napalm and crop destruction were authorized. There were

plenty of atrocity stories, but no reaction, because it was considered entirely legitimate for us to invade and attack another country
and to terrorize its civilian population.

It was not until the mid-1960s that resistance on campus was
mobilized, and even then of course the level of awareness and
activity differed enormously from one university to another. In fact,
I had the opportunity to observe this difference firsthand since, in
those years, I worked at both Harvard and MIT.

Despite its connections to the Pentagon, MIT was in fact much
more active in opposition and less hostile to dissent on campus
than was Harvard. Most anti-Vietnam War efforts on the area were
centered at MIT. Salvador Luria, who was at MIT, was a refugee
from Fascist Italy and remained a committed, militant leftist. He
initiated a lot of activity. If you take a look at national faculty ads in
the *New York Times*, you will find that MIT initiated most of them,
with some Harvard participation, but that was much more marginal. I do not doubt that you would find the Harvard faculty to be
more liberal, again by usual standards, than the MIT faculty in
those years. But the freedom to be an open, outspoken, dissenting, intellectual and political activist has been greater here
than at Harvard, in my experience. That is why it is not only faculty
peace activities, but also other activities, that are usually centered
at MIT, even public meetings on issues of the day, at least those
with grassroots initiative and participation. Take, for example,
Resist, a national funding support group for various movement
activities, which got started around 1967. In large measure it grew
out of MIT. If one were to look at the list of people directly
involved, people on the board, you would find lots of MIT people.
From the beginning up until today, there have scarcely been any
Harvard faculty. That has been a fairly consistent difference. It is
not 100 percent, obviously, but the tendency is real.

The general difference between MIT and Harvard was probably
due to the fact that MIT was a science-based university, and hence
the ideological constraints were much less. I do not think that I
could have survived at Harvard. I have had no problems at MIT,
never did—even though I was very visible and I am sure causing

them plenty of problems—I was involved in the resistance, in and out of jail, and all sorts of things. And this was virtually Pentagon university. Aside from two military labs that it ran, about 90 percent of the budget came from the Pentagon. But the academic freedom record was quite good by comparative standards. I never heard a word. If the administration was getting pressure from somewhere, I never heard of it. And the same was true of others; I would not say it was perfect, but one of the best in the country. Much better than other universities that I know about, where there was plenty of repression, and persecution of activists and people on the Left. There were things here that should not have happened, but by and large their record was quite good—and remains so.

When I came here in 1955, MIT was heavily military. The building I work in was the Research Lab of Electronics, which was funded by the three armed services. Everyone routinely underwent security clearance. I refused clearance, and I was told that I was the only person to have done that then. Nobody cared; people considered it mostly silly. All I was doing was turning down free trips on military air transport and other amenities. I simply made it clear that I refused to undergo clearance, and I do not recall anyone noticing it. I was very upfront and outspoken about my political views, but it simply was not an issue.

The undergraduate population at MIT was very passive. Until the fall of 1968, very little student activity existed. There was a small group of students who formed the Rosa Luxembourg Collective around 1965 or 1966. Louis Kampf and I were their faculty advisors, and by then we were teaching courses on our own time, big undergraduate courses on these issues with hundreds of students, so the interest was beginning to develop. But it was not until the fall of 1968 that it crystallized. A lot of these students, incidentally, are still among the most active and effective on the Left up until today. One of them, Mike Albert, who was elected student body president and then was thrown out (though we were able to have him reinstated partially), went on to help found South End Press, later Z Magazine. A lot of writers, like Steve Shalom, come from that background, too. So it was quite a lively and very good group, still quite active—some of the best people around.

But they were very much on the margins at MIT until the fall of 1968, when this small group proposed to set up a sanctuary for an army deserter, the kind of thing that people were doing at the time. The guy in question was a working-class white deserter from downtown Boston. The students involved had talked to him. He had thought it through carefully, knew the consequences, and decided that he was going to desert publicly. It was a hard decision to make. He would announce it publicly in the sanctuary, where people would stay with him until the FBI came. I was opposed. I thought it would get no support from the student body. But the students went through with it anyway, and I was dead wrong. They had a news conference at the student center, and within no time MIT had practically shut down. Practically the whole student body was over there, thousands of people, twenty-four hours a day. There was an endless stream of everything from political seminars and meetings to rock music and the rest of what went on in those days. It just turned the whole Institute around.

After that came a lot of initiatives, including the first serious inquiry into the MIT-government relationship, the questions about the social role of science and technology and what considerations should go into it, and much else. On March 4, 1969, a big, full-day meeting took place, in which the whole Institute shut down. It had plenty of impact, which lasted. The place really has not been the same since.

The funny thing is, around that time, MIT was still thought of as entirely passive. In 1968, when there was a business-initiated decision to stop the escalation of the war and move toward negotiations and eventual withdrawal, one thing that was done was to try to calm down the universities, to say, "Okay, it is all over, we're all on the same side now." McGeorge Bundy, who had been national security advisor and a former Harvard dean, was sent on a "peace mission" around the country to tell everybody, "Let's be friends and make up, it's all over." As a trial balloon, he was sent first to a very quiet place, De Paul University, I think, simply to see how that would work. And it worked well—there was a big story in the *New York*

Times about it. I think the second place on his tour was MIT, which was presumably picked because it was so quiescent and passive, and therefore it would be safe. What happened was a bit of a surprise to everyone, which I will not go into. But anyway that ended the tour.

Going back to the question of government money, I think there is a considerable difference between the natural sciences and the social sciences. Although the natural scientists were pretty supportive of government policy, I would say, I do not think this was because of military funding. I believe my experience is quite typical in that regard. But if one were to look at the social sciences, it is different. What is now the Political Science Department at MIT was under economics until around 1960; MIT was an engineering school, it had very few departments in other fields. Not until the 1960s did it become a university in the usual sense. So around 1960, the Political Science Department separated off from the Economics Department. And, at that time, it was openly funded by the CIA; it was not even a secret.

No one saw any reason to keep it quiet. I do not see any reason either, frankly. In the mid-1960s, it stopped being publicly funded by the Central Intelligence Agency, but it was still directly involved in activities that were scandalous. The Political Science Department was, as far as I know, the only department on campus which had closed, secret seminars. I was once invited to talk to one, which is how I learned about it. They had a villa in Saigon where students were working on pacification projects for their doctoral dissertations and that sort of thing. In that framework, I do not doubt that relation to the government was very strong in shaping political attitudes or maybe selecting faculty and students. I do not know how long that lasted. Certainly, nothing like that is true now; it is a much more open department. But I thought there was a pretty dramatic difference between the Political Science Department and the Institute as a whole. Now if you had given people a questionnaire, you probably would have found the Political Science Department to be more liberal than the Engineering Department, by usual standards. But that is independent.

The fact of the matter is that there was very little secrecy even then. In 1969, I was on the committee that looked into the M IT budget in the aftermath of the events I mentioned. This is public, so you can find the data. My recollection is that the M IT budget was something over $200 million a year, half of it straight to big military labs that M IT ran, Lincoln Laboratories and the Instrumentation Lab, now called the Draper Lab. Of the other half, the academic budget, my recollection is that 90 percent was Pentagon-based. That shifted over the years, partly because of changes in the sciences, because biology grew and developed after that period. So by now it is nothing like 90 percent, though it has been substantial. But I think very little secret work was being done.

There was supposed to be a library somewhere of classified material in the sciences. If so, the material was marginal and unlikely to have survived this period. The decision was made at that time to cut off all classified work, and I doubt that there has been any secret work since. On the other hand, as you move away from government funding and toward corporate funding, then secrecy increases. Corporate funding is much more restricted and narrow than Pentagon funding, in general. The Pentagon funded basic science. The Pentagon, in fact, has been the cover for U.S. industrial policy. It was set up this way in the late 1940s to be a device for public funds to be used to subsidize advanced sectors of industry—that was completely public. It was in the business press; no secret was made about it at all. So, for example, through the 1950s about 85 percent of electronics research was Pentagon-funded—by Pentagon I mean the whole system, the National Aeronautics and Space Administration, the Department of Energy, and so on; what is euphemistically called "defense." A large part of it, and one of the reasons it stays at roughly Cold War levels, is that it is the system of public funding of advanced sectors of industry. And that meant that the Pentagon was funding basic science without concern for short-term payoff. The Pentagon would fund fundamental science in the expectation that sooner or later something will come out that would be useful for private power. The history of computers is an example of such an arrangement.

They were unmarketable in the 1950s, because they were too big and clumsy. So public funding was at about 100 percent through the Pentagon. By the 1960s, computers became marketable, so the Pentagon handed it over to what is called "private enterprise" (public subsidy, private profit), and then the public share gets to be about 50 percent. The story is similar in other fields.

It is hard to find a sector of the American economy that did not then and does not now live off something like this. Right through the 1980s, the Reaganites—statist reactionaries, nothing conservative about them—apart from greatly increasing protectionism, also took the initiative to fund the big development in computers and related technologies at that time. It was partially funded by the Defense Advanced Research Projects Agency, the Pentagon research agency, that set up the startup companies of the Silicon Valley type, which became the leaders in this field. "Star Wars" was pretty much the same. That has been the case for almost fifty years.

On the other hand, business does not want to fund basic science for the same reasons Ford Motor Company does not give its technology to General Motors. Anyone can use basic science. They want to fund things they can profit from. So that means very narrow funding, short-term applied work and secrecy, because they do not want anyone to know about it. Now they cannot impose secrecy, but they can make it known that renewal of funding depends on it. The effects can be felt, as the universities shift toward more corporate funding, away from government funding. The Pentagon was in many ways the freest of all the funding institutions. The Pentagon did not have Senator Proxmire looking over its shoulder to see what it was doing; the National Science Foundation (NSF) did. So the Pentagon was much freer in the kind of the funding it would do. It simply regarded itself as the nanny state for the rich, for advanced sectors of industry; so funding could be provided for anything that might ultimately be useful, maybe years down the road, without much supervision. The NSF was much more bureaucratic—it was being monitored, and corporations are micromanaged, they have their own short-term interests. This has reached a sufficient scale for *Science* magazine to have a news article about it recently, discussing the nationwide effects of narrowing the scope of research, and also increasing secrecy—at least on willingness to share information—with the shift to corporate funding.

Vietnam and the Intellectuals

To this day, the fact that the United States attacked South Vietnam has not penetrated American scholarship, intellectual life, or, indeed, most of the Left. It is hard to imagine a more dramatic example of discipline and subordination of the intellectual class than the fact that we cannot recognize the elementary truth that we attacked South Vietnam—certainly in 1961—and that South Vietnam was the main target of our attack right to the end of the war. One example of how this has been treated can be illustrated with Robert McNamara's book, which is now a major phenomenon, and everybody has reviewed it and discussed it.

McNamara was involved in two major decisions. The first was in 1961, shifting from state terrorism to direct attack against South Vietnam. The second major decision of the war was in January-February 1965: not the decision to bomb North Vietnam and not to send American troops to South Vietnam, but to bomb South Vietnam at triple the scale of the bombing of North Vietnam, and at a level that no area had ever been subjected to before. That is virtually a direct quote from Bernard Fall, who was the very hawkish French military historian and expert, also a very valued U.S. advisor—he went on missions in the field and so on. McNamara does not quote him, but he cites the article from which I just quoted. In fact, Fall is the only outside expert who is cited seriously in the book. McNamara cited his articles as "encouraging news." The context is McNamara's explanation of why it made sense to escalate the attack and bomb South Vietnam. He says that we were getting encouraging news from the ground. The article of Bernard Fall's that he cites says exactly what I mentioned; that the major decision of the war was to bomb South Vietnam at a level that no area had ever been subjected to. McNamara never discusses the decision to bomb South Vietnam in 1961 or in 1965.

The bombing of the south carried no cost—so it was uncontroversial and unimportant. Furthermore, Fall goes on to say that the United States is using so much military force that it cannot be militarily defeated in the short run. The United States was going way beyond anything the French ever did—so it cannot be militarily defeated any more than the French were in Algeria. But the Vietnamese will suffer the same fate, Fall says. That is McNamara's "encouraging news" from Fall. Fall was a hawk but he cared about the Vietnamese. He goes on to describe horrible war crimes, torture, combat missions in which the United States is massacring peasants, bombing hospitals, and so on. That is the "encouraging news." It is costless to us, so irrelevent.

Then McNamara has a footnote, in which he says that two years later Fall changed his mind and departed from his optimistic views, coming to think that perhaps U.S. force would not prevail. McNamara's referring to articles that Fall wrote in 1967 in which he expressed his concern that American forces might prevail. What he says in these articles is that Vietnam as a cultural and historical entity is in danger of becoming extinct under the blows of the most massive military machine ever directed against an area of this size. To McNamara, that means he changed his views from optimism to pessimism as to whether the U.S. force would prevail.

Well, the fact that McNamara interprets it that way is of no interest; he is an insignificant technocrat who barely understood what was going on. But what is of interest is the reaction to this book across the spectrum. Take a look at the reviewers. No one thought there was anything odd about McNamara citing Bernard Fall's bitter condemnation of U.S. atrocities as "encouraging news," and saying that he changed his mind on the "encouraging news" because he thought the United States was going to drive the country to absolute extinction. One would have to work pretty hard to find a counterpart to this in the Nazi archives. And that is across the spectrum!

I bring this up to show the inability of American intellectuals, including most of the dissidents on the Left, to break out of the constraints of the propaganda system. To this day, we cannot face the elementary fact that the United States attacked Vietnam. In fact, the United States carried out what must be the most amazing propaganda achievement in history. They managed to transfer the blame to the Vietnamese: we were the injured party. So from the end of the war up till today, the operative question is whether Vietnamese behavior has been good enough for us to allow them to enter the civilized world. When George Bush was president, a front-page story appeared in the *New York Times* that quoted a speech he gave in which he said that Hanoi must understand that we do not seek retribution for the crimes they have committed against us; we just want them to give an honest accounting of what they have done. This article appeared next to another, one of dozens of articles, noting with a kind of amazement that the Japanese have some flaw in their character; they seem to be unable to confess to the crimes they committed during World War II. I doubt that you would find such behavior anywhere else, even in Brezhnev's Russia. There, people knew that they were invading Afghanistan, that Russia was not the injured party. Here, the reversal passes smoothly, virtually without comment, probably even without awareness.

There was a story in the *Times*, another one of Nicholas Kristof's innumerable stories about the Japanese character flaw, in which it says that the Japanese finally did express remorse, but they used a word that does not mean "apology" but means "regret." What follows is a kind of philological analysis of the characters right there on the front page. And, furthermore, when the Japanese referred to their atrocities, Kristof argues, although they did make a strong statement about the fact that Japan had caused terrible suffering to the people of Asia, they did not really come clean. They were still trying to evade their guilt by putting it in the context of other aggression and colonialism. Obviously, that is absurd, nobody but the Japanese carried out colonial atrocities or aggression in Asia. Certainly, the Dutch never did, the British never did, the French never did, and we never did. How could anyone imagine that when we conquered the Philippines and killed a couple hundred thousand people it was anything but a welcoming party? As for Vietnam, four million Indochinese may have been killed, but it is the fault of the North Vietnamese, not our fault. And this is right in the same paragraph! The report quotes *Asahi Shimbun*, sort of the *New York Times* of Japan, to show that not everyone is willing to go along with this Japanese unwillingness to apologize; *Asahi* had a strong editorial condemning the outrageous refusal of Japan to apologize fully. Has the *New York Times* ever "apologized fully" or condemned the United States for not apologizing fully for the war in Vietnam, or for anything else for that matter? If you look at McNamara's book, he does apologize—but to the American people for what was done to Americans. If you now look at the reviews, that is considered very courageous and honorable.

Big changes took place in the whole culture in the 1960s, and the university was in many ways involved in it. There were major changes in attitudes toward everything, and these changes affected the entire society: in personal relations, in attitudes toward women, toward the environment, respect for other cultures —across the board there has been a very substantial change.

Even the *Times* has changed, because any institution reflects public attitudes to some extent. Even the Kremlin reflected public attitudes to some extent. So, as a result, the *Times* is much more open than it was in the 1960s. You wouldn't have had Bob Herbert writing in the *Times*. In fact, the *Times* was very prowar. Anthony Lewis was maybe the first person that I recall at the *Times* to criticize the war—though what it called "criticism of the war" was to say that the United States might not win at an acceptable cost. So, David Halberstam was "critical," and the editorials were "critical," on the grounds that the United States was following bad tactics and probably would not win, or maybe it was costing too much so we should try some other way. Even Lewis's belated criticism was very mild; it was that we began with bungling efforts to do good but it turned into a disaster and was costing too much. That was called "criticism" back in the 1960s and 1970s.

The students are not all that different from the general culture, nor were they at the time. But let us take something very remote from this topic—Native Americans. The original sin of American culture, after all, is what happened to the native population. That was not part of popular culture, not part of intellectual culture, not even part of academic anthropology. It was not until the late 1960s that the issue finally entered understanding and attitudes, and there was a willingness to notice that something happened to several million people who are not here anymore. That is when the scholarly research began in a serious way, some of it initiated from outside the academic profession, though it gradually got in. Public attitudes changed, too. By 1992, an attempt was made to carry off a celebratory quincentennial, liberation of the hemisphere. It was impossible. Not because of the colleges; the public would not accept it. They would not accept this as liberation of the hemisphere. And this change extends to almost every issue.

Again, you can see this dramatically with regard to Vietnam. Polls have been taken on public attitudes toward the Vietnam War since 1970 or so, and the responses are dramatic. The latest one that I know of was done in the early 1990s, I think. From the time they began in the 1970s until the early 1990s, about 70 percent of the general public describe the war as "fundamentally wrong and immoral," not "a mistake." But virtually none of the intellectuals have ever described it that way. The most they will say is "a mistake," and that is true of a good part of the Left. In Charles Kadushin's *The American Intellectual Elite*, published in 1974, he asked 200 "elite intellectuals," many of whom could be considered as left or left-liberal, what their attitudes were to the Vietnam War. These interviews, incidentally, were done in April 1970 or so, right after the invasion of Cambodia, which was the peak period of opposition to the war—colleges were closed down, everything was collapsing. This is from memory, so I may not have it exactly, but as I recall, he divided them into three categories. There were those he called "pragmatic" opponents of the war, such as Anthony Lewis, who basically said we are not going to get away with it, and it is costing us too much. Then there were what he called "moral opponents," who basically said, look, it is getting too bloody; napalming one hospital was okay but not ten hospitals. So that is "moral" opposition. The term is interesting. Then he had what he called the "ideological opponents," who said aggression is wrong. I think there were two out of two hundred—I'm not sure who the other one is, but every statement he quoted I recognized as my own.

Now, Kadushin did not do it, but suppose he had asked people what they thought of the Russian invasion of Czechoslovakia. That was bad enough, but they did not kill millions of people; they killed virtually no one. Well, everyone would have been an "ideological opponent," but he or she certainly would not have called it "ideological"—that would have been simply normal decency. On the other hand, among the American intellectual elite, at the peak period of opposition to the war, virtually no one opposed it on principled grounds, and those few are dismissed as "ideological," not really serious folk. At that time, about two-thirds of the public were condemning the war as immoral, and in a few years you get this stable result: "fundamentally wrong and immoral and not a mistake." Now that is one of many, I should say, reflections of a cultural split between the general public and the intellectual elite, which I think is pretty noticeable.

The universities have changed because the people in them have changed. When I say that the intellectuals have not changed, I mean the *public intellectuals*, people who are in the public arena who make profound statements about the world and so on—I do not think they have changed a great deal. To the extent one can measure it, the change is less dramatic than in the general public.

In any society, the respectable intellectuals, those who will be recognized as serious intellectuals, will overwhelmingly tend to be those who are subordinated to power. Those who are not subordinated to power are not recognized as intellectuals, or are marginalized as dissidents, maybe "ideological." Societies differ, however, and it is never 100 percent. But the tendency is just as obvious as the fact that corporate media serve corporate interests. This goes back through all of history, as far as I know. An example can be found in the Bible. Who were the respectable intellectuals and who were the dissidents? The false prophets were the respectable intellectuals. Centuries later they were labelled "false" prophets, but not at the time. At the time, who were the people that were imprisoned, reviled, and driven over the desert? They were the ones who were called "prophets" hundreds of years later. The reason was that they were giving both a moral and a geopolitical critique: that the leaders were going to drive the country to destruction, people should care about widows and orphans, and other such deranged fanaticism. Such people are going to be treated harshly, how harshly depends on the nature of the society. In Brezhnev's Eastern Europe they might be imprisoned or exiled. In a typical U.S. dependency such as El Salvador, they might have their brains blown out by U.S.-trained elite battalions or be cut to pieces with machetes, or they might simply flee for their lives. But such people are unikely to gain much respect in the respectable mainstream.

This is not something that is peculiar to our society by any means, far from it. Our own society is an unusually free and open one, and relatively privileged people—which means a lot of people —may undergo many kinds of unpleasantness, but not much by comparative standards.

The tendency to marginalize dissidents is always there and will always be there as long as grave inequalities in actual power and domination exist. When the actual power to make decisions is narrowly concentrated, then that power will be exercised in the doctrinal institutions as well.

John Dewey once described politics as the shadow cast by big business over society. The same is true of the universities and the doctrinal system generally, to no slight extent. Of course, one can struggle against that and change it, as in the 1960s and since. The situation in the universities or in the country generally is not what it was forty years ago. The change in the way blacks are treated in the South is dramatic, to mention one example. I was in Hattiesburg, Mississippi, a couple of years ago and the difference from the early 1960s is day and night. These changes were not a gift. They came from brave and dedicated struggle. And the same is true of everything else. Furthermore, it is an ongoing struggle. Those who are trying to roll the situation back to what it was will never stop. They are always engaged in that effort; they have plenty of resources, and unless people resist, they will win.

The changes cannot be rolled back easily, but they can be rolled back. The history of the labor movement is an instructive case. In every modern society, it has been a leading force for democratization and human rights. The United States happens to have an unusual labor history. This is a business-run society, to an unusual extent, and American labor history has been unusually violent and harsh. Not until the 1930s did American workers obtain the rights that workers had gained long before even in quite reactionary industrial societies. May Day was originally a day of solidarity with American workers; it is a dramatic reflection of the prevailing culture that this is one of the few societies where hardly any people know anything about May Day, let alone participate in it.

When the United States entered the mainstream of industrial society sixty years ago, the business press warned of the "hazard facing industrialists" in "the political power of the masses," and the need to "direct their thinking" to more proper channels and to roll back the rights that had last been won. After the war, the counterattack began in force. It was quite astonishing in scale and dedication, and class consciousness, with business leaders calling for a huge effort to win "the everlasting battle for the minds of men" and to "indoctrinate citizens with the capitalist story."

Forty-five years of intense propaganda has had an enormous effect. One result is that attitudes toward unions are very critical. About 80 percent of the population thinks working people ought to have more of a voice in public affairs, but about half that number think unions have too much of a voice. That is a reflection of extremely successful propaganda, everything from advertisements to the entertainment industry, where business propaganda presents the image of honest workingpeople fighting their enemy, the union. Demonizing unions has been one consciously designed theme of business propaganda from the late 1930s and by now it has had an effect. Another theme holds a certain picture of government, one that supports a huge welfare state for the rich through the Pentagon system and other devices, while

engendering fear and dislike of those aspects of government function that reflect popular interests and concern—and of course
concealing Dewey's truism. That's true quite broadly. For example,
why are the deficit and the debt a big issue? Are they an issue
because people are worried about the fact that the debt is well
within the historic range, relative to gross national product? They
are issues because it is driven into people's heads, day after day,
that this is our biggest problem.

The reasons are simple: the business world, particularly financial
interests, want the budget balanced, and also see that they can use
that project as a device to undermine the social programs that they
have always regarded as at best a tolerable luxury. As for the public,
here the polls are interesting. Typically, two kinds of questions are
asked: one set for the headline writers; the other for people who
are fighting "the everlasting battle for the minds of men" and,
therefore, want to keep their finger on the public pulse so that they
can package their agenda properly. For the headlines, the question
is: Do you want the budget balanced? The expected answer: Sure—
as if you were asked whether you want your household debts mag-
ically cancelled. Then comes the sensible question, on a par with
Do you want your debts cancelled if you lose your house, your car,
your children's education?—in this case, Do you want the budget
balanced if it means cutbacks in spending for health, education,
enivronmental protection? Then support drops radically, to 20 to 30
percent, depending on just how the question is asked.

But the business-financial world has spoken, and the shadow
obeys. Both political parties are adamant that the budget must be
balanced, and the media ram home the message constantly,
telling the public that it demands a balanced budget and it has
voted for it. A fabrication, but by dint of endless repetition, it will
probably come to be internalized, maybe even believed. The idea is
that if you drill something into people's heads long enough, their
attitudes will change, or at least what people think are their attitudes. Lacking any support in a depoliticized society in which popular organizations that might sustain a functioning democracy
have largely eroded, individuals are in a difficult position, often

unable to come to understand what they think, believe, and want —not an easy task under the best of circumstances. They sometimes react in irrational ways, which is no problem, as long as it does not threaten privilege.

The same is true of other propaganda campaigns. The "drug war" is just one example. Until Bush dramatically announced a "drug war" (once again—it is periodic) in September 1989, the drug problem was low on the list of public concerns. Out of curiosity, I monitored the media that month. The Associated Press wires had more on drugs than the whole international scene combined. On television and in the press, everything was drugs, drugs, drugs. By the end of the month the drug problem had shot way up to the leading issue of public concern. Was it because the problem had increased? No, simply very successful propaganda.

Again, these are natural features of a business-run society, that is, a society based on marketing and advertising—essentially, forms of manipulation and deceit. And these things have their effects, though they are sometimes slow. The United States came out of World War II as pretty much a social democratic society. Right through the 1980s, in fact, and even today, New Deal-style attitudes have remained deeply engrained, despite half a century of intense propaganda using every available medium to drive such ideas out of people's heads. It takes time, but there can ultimately be an effect, even if it is only confusion and demoralization, which is as good as actual thought control for those who want to ensure that the shadow remains obedient to the substance that casts it, and that democratic forms do not function significantly to undermine the power of the private tyrannies.

In my opinion, one leading current tendency is an extension of the traditional effort to reduce the threat of democracy, and to establish more firmly the Madisonian principle on which the country was founded: that the prime responsibility of government is "to protect the minority of the opulent against the majority," as Madison put it in the debates of the Constitutional Convention. The public is aware of the erosion of democracy. There is a regular Gallup Poll question asking people who they think the government works for. For a long time about half said "a few big interests looking out for themselves." Now over 80 percent say that the government is working for the few and the special interests— though what the public thinks the "special interests" are after years of intense propaganda is another question.

Such results, which extend rather broadly, reflect a general sense that we do not have a functioning democractic society, even if the reasons are not understood. In such a situation, a small group of dedicated fanatics with plenty of money behind them can make many changes, whatever the public prefers. A look at the Heritage Foundation budget proposals reveals such a possibility. It calls for severe cuts in social spending (in sharp opposition to the public will) and for an increase in Pentagon spending (overwhelmingly opposed by the public).

Where this will lead it is hard to say. It depends on whether, as often in the past, people can find ways to organize and respond constructively, defending at least a minimal social contract and recovering what was common understanding among a very large part of the population not too long ago: that concentration of decision making in the hands of unaccountable institutions of a basically totalitarian character is completely unacceptable, and that no decent human being should tolerate "the New Spirit of the Age" denounced by the popular working-class press in the mid-nineteenth century: "Gain Wealth, forgetting all but Self."

If they choose, privileged intellectuals in the universities and elsewhere can contribute to protecting and advancing democracy, freedom, and human rights. That is unlikely to win them many plaudits, but it brings rewards that are immeasurable.

Notes

1. This essay was extracted from an interview with Professor Chomsky.

(Immanuel Wallerstein)

The Unintended Consequences of Cold War Area Studies

In 1943, the Committee on World Regions of the Social Science Research Council (SSRC) (the coordinating council of the seven major U.S. social science national associations) wrote an internal report entitled "World Regions in the Social Sciences." The report opens with geopolitical considerations:

> The present war has focused attention as never before upon the entire world. Interest in foreign regions has been intensified and sharp attention drawn to areas over which we have felt little or no concern.

> The immediate need for social scientists who know the different regions of the world stands second only to the demand for military and naval officers familiar with the actual and potential combat zones. Since few overseas areas have hitherto attracted research, we lack the regional knowledge now required; and traditional curricula and methods of instruction have left inert much of such information as we possess. Travel and individual study have supplemented formal training but failed to correct the deficiency, and immigrants have learned more from us than we from them. The consequent scarcity of professional and scientific personnel combining linguistic and regional knowledge with technical proficiency seriously hampers every war agency. The supply of social scientists familiar with important

areas is so limited that highly trained specialists who possess
the requisite regional knowledge now occupy key positions that
make little or no use of their professional skill and require
thorough competence in a quite different social field. Our need
for comprehensive knowledge of other lands will not end with
the armistice or reconstruction. No matter what shape international organization may assume, the United States will enjoy
unexampled opportunities and face heavy responsibilities.
The ease, speed, and cheapness of communication and trans-
portation will tend to promote economic, political, and cultural
relations among nations. Trade, shipping, air lines, the press,
mining, the production and distribution of petroleum, banking,
government service, industry, and communications will require
thousands of Americans who combine thorough professional
or technical training with knowledge of the languages, economics, politics, history, geography, peoples, customs, and reli-
gions of foreign countries. In order that we may fulfill our
postwar role as a member of the United Nations our citizens
must know other lands and appreciate their people, cultures,
and institutions. Research, graduate teaching, undergraduate
instruction, and elementary education in world regions will be
desirable as far as one can see into the future.[1]

After reviewing the paucity of existing (non-Western) "regional
specializations" (with the limited exception of Latin America), the
committee takes the view that: "in permanent interest to the
United States no region outranks [the Far East (China and Japan)
and Latin America]."[2]

Toward the end of the report, the committee speaks to the epistemological questions that would become central to the practice of
area studies:

The primary task of the social scientist is to master and
contribute to his discipline. Since the scarcity of thoroughly
competent personnel (in this country and everywhere)
obstructs human progress, one may seriously question whether
we can spare the energies of accomplished and potential
scholars for regional study. But the laws and generalizations of
the social sciences are relevant to time, place and culture; and
much can be gained by the concreteness derived from the
regional approach. Some of the most fruitful results have been
obtained through the comparative method, and more precise

regional data will greatly extend and improve its use. Regional study offers the same advantages as the case method and reduces the temptation toward vague generalities—one of the besetting sins of the social scientist. Concentration on regions may conceivably open the road to one of the major and most distant goals of many outstanding social scientists: a weakening of the rigid compartments that separate the disciplines.[3]

That same year, the Joint Committee on Graduate Instruction of Columbia University appointed a Committee on Area Studies, which issued its preliminary report on December 17, 1943. There, too, the committee opened with geopolitical considerations: "It is clear that we have come in this country to [the] end of isolationism.... There will be need of many Americans who are thoroughly, exhaustively, and scientifically informed about particular neighbors."[4] The committee refers to

[T]he comment of a high officer in one of the great oil companies to the effect that for the Far East his company will have to recruit entirely new staffs since he does not believe it would be possible to send back to Asia men who had lived there in the era when white superiority and arrogance were the accepted thing.[5]

In discussing the pedagogy of area studies, the Columbia committee comes up with what would become the general pattern: graduate study in a standard discipline (or in one of the professional schools) combined with training in "general knowledge of a region." The committee suggests a metaphor: "An appropriate image would be that of a mine with numerous lateral shafts and one deep vertical shaft."[6] In tandem with the SSRC, it, too, suggests priority for Latin America and China and Japan.

Background to Area Studies

How did U.S. social science get into the situation out of which these two committees sought to extricate it? The fact that the United States had no "regional specialists" in 1943 was the direct consequence of how the social sciences were institutionalized in the period 1850 to 1914 in the five key countries of the process: Great Britain, France, Germany, Italy, and the United States.

Differentiation of the generic interest in social inquiry began to seem important in the eighteenth century, grew central after the French Revolution, and took institutional form in the second half of the nineteenth century.

This differentiation was built around three principal cleavages. The first was a cleavage past/present between "idiographic" history and the "nomothetic" social sciences (principally three: economics, political science, sociology). All four of these emergent disciplines concentrated their energies virtually exclusively (with quite rare exceptions) on the Western world. As Paul Buck noted, just before he took up his post as Director of Harvard University Library in 1959: "In 1903 not a single Harvard thesis dealt with anything beyond the limits of Classical Antiquity, Western Europe, and the United States."[7]

The second was the cleavage West/non-West. While the above four disciplines concentrated on the Western world, the non-Western world was studied by two different disciplines: anthropology for the "tribal" ("primitive") peoples, and Oriental studies for non-Western "high civilizations"—most notably, China, Japan, India, Persia, and the Arab-Islamic world. (If Latin America was a limited, partial exception, it was because it seemed to fall between stools.) The third cleavage was that of state-market-civil society, which established the boundaries for political science, economics, and sociology.[8]

In terms of the lack of "regional" experts in 1943, the key problem was the second cleavage. There were "experts" available (anthropologists, Oriental scholars, and a small cadre of geographers), but these "experts" were not what the SSRC or the high officer of the oil company adverted to in the Columbia report were looking for. The reason seems clear. Both anthropology and Oriental studies had been built on the nonhistoricity of the peoples and regions they were studying. Traditional ethnography sought to reconstitute the timeless patterns of the peoples prior to "culture contact" with the Western (colonizing) world. And Oriental studies was based on the not-too-hidden premise that the high civilizations they were studying were frozen historically, that is, that they were incapable of proceeding autonomously to modernity.

In fact, during World War II, the U.S. Army conducted "area training programs" of two kinds: Foreign Area and Language Curricula of the Army Specialized Training Program (ASTP-FALC) for enlisted personnel (located in fifty-five institutions) and ten Civil Affairs Training Schools (CATS) for officers; and in 1946, William Nelson Fenton of the Smithsonian Institution evaluated the ways in which and the degree to which geography and anthropology were integrated in these programs. (He makes no mention of Oriental studies, and I have no reason to believe such specialists participated at all in the army programs.)

Fenton argues that "geography is the regional science par excellence; it should be central to area study." Nonetheless it was not found to be "essential" in these courses.[9] The geographers were reduced to being providers of physical descriptions, as the anthropologists were to teaching "so-called customs...as unique phenomena without any feeling of cultural relativity."[10] Fenton was clearly dismayed by the pushing aside of what was called at the time ethnogeography:

> It may be argued fairly that Army area training programs did not summon real anthropology and real geography. But the concept of integrated area study drew upon the geographer's concept of region and the anthropologist's concept of culture. The training, however, stressed content without scientific principles. It was descriptive ethnogeography of a superficial and "pragmatic" variety.

He concluded with wistful hope for better days:

> The War and the Armed Forces reawakened students to study geography and to learn about the "funny people" of the world. We may expect an unforeseen demand for these subject matters in the postwar curriculum, and should not be amazed if courses in anthropology and geography are disproportionately large.[11]

Robert B. Hall, in a 1947 SSRC report, took a similarly dim view of the wartime experience:

> The war brought acceleration in and enthusiasm for area studies, partly through such devices as the Army Specialized

Training Programs and the Civil Affairs Training Schools in area and language. Governmental research in Washington and abroad was largely organized upon a regional basis, and many university professors in their war service had their first experience in the area approach and were converted to it....

Nevertheless, much of the effect of the war was harmful to a sound development of area studies, rather than beneficial. The A.S.T.P. and C.A.T.S. programs were devised to train people quickly to do specific and limited jobs. Area instruction was of necessity largely makeshift. Language, which on the whole was well taught, gradually came to be the one important aim in many institutions. The wartime area program is certainly not to be taken as the model for a liberal education or for training for research.[12]

But the army experience did serve nonetheless as a portent, both in its pushing aside of ethnography and in its emphasis on language training (which was later to become the major justification for postwar U.S. governmental financing of area studies). The army was reflecting the pragmatic concerns of the extra-university sponsors. After all, it seemed quite clear in 1943 that there was or would soon be much political turmoil throughout the world. It was not very helpful to U.S. diplomats, military officers, businessmen, or any others engaged in ongoing relations with these areas to know about preculture-contact patterns or the classical texts of frozen civilizations, and it was only marginally important to know about physical geography. They needed to know about the contemporary dynamics of areas that seemed to be going through at least as much change as the Western world.

Cold War Concerns

If this need was already felt during World War II, it of course became all the more urgent after 1945 when the world-system rapidly became structured in geopolitical terms by what came to be called the cold war. The United States believed it needed to know about current dynamics in non-Western areas not merely "to promote economic, political, and cultural relations among nations" (in the words of the SSRC report) but in order better to understand the functioning of those that already had communist regimes and to help prevent other areas from "falling into the hands of the communists," a theme that was central to U.S. official rhetoric for over forty years. As Harry Eckstein would write:

> We need not dwell long on what made non-Western societies obtrusive during the war, especially in the Middle East and Asia; a nucleus of people competent to study them had in fact been generated by special military training programs and work in the wartime and immediate postwar intelligence services. [Note: It would be interesting to do an analysis of the early staffs of the area programs from this point of view. Their nuclei, I would suppose, came chiefly out of the military ASTP programs and organizations such as the Office of Strategic Services (the predecessor of the Central Intelligence Agency).] They became more conspicuous as a result of decolonization and the accelerating growth of new nations. And the intrinsic appeals of studying exotic peoples and social structures and being *au courant* with rather dramatic current events were hardly lessened by the fact that the market for expertise in non-Western societies was bullish, especially, of course, in Washington. It need only be added that the most obtrusive and most marketable aspects of non-Western social life were political, or highly tinged with politics. There was a manifest need to diagnose and adapt to likely political trends in the Third World; and most of what was "new" in the new nations was either directly political (the appearance of nation-states or of parties of national "mobilization") or engineered by political structures (e.g., attempted industrialization, land redistribution, and so on).[13]

By the end of 1945, just after the conclusion of the war, when Harvard's committee made its report, the priority areas had already shifted. Latin America and Japan moved to the background. The priorities had now become the Soviet Union and China:

> The selection of the Soviet Union and China for regional study reflects various considerations. For an indefinite period, knowledge and understanding of Soviet Russia will probably be the most important single concern of our foreign policy. A continuing program of research in this field is of capital importance, although this Committee is well aware of its difficulties. Harvard can provide, from its existing resources, a strong nuclear team for work on Soviet Russia.

China will also loom large in the interests of this country in the coming decades. China is still in many respects *terra incognita* and presents an exceptional challenge to research. Trained personnel for China will perhaps be even more in demand than for Russia. The very remoteness of her civilization makes the study of China an unusually interesting one from the standpoint of liberal education. Here again Harvard can provide from her present resources a strong team.[14]

When the Committee on World Area Research of the SSRC (chaired by Robert B. Hall), successor to the earlier Committee on World Regions, made its case for area studies, it took the precaution of summarizing separately the arguments for and against area studies. It is interesting to note what these arguments were and in what order of priority they were placed. The first argument for area studies was once again geopolitical:

Those who hold most strongly to this view contend that the universities have an obligation to the nation. National welfare in the postwar period more than ever before requires a citizenry well informed as to other peoples, and the creation of a vast body of knowledge about them. The provincialism of the American public, so often bemoaned, is in no small way the fault of the American university....

The great danger here is that we forget so easily and insist upon the hardest road to learning. With and immediately after World War I there was a flurry of academic interest in Latin America. But the lesson was not learned. Forgetfulness soon came, with the emergency past, and we approached the next war under the same shroud of ignorance. During the war we spent untold millions in an attempt to make up for lost time. Already there are signs of lapsing again into the old and comfortable ways. Is man's judgment necessarily less realistic in time of war than in the tranquillity of peace? There were few academicians who were not convinced, during the war, that we must somehow break out of our shell of provincialism. Many of them today are opposed to any change in the academic status quo. We expend every effort to win a war, but we let the peace look out for itself. No wonder it fails to endure! Can we longer doubt that total peace is the direct counterpart of total war? A vast understanding and continued interest in all other lands and in all other peoples is mandatory if we are to gain that peace. Is this not at least a partial respon-sibility of our universities?[15]

The second and third arguments were more purely scholarly. Area studies would repair the fact that the social sciences "lack univer-sality." And they might help to overcome overspecialization:

> [T]he vertical pillars of knowledge, which are the largely self-isolated disciplines of today, leave between them both twilight zones and roles of complete ignorance. The cooperative attack upon the whole knowledge of an area is one way in which parts of these voids can be filled.[16]

The case stated against area studies does not seem very strong. One was the doubt that area studies has a "hard core." The second was that area specialists would have a hard time getting jobs. The answer the committee offered was that competence in the "traditional disciplines" would still be required, that is, the stu-dents would still get a Ph.D. in a discipline; and having this, he could presumably still get a job.

In conclusion, the committee returned to geopolitics. After surveying what kinds of areas studies existed as of then, it asked the critical organizational question: how much is needed? Here is the response:

> How shall we build this national program for area studies? First, we must work toward complete world coverage. This is necessary for several reasons. In terms of the national good, we must not gamble. The consensus of judgment might indi-cate that the critical areas for study are, let us say, the Far East, Russia, and Latin America; and still we might conceivably face our next great crisis in Africa or the Near East. Obviously, we need complete world coverage if we are to gain the full benefit of area studies academically. Since we cannot at once develop first-class centers of study for every area, it would seem prac-tical to attack the critical ones first. Of course, motivation for the development of programs is not uniform for all areas; it differs in both character and strength. The relative power of an area is one important consideration. Does the area in ques-tion generate an excess of power; does it approximate an equi-librium in this regard; or does it simply submit to the power exerted from other areas? Another consideration lies in the

level of culture existing in an area. Presumably we have more to gain from the study of China or India than we have from, say, the Congo Basin or New Guinea. Nevertheless, the long-run aim should be that once the more important areas are taken care of, or at the same time where opportunity is favorable, we should move rapidly toward filling out the map.[17]

It is fascinating to compare the SSRC report of 1947 with one issued the same year in Great Britain. There the committee, headed by the Earl of Scarborough, had been appointed by the Foreign Office in 1944, and was an interdepartmental committee primarily composed of representatives of many governmental ministries and including only two university-related persons out of fifteen, and these two the chairman and the secretary of the University Grants Committee. The terms of reference of this group, whose name was the Interdepartmental Commission on Oriental, Slavonic, East European and African Studies, were:

> To examine the facilities offered by universities and other educational institutions in Great Britain for the study of Oriental, Slavonic, East European and African languages and culture, to consider what advantage is being taken of these facilities and to formulate recommendations for their improvement.[18]

This commission too started by noting the problem of lack of specialized skill but then found a quite different solution. Whereas the Hall committee in the United States took no note whatsoever of Oriental studies, as though they did not exist, the British Scarborough report was *entirely* devoted to Oriental studies. It opened by reminding the reader of an English tradition of Oriental studies going back to Adelard of Bath, tutor of Henry II, who trans- lated a number of Arabic texts into Latin. It deplored the fact that nonetheless, as of 1939, there were more teaching posts in Oriental studies in France, Germany, Italy, the Netherlands, the Soviet Union, and the United States than in Great Britain. And the entire report is devoted to how to strengthen the structures of Oriental studies in Great Britain, restraining any criticism of it to two mild remarks: that "there is a disposition to overlook the fact that the languages in question are living and not historically embalmed," and that sometimes "the portrayal of the living present has been neglected and teaching has tended to concentrate on the classical past," which the committee fears "may have had some deterrent effect upon potential students."[19]

Area studies rapidly became accepted as a major innovation in the leading U.S. universities. It obtained the strong support of the SSRC. The basic premise was clearly laid forth in Charles Wagley's report of the SSRC National Conference on the Study of World Areas in 1948, which brought together a stellar cast of over 100 leading academics. Wagley tells us the group claimed that the objectives of area study were those of all social science, "namely the development of a universal and general science of society and of human behavior." The argument was that area studies could make "an unusually direct contribution to this ideal":

First of all area study calls for cooperation among the various disciplines of the social sciences and makes each specialist aware of his dependence upon specialties other than his own. Both Pendleton Herring and Talcott Parsons drew an analogy between area study and the science of medicine. There is no single science of medicine. Medicine is a most important field of application of a number of sciences: anatomy, physiology, biochemistry, bacteriology, and even psychology and some of the social sciences. Medicine calls on all these sciences to contribute to the understanding of the practical problems of the total human organism, to the whole man. In a similar way the study of an area, its culture, and its society calls for the contribution of many sciences, and the area provides a concrete focus for the disciplines of the social sciences and related fields of the humanities and natural sciences. Teamwork is absolutely necessary in area study, as in medicine. No single person, or even science or discipline, is capable of dealing with the complexities of the culture and environment of an area. The geographic limits of an area induce the specialists to pool their knowledge and prevent them from ignoring the relevance of factors which are outside the domains habitually considered by any one of them. The area approach induces the participants to cooperate. "In trying to advance knowledge within a definable context [area studies] may have a profound effect upon the development of social science research."[20]

The second SSRC conference, held two years later, reaffirmed these views, but worried about the financial implications of overcoming campus opposition to area studies:

> There are many other factors, perhaps less dramatic but nonetheless fundamental, which bear upon the present position of foreign area studies. To mention but one, the goals, methods, and support of American higher education continue to arouse protracted and sometimes anxious consideration. The American educational structure is still almost as centered on Western Europe as it was when Cathay seemed almost as far away as the moon. With the best will in the world, one commentator noted, the individual institution cannot do enough to give our education a world perspective. "The job is so big and time is short. Only a great Federal program can do it. The problem is to find out on what terms Federal aid is possible without Federal control."[21]

In 1952, UNESCO's *International Social Science Bulletin* devoted an issue to area studies. It opened with an somewhat acerbic, French view of the "problems of method" by Jean B. Duroselle, which considered area studies less a contribution to the "science of society" than to the pursuit of foreign policy:

> The expression "area study" is becoming the fashion in the United States. For some years now, doubtless as a corollary to the rapid development of an American foreign policy on a world scale, a large number of scholars, generally working in teams, have been instituting a form of enquiry whose aim is to spread a scientific knowledge of the problems raised by certain territories, States or groups of States in the world. Perhaps this is an instinctive reaction against the almost complete ignorance about everything that did not concern their continent from which American diplomatic circles suffered in the isolationist period....
>
> Is this method entirely new? Does its development, which is a characteristic phenomenon of present-day American science, represent a sensational bound forward in the history of the human-mind, one of those abrupt mutations which occur only once or twice in a century? Such a claim would be somewhat naive....
>
> No one will be surprised that we class area studies in the very well-defined field of the study of international relations. A simple consideration of the nature of these studies reveals

the direction given them, consciously or not, by their authors. Take as an example a collection which has already created some stir, *Modern France*, a symposium edited at Princeton by Professor Edward Mead Earle, with contributions from 28 American scholars and one Frenchman, Mr. André Siegfried. Taken together, the studies, which might be disparate if they had been juxtaposed, converge towards a well-defined aim: to help the educated public, particularly American scholars and statesmen, to understand the real situation of France. Yet, setting aside a purely abstract curiosity, what can be the interest of a precise knowledge of the French situation if it be not to evaluate the place and the role of France in the world? The mere fact of examining scientifically the various factors in the situation of a given country or group of countries implies that the chief aim is to assess the relationship between the geographical area under consideration and the rest of the world. It can, indeed, be said that a study of an area which treated its subject in the absolute and failed to regard it as essentially an element in the human universe, would be pure verbiage, without any scientific value....It is finally possible to imagine—and it would not be such a very extravagant flight of fancy—area studies being commissioned by the Defence Ministry or the Foreign Affairs Ministry of this or that country, with a militarist or imperialist aim.

It is thus clear that an area study is essentially a contribution to the study of international relations.[22]

Hans Morgenthau's views, in the same issue of the journal, were not too different:

Practical needs, if on a higher intellectual level, still provide one of the major arguments in favour of area studies; they are also apparent in the selection of the areas most frequently studied. Russia and the Far East vie with Latin America for the attention of students and the commitment of resources. It is not by accident that it is with those areas that American foreign policy is primarily concerned and that, at least with regard to the first two of them, knowledge is fragmentary and the supply of experts available for government service falls drastically below demand. Nor is it an accident that the areas around which area studies are centered are generally defined in terms which coincide with the areas of political interest.

Aside from the training of prospective government officials, area studies are frequently motivated by the recognition of America's predominant place in world affairs, which necessitates a knowledge of the world with which the United States must deal as friend or foe. This higher level of practicality entails the desire to learn all the facts about all the regions of the world. Since the regions of prime political importance seem already to be adequately covered, late comers among university administrations have been known to search for empty spaces on the map which they might cover with an institute for area studies. Underlying this tendency is the conviction that knowledge of unknown areas is useful in itself and that the more knowledge of this kind there is, the better will we be able to understand the world and discharge our responsibilities towards it....

[A] non-directive, "objective" social science is a contradiction in all terms. All social sciences, in so far as they deserve the name of science at all, cannot fail to reflect both the social *Standort* and the particular intellectual interest of the observer. A social science which strives for unattainable objectivity can at best collect the raw materials of science in the form of a mass of unrelated or but superficially and irrelevantly related facts. Social science is of necessity science from a certain point of view, and that point of view is determined by the general factor of the over-all outlook of the scholar as well as by the special factor of the particular interest with which the scholar approaches the segment of social reality which he intends to investigate.[23]

By the 1950s, area studies had become well instituted in U.S. universities.[24] Support was coming from the major foundations. Rockefeller was the pioneer, having given grants for non-Western studies as early as 1933. Rockefeller also provided the initial funds after 1945 for the Russian Institute at Columbia, which many considered to be the model for other area studies programs. Carnegie soon followed, giving a very large grant to Harvard's Russian Research Center in 1948. But it was the newly established Ford Foundation that was to have the widest, longest impact, beginning in 1952 when it instituted its Foreign Area Fellowship Program, which was administered directly until 1962 and since then via Joint Committees of the SSRC and the American Council of Learned Societies (ACLS). These fellowships paid for doctoral training and field research of a very large number of the most well-known U.S. area specialists. (I myself was an early recipient of one of their Africa grants in 1955–57.)

The Soviet Union made a spectacular contribution to U.S. area studies by launching the first Sputnik on October 4, 1957. This enabled the Eisenhower administration to persuade Congress of the urgency of passing the National Defence Education Act (NDEA) in 1958. Under Title VI of NDEA, aid was given to area studies centers throughout the United States for more than twenty years.[25] In the process, not only were the faculties and training programs internationalized but so were the libraries.[26] When Richard D. Lambert did his SSRC survey of the situation in 1973, he observed a spectacular growth in area studies:

> We only need to note that thirty years ago the American scholarly experts on many of the world areas could have been assembled in a small conference room and that today all the world areas are represented by flourishing scholarly associations with memberships running, in some cases, into the thousands. Similarly, comparing the course offerings in any major university in 1941 with those in 1971 will show the success of language and area studies in broadening the curriculum. While there are no figures quite comparable for an earlier period, the scale of the enterprise is now striking. In 1969, some 3,803 language and area specialists in 203 organized graduate-level programs taught 8,890 substantive courses dealing with the various world areas to 65,243 graduate students, of whom 3,014 were training specialists, and 227,541 undergraduates. Language courses given by these programs had an enrollment of 91,029. On each campus, language and area studies have made great strides in growth, in institutionalization, in winning student clientele, in gaining administrative support, and in placing one faculty member after another in the various academic departments. Several generations of students have been trained, graduated, and placed in fruitful and often prestigious jobs. Research has become theoretically and methodologically more sophisticated as scholars have become more competent in dealing with their areas. In several disciplines, many of the more promising young men are working on non-Western areas; furthermore, many cross-disciplinary specializations—such as anthropology and law, sociology and history, economics and sociology, political

science and anthropology, art and music, philosophy and religion—are developing largely in a non-Western context.

The centers and their faculties provide a repository of expertise on which government can and does draw for research, consultants, or temporary employment. The graduate students produced at the centers are an important recruitment source for the foreign affairs agencies. Much of the literature which stocks international agency libraries is produced by individuals in these centers. The government also uses these centers for the training of current employees.[27]

Unintended Consequences

If the primary purpose of area studies was to produce a large supply of skilled specialists available for public service and private business, it was no doubt a great success. By 1974, a skeptical Congress, faced with further appropriations requests, was already wondering about an "oversupply." It required the intervention of "academics close to Nixon (viz., Daniel Moynihan and Henry Kissinger)" to save Title VI.[28]

If, on the other hand, the primary purpose of area studies was to demonstrate a new model of university research and teaching, we may be more skeptical of its effectiveness. Lambert admits that he is "a bit puzzled by the force of negative feelings towards area studies of some non-area-oriented American scholars, particularly in sociology, political science, and economics." He cites James Rosenau's reassertion of the virtues of the "disciplinary generalist" as against the area specialist, "the former presumed to be distinct from the latter-and-presumed to have superior theoretical and methodological—especially quantitative—skills."[29]

The quarrel could be put down to one over resources, or a rehash of the *Methodenstreit* between nomothetic and idiographic epistemologies, and of course in part it was. But the stakes were in fact greater, because the quarrel was in fact over the future organizational shape of the social sciences. The fact is that area studies had no clear epistemological position and stood de facto, but not intentionally, in an uncertain middle ground in the *Methodenstreit*. This story must be told twice, before 1968 and after 1968.

It was clear, as we have already noted, that area studies threatened the basic justifications of both Oriental studies and anthropology in their dominant pre-1945 versions. Of the two, the impact was greater on Oriental studies since it had claimed to be studying large regions that were often not too different in geographic or cultural scope from the areas encompassed in area studies. It was not an overlap that could be ignored. Oriental studies really only had two choices when faced with area studies: it could resist; or it could surrender, hoping to turn area studies into its avatar.

In 1955, Wilfrid Cantwell Smith, addressing the American Oriental Society, called for resistance. He staked his ground on the "pursuit of truth" by the humanities, which he saw as disinterested and intent on "increasing human knowledge" via the "peculiarly Western" characteristic of "boundlessly inquisitive curiosity" (with which he identified Oriental studies) as contrasted with "the pragmatic reflection of the scientist, especially the applied scientist" (represented for him by the area studies specialists):

> [T]here is the more recent, more practical, more sudden task to which the universities have addressed themselves, chiefly through the emergence of "area studies" centers. These have arisen not primarily out of the inner impetus towards disinterested knowledge, but in response to a stringent practical demand—the need for "experts," for men who can deal with concrete and specific problems that have arisen because of inter-cultural activity, particularly at the governmental level. And here comes into play that brilliant and dangerous Dewey-esque half-truth, according to which "thought is interrupted action." This, of course, is an oversimplification. It leaves out too much; specifically, it leaves out thought in the humanities tradition....
>
> When an unexpected problem, unfamiliar obstacle, confronts an on-going activity, the universities are called upon to solve that problem, to manipulate that obstacle.
>
> It would be idle to deny that this principle underlies, and doubtless will continue to underlie, the stark and perhaps exhilarating expansion of oriental studies in our day. It is the source of money, of students, of whole new programs. But it would be equally idle to deny that it is full of danger, both to our studies and to the world. There is the danger of "being used"; of subordinating

knowledge to policy, rather than vice versa. There is the subtler danger of acquiring seeming knowledge that is, in fact, false. For it happens to be a law of this universe in which we live that you cannot understand persons if you treat them as objects. You misinterpret a culture if you approach it in order to manipulate it. A civilization does not yield its secrets except to a mind that approaches it with humility and love. Knowledge pursued *ad majorem Americae gloriam* will, in the realm of oriental, as indeed in all human studies, fail to be sound knowledge....

Another point in this connection that it would take far too long to develop here in full but on which it seems to me imperative to enter at least a passing protest, concerns the concept of "discipline." As an academic divisional concept this has to a considerable degree in American universities replaced the quite different notion of "subject." It had done so largely because of the preoccupation with the technique and method rather than with the object of study, and, correspondingly, with manipulation and control rather than appreciation. The recent emphasis on interdisciplinary study is a backhanded recognition of the inadequacy of the whole procedure; but it is no solution. Also, the confusion in our studies over the question of "discipline" versus "area specialty" has in part arisen, I suggest from the inadequacy, I would even say invalidity, of the presuppositions on which the "discipline" idea rests; and, in my submission, accordingly of the whole manipulative approach to the cultures of the Orient....

In this matter, as in the matter of reverence and humanity, the fact is that any student mind must, to operate effectively, have a loyalty that transcends its immediate group, whether professional or cultural. In oriental studies, it must transcend both professional and cultural at once; and there's the rub....

To learn to understand, with imaginative sympathy and objective validity, the other cultures of the world must not be at the expense of appreciating our own culture, or keeping loyalty to it. On the contrary, it must be grounded rather in the recognition that it is of the genius of our culture (and in this it would seem to be alone among man's systems) to understand the world in which we live, including the civilizations which have preceded and those which surround us. And on the practical side also, it is only so that we can serve our culture; for only so can our society learn to live with (not to dominate) the others who share the planet and its problems with us....

The over-all problem should perhaps be worded: "The role of university in a multi-cultural world." The problem of oriental studies in a university is the problem of the emergence of that new kind of university that will be apt in our new kind of world.[30]

It is worthy of more than passing note that this very tradition-alist, deeply conservative defense of the humanist tradition and of Oriental studies ended on the theme of a multicultural world. What is striking about this declaration is its political stance. It was clearly not in tune with the founders and sponsors of area studies, with the idea that the university must urgently serve the national interests of the Western world by training the personnel who can run the world. But neither was it in tune with the contemporary elites and mass movements in the areas of the world it was studying. If William Cantwell Smith did not wish to serve as an expert for John Foster Dulles, he did not wish to be one for Jawaharlal Nehru either. The world he was defending was an Orient that had been.

There was another road possible for Oriental studies, the road of accommodation. In 1959, the University Grants Committee of the United Kingdom decided to review the scene previously ana-lyzed in the Scarborough Report. The so-called Hayter Subcommittee reported in 1961, and its tone was very different from that of the Scarborough Report. Its three key findings were:

4. The Sub-Committee regards the overall pattern of
development of Oriental and Slavonic studies as disappointing.
Progress in studies related to countries within the Commonwealth has been rather more encouraging, but by and large
interest in eastern Europe, the Middle East,
South-East Asia and the Far East is confined to the language
departments. The study of these regions barely enters into the
work of the non-language departments. Within the language
departments themselves the proportion of work devoted to
modern studies is small, and there is little attention given either
at undergraduate or post-graduate level to these countries as
living societies. In some departments interest in modern
languages has grown very slowly although there has been some
improvement in the last year or two. (Chapters VI and VIII.)

5. Great changes have come over the world in the last 15 years.
The political centre of gravity, which up to 1939 was in western

Europe, has now moved outwards, east, west and south. The British educational system has taken little account of this move and is still centred on western Europe, with an occasional bow to North America and the Commonwealth. This seems to the Sub-Committee anachronistic. It is the central point of the Sub-Committee's recommendations that the universities should now be encouraged to pay more attention to studies related to Asia, Africa and eastern Europe. (Chapter VII.)

6. The Sub-Committee does not think that the main expansion of these studies should be in the language department. It is in the history, geography, law, economics and other social science departments and faculties that the new developments should take place.[31]

But they go even further:

All our recommendations are conditioned by our belief that this country must be better equipped to understand and to contribute to developments in Asia, Africa and eastern Europe. The new and growing importance of these regions with their vast populations has so changed the balance of power and the inter-action of ideas that the civilisation of western Europe has no longer an undisputed pre-eminence. Its importance continues, but it must accommodate itself to other powerful and creative influences outside.[32]

Shortly thereafter, in 1963, Sir Hamilton Gibbs, a leading British Orientalist who had become the director of a U.S. area studies center, the Center for Middle Eastern Studies at Harvard, addressed the School of Oriental and African Studies of London University on the subject of area studies:

Gibbs acknowledged "the limitations of classical Orientalism":

Briefly stated, its subject has been the study of what is now generally called the "great culture," the universal norms expressed or predicated in literature, religion and law, recognised as authoritative and paradigmatic by all its adherents, but rarely more than loosely approximated in their diverse local groups, at grips with the actualities of their existential situations. It is the impact of this realisation that is bring about a revolution in contemporary orientalism. More intimate and prolonged contacts with these diverse peoples and groups have opened our eyes to the facts of diversity, of the multiplicity of "little cultures," existing under the shadow of the "great culture," each with its own specific relation to and interpretation of the "great culture", its own tradition, and its own reactions to local events and circumstances that affect its manner and means of livelihood. This does not mean the long-established and deep-rooted ideals and emotional stimuli of the "great culture" have ceased to influence their attitudes and aspirations; but it does mean that they are interpenetrated, and sometimes in competition, with other influences deriving from the more immediate local factors.

The revolution does not, however, end with this growing interest in contemporary societies. Rather suddenly the orientalist has come to realise that diversity is not just a modern phenomenon—on the contrary, it has always been there, a permanent feature of social life and organisation under the overarching unity of the "great culture." The Indianists have been aware of this for a long time, but it has only comparatively recently entered into the perspectives of Far Eastern and Near Eastern orientalism. With this discovery, the range and function of classical orientalism have been correspondingly not only enlarged, but made immensely more complex and difficult.[33]

Having conceded the limitations of classical Orientalism, Gibbs proceeds to find it a place *within* area studies:

The essence of an Area Studies programme (and the feature that sometimes renders it suspect in the eyes of academic purists) is that it must be in some degree "interdisciplinary." The term may perhaps sound rather pretentious, and in any case calls for definition. In practice, what it amounts to is an awareness that social reality is both specific and multi-dimensional, and that the methods of analysis employed by each specialist in a given area must be gradually redefined and their findings adjusted, and in a sense controlled, by correlation with the analyses and findings of the others. The problem that it sets, therefore, is one of intercommunication, which in turn calls for a substantial foundation of mutual understanding. No doubt each social scientist must be able to communicate with his own kind, economists, political scientists, sociologists, linguists, etc., in the peculiar technical notation of his "science," but at the same time, in the context of Area Studies, he must in some respects change his frame of reference. It needs no proof that to apply the psychology and mechanics of Western political institutions to Arab or Asian situations is pure Walt Disney....

I must underpin my statement that the role of the orientalist is central in area studies. One might say that it is central in the sense that it is a part of his function to bring together and correlate the findings of the separate special studies. Yet the mere juxtaposition or interweaving of these findings might be done by others. The important thing is that, if any such synthesis is attempted, it is significant and valuable only if the various data are related to a central core. The orientalist's function is to furnish that core out of his knowledge and understanding of the invisibles—the values, attitudes and mental processes characteristic of the "great culture" that underlie the application even today of the social and economic data—to explain the why, rather than the what and the how, and this precisely because he is or should be able to see the data not simply as isolated facts, explicable in and by themselves, but in the broad context and long perspective of cultural habit and tradition.[34]

A good example of how Oriental studies could accomodate to being an area studies center is the Department of Uralic and Altaic Studies of the University of Indiana, founded itself as an outgrowth of an ASTP-FALC during World War II. Although theoretically defined in terms of a linguistic grouping of studies, de facto it redefined itself as a center of "inner Asian" studies, including the study of Tibetan, which is neither a Uralic nor an Altaic language. In 1967, the then chair of the department justified this inclusion in the following fashion:

The explanation [of including Tibetan] lies in the Department's concern for high standards of scholarship, permitting an understanding in depth of the civilizations falling within the scope of the instruction given. Political and religious ties linking Mongolia and Tibet have, for centuries, been very close. For instance, virtually the whole body of the Buddhist sacred books written in Mongolian were translated from Tibetan, or to take another example, the Tibeto-Mongol treaty of 1913 was a political instrument of great importance....

In the minds of the public influenced by newspaper headlines, Asia tends to be equated with East Asia where, in the last three decades, the United States has fought three wars. Troubles in

THE UNINTENDED CONSEQUENCES OF COLD WAR AREA STUDIES

the Middle East and famines in India receive their fair share of interest, but very little is heard of the huge empire of the Soviet Union which, together with Tibet, Afghanistan, and Chinese Turkestan form what is conveniently called Inner Asia. The absence of sensational news should not let us forget the importance of the region. The Asiatic parts of the USSR cover an area far greater than that of the United States, and its land boundary extends over eight thousand miles. This land frontier is not only one of the longest in the world, it is also one of the most peaceful. A fact which, if not overlooked, is usually surrounded by a conspiracy of silence is that among the "white" nations of the world, the Russians alone have maintained themselves in Asia without encountering serious difficulty. As the living standards of the Asiatic parts of the Soviet Union are undeniably superior to that of the surrounding countries, the study of the relationship between populations living on both sides of the border is extremely rewarding.[35]

Did Gibbs's hope that the Orientalist should be central in area studies come to fruition? It did not, and in 1973, the International Congress of Orientalists changed its name to the International Congress of Human Sciences in Asia and North America. To be sure, this was after heated debate, and ten years later, the group sought to restore the balance slightly by a further change of name to the International Congress for Asian and North African Studies. But the term Orientalist was not resuscitated.

What happened to the anthropologists was parallel. Before 1945, they were virtually alone in studying the peoples they were studying. Not only were they alone collectively, but also were alone individually. The combination of a paucity of numbers and a certain informal tradition made it that few "tribes" or "peoples" had ever been studied by more than one anthropologist, especially those that were located in remoter areas. Anthropologists tended to see themselves as the sympathetic spokespersons of their peoples before a world that was ignorant and often hostile in ways parallel to the sense of the Orientalist who could empathize with his or her "great civilization" in ways that most Westerners failed to appreciate. The moral stance of most anthropologists was that of the defender at court.

With the rise of nationalist movements in the colonial world, the anthropologists began to be considered by these movements as anachronistic and unfriendly insofar as they seemed to deny the reality of *national* sentiments and aspirations in the colonies. Far from being defenders at court, they seemed to be denigrators at court of the new movements. Meanwhile, with the advent of area studies, all sorts of other social scientists came to study these areas. Those who concentrated on the present (the nomothetic trio, for example) tended to concentrate on urban, national phenomena, and hence were in tune with nationalist premises and quite often with nationalist aspirations. Even the historians seemed in tune, since one of the things nationalist movements wanted most urgently to demonstrate was that their countries had a history, and that if German history could be traced back to the Huns and French history to Vercingetorix, then Gold Coast history could be traced back to the ancient kingdom of Ghana.

Suddenly, anthropologists who had often been in trouble with colonial officials because they were considered too friendly to the "natives" saw themselves lumped by the nationalists with the more retrograde sector of remaining colonial officials. In any case, anthropologists lost their geographic monopoly and were forced to rethink their object of study. The pristine patterns of preculture-contact peoples was of limited interest when the new cadre of historians, linguists, and archaeologists were demonstrating how continually changing had been these patterns.

On the other hand, anthropologists had joined the movement for area studies with considerable enthusiasm, since almost all of them were immediately eligible as area specialists. And area studies promised to be a source of funds for anthropologists who had few such sources previously. Therefore, anthropologists were not in general going to allow the mere fact that they had lost their geographic monopoly, their relatively favorable image in the regions, and their underlying rationale stop them. They sought to salvage the situation by emphasizing their traditional strengths—the concern with "culture," the concern with the "local," the search in the specificities of each culture for alternate forms of rational behavior. How and why these concerns added up to a distinctive "discipline" of the social sciences was seldom addressed, but anthropology continued to display organizational vitality by assembling many who felt uncomfortable with the more nomothetic social sciences.

Meanwhile, as Oriental studies and anthropology (the "non-West" social sciences) were losing their clearly defined niches and even their underlying premise of ahistoricity, the "Western" social sciences—history and the nomothetic trio of economics, political science, and sociology—were being corroded by area studies. I use the word "corroded" deliberately because the best metaphor is that of a rust that was formed by contact with reality which began to eat away at these four disciplines. Gibbs, in his lecture, described the key element quite well:

> The fourth, and not least important, function of Area Study Centres is to play the part of Trojan horse, that is, to awaken and stimulate within the general academic community a growing interest in and concern with non-Western civilisations in the disciplinary departments and faculties. Instead of being cloistered in some separate nook or cranny in the university complex, each specialist member of their staffs is expected to take, and generally does take, his proper share in the normal activities of his own department; thus collectively they radiate a knowledge and understanding of specific aspects of non-Western cultures among a much wider range of undergraduate and graduate students—as well as (it is to be hoped) among their departmental colleagues.[36]

In 1945, in the average department of history in a U.S. university, at least 95 percent of the members were concerned with U.S., European, and Greco-Roman history. The figure for the trio of nomothetic departments was more likely to be 100 percent. By the 1960s, as many as a third of the members of any major history department were working on and usually teaching "non-Western" history. The figures were a little lower in political science but still substantial. Sociology was lower still and economics lowest of all, but there were some. And the percentages continued to grow in the 1970s. The impact of this has never been really studied, but the image of a Trojan horse is well-taken. Once the demography of the faculty was changed, the curriculum was changed and above all the legitimacy of topics for study was transformed. The narrow set of legitimate objects of study was breached. The initial breach was only geographic. But it was crucial, since it crossed the West/non-West, civilized-barbarian divide. Once the breach was made, everything else could follow; and follow it did, after 1968.

The Cold War Eats Its Own

In the 1960s, a famous scandal erupted in area studies—Operation Camelot—which led to the first serious debate in the U.S. social science community about the use and misuse of area studies.[37] Operation Camelot posed "a crisis of ethics."[38] The story itself is rather simple. In 1964, the Special Operations Research Office (SORO) of American University, an agency funded by the U.S. Department of the Army, received a grant for something called Project Camelot. On December 4, 1964, the organizers sent out to potential participants in a planning conference this description of their intentions:

> Project CAMELOT is a study whose objective is to determine the feasibility of developing a general social systems model which would make it possible to predict and influence politically significant aspects of social change in the developing nations of the world. Somewhat more specifically, its objectives are:
>
> First, to devise procedures for assessing the potential for internal war within national societies;
>
> Second, to identify with increased degrees of confidence those actions which a government might take to relieve conditions which are assessed as giving rise to a potential for internal war; and
>
> Finally, to assess the feasibility of prescribing the characteristics of a system for obtaining and using the essential information needed for doing the above two things.
>
> The project is conceived as a three to four-year effort to be funded at around one and one-half million dollars annually. It is supported by the Army and the Department of Defense, and will be conducted with the cooperation of other agencies of the government. A large amount of primary data collection in the field

is planned as well as the extensive utilization of already available data on social, economic and political functions. At this writing, it seems probable that the geographic orientation of the research will be toward Latin American countries. Present plans call for a field office in that region.

By the way of background: Project CAMELOT is an outgrowth of the interplay of many factors and forces. Among these is the assignment in recent years of much additional emphasis to the U.S. Army's role in the over-all U.S. policy of encouraging steady growth and change in the less developed countries in the world. The many programs of the U.S. Government directed toward this objective are often grouped under the sometimes misleading label of counterinsurgency (some pronounceable term standing for insurgency prophylaxis would be better). This places great importance on positive actions designed to reduce the sources of disaffection which often give rise to more conspicuous and violent activities disruptive in nature. The U.S. Army has an important mission in the positive and constructive aspects of nation building as well as a responsibility to assist friendly governments in dealing with active insurgency problems.

Another major factor is the recognition at the highest levels of the defense establishment of the fact that relatively little is known, with a high degree of surety, about the social processes which must be understood in order to deal effectively with problems of insurgency. Within the Army there is especially ready acceptance of the need to improve the general understanding of the processes of social change if the Army is to discharge its responsibilities in the over-all counterinsurgency program of the U.S. Government. Of considerable relevance here is a series of recent reports dealing with the problems of national security and the potential contributions that social science might make to solving these problems. One such report was published by a committee of the Smithsonian Institution's research group under the title, "Social Science Research and National Security," edited by Ithiel de Sola Pool. Another is a volume of the proceedings of a symposium, "The U.S. Army's Limited-War Mission and Social Science Research." These proceedings were published in 1962 by the Special Operations Research Office of the American University.

Project CAMELOT will be a multidisciplinary effort. It will be conducted both within the SORO organization and in close collaboration with universities and other research institutions within the United States and overseas. The first several months of work will be devoted to the refinement of the research design and to the identification of problems of research methodology as well as of substance. This will contribute to the important articulation of all component studies of the project toward the stated objectives. Early participants in the project will thus have an unusual opportunity to contribute to the shaping of the research program and also to take part in a seminar planned for the summer of 1965. The seminar, to be attended by leading behavioral scientists of the country, will be concerned with reviewing plans for the immediate future and further analyzing the long-run goals and plans for the project.[39]

The project was designed primarily to study Latin America as the letter indicates. But the list of countries recommended for initial research included not only twelve Latin American countries but also three in the Middle East, four in the Far East, one in Africa, and even two in Europe (France and Greece). The project combined the U.S. government's interest in learning how best to "counter insurgencies," but also presumably a social science interest in developing substantive knowledge about "social conflict theory."

What undid Camelot was also quite simple. SORO asked a Chilean scholar who had become a U.S. citizen, Hugo Nuttini, to make a trip to Chile to explore possibilities of cooperation by Chilean scholars in the project. Nuttini exceeded his mandate and actually invited participation. At the very same time, Johan Galtung, a Norwegian sociologist who was teaching at FLACSO in Santiago, received an invitation to SORO's meeting on the project which indicated the U.S. Army's role in sponsoring the study of counterinsurgency. He declined to go, on principle. What principle? In reply to a later article by Alfred DeGrazia critical of his actions, Galtung explained his attitudes:

> DeGrazia's editorial contains a sentence: "A Norwegian pacifist named Johan Galtung egged on a Chilean communist paper to agitate South American antiyanqui jingoism among a few professors etc.," which is a rather incorrect description of what happened. Although it is true that I am a pacifist, this is irrelevant: I see nothing wrong in general in Defense Department

sponsored research and fully appreciate the role of the armed services in sponsoring important behavioral science research. Being Norwegian is more to the point: Project Camelot looks different from the point of view of a small nation than from the point of view of the top nation in one of the power blocs. What is completely untrue is that I "egged on a Chilean communist paper." What happened was that I (working in Chile as a UNESCO professor) had been invited by the late project director to participate in the project, rejected the generous offer because I had misgivings about it, received no satisfactory explanation from the project directors about the issues I raised (the same as the issues discussed in the present article), and only then made the information I had about the project available to Latin American colleagues. I can assure DeGrazia that more than "a few professors" were appalled by the project and refused indignantly to participate in it; in fact, there have probably been few issues that have united empiricists, phenomenologists and Marxists alike as effectively. That all this later (in fact almost two months later) reached a local communist paper (*El Siglo*) will surprise nobody, nor that it was exaggerated into accusations of deliberate espionage or almost military intervention. Also blatantly untrue is the assertion that the project was "supported by some of the best foreign scholars in Latin America."[40]

In any case, Nuttini plus Galtung seemed to be enough to arouse considerable discussion in Chile, an intervention by the president of Chile with the U.S. State Department, debate in the U.S. Congress, and cancellation of the project worldwide.[41] More importantly, it stimulated a major debate within the United States and elsewhere about the propriety of collaboration by scholars with U.S. government projects. It will be no surprise that there were many different views expressed on this subject on the part of both scholars and public figures. The range of statements on this particular project may be found in a collection edited by Irving Louis Horowitz.[42]

Project Camelot had the consequence of directing systematic attention to the Cold War side of area studies, which now became the object of general discussion, the occasion for individual and organizational statements of ethical-political positions, and an increased wariness of many governments about the role of U.S. scholars doing research in their countries.

The revolution of 1968, which subjected the general role of the universities in relation to Cold War politics to a very great criticism, was now at hand. We need not here review the implications of this revolution for the world-system as a whole[43] but merely its implications for area studies. It was a case of innocence lost. Area studies had basked in a self-congratulatory aura of beneficent empathy akin to the attitude of anthropologists before the rise of anticolonial national movements. Now area studies, which in a sense repeated the role of the anthropologists in a new form in the period of decolonization, came under attack by those being studied on the very same grounds, of being in Galtung's phase "scientific colonialism," which he defined as "a process whereby the center of gravity for the acquisition of knowledge about the nation is located outside the nation itself."[44]

What happened subsequently was that the rationale for area studies began to fritter as it came under attack for its sociopolitical role as well as for its intellectual limitations. In a celebratory report of the Office of Education, written in 1964, Bigelow and Legters state of the NDEA Language and Area Centers:

> Language and area centers have been described as a product of the well-nigh revolutionary awakening of American higher education to the non-Western world.... Perhaps the greatest gain, difficult to measure at this stage of history, has been the effect of both the center concept and the centers program on non-Western studies generally and, in turn, on the liberal arts.[45]

In 1964, these programs were still basking in a glow of self-congratulatory liberal internationalism. The Vietnam War and the university turmoil of 1968–1970 put another gloss on these programs. A mere ten years later, Lucian Pye was writing:

> The record of relations between developing countries and Western scholars, whether discipline or area specialists, has not been a steady or an easy one. As disillusionment about the prospects for rapid development spread among the leaders and the intellectuals of such societies they came increasingly to resent the presence of foreign scholars, particularly those engaged in empirical investigations. Often there was a reversal in attitudes and foreign researchers were denounced for not

knowing the local languages and cultural patterns. Scholars interested in earlier times and "safer" subjects became more acceptable, while those concerned with contemporary and emerging trends were suddenly suspect and questions were often raised as to their possible political motivations. By the early 1970s events in much of the ex-colonial and developing world pointed to a closing down of research possibilities.[46]

What Pye is discussing is the question of "access" by U.S. area studies specialists to their "areas" for "field work." Obviously, the changed political atmosphere—the emergence of a nonaligned movement in political response to the Cold War—combined with the political power of these areas resulting from decolonization and multiple forms of revolution, involved a certain distancing from U.S. scholars, often considered to be agents, if not always wittingly then unwittingly, of U.S. governmental interests. There were two principal ways U.S. scholars could react. For those who regarded the new suspicion with dismay, a possible road was prudent retreat (to which Pye adverts). For those who found many of the suspicions well warranted, a possible road was the redefinition of their role. Either road led away from area studies as it had been conceived theretofore.

The impact of the decisions of the more conservative group on the structure of the university was in fact small. They simply took up relatively traditional, "disciplinary" stances, critical of the "normative" perspectives of the second group. According to Pye:

> At this stage when area specialists were rejecting Western concepts they frequently ran into new difficulties because they at the time accepted the rhetoric of politics in their region, which often turned out to be as self-serving to the political classes of these foreign countries as the Western language of politics was to actors in the American and liberal Western systems. Justification of foreign practices often went hand in hand with the de-idealization of Western norms. Confusion often reigned because inadequate distinctions were made between analytical concepts and normative models. Ultimately there was a clear need for new paradigms. The crisis in both values and analytical rigor was dramatized when scholars simultaneously questioned the appropriateness of the pluralist

model for American politics while defending the concept of
one-party or even military rule for Africa. To criticize the rule
of an elite in the United States while justifying authoritarianism
abroad represented a bankrupt form of ethnocentrism which
inevitably challenged the integrity of political science. By the
early 1970s the discipline was in crisis as it sought to untangle
its normative and analytical perspectives.[47]

Those who did not share Pye's perspective moved in quite different directions—to a critique of modernization theory which had
informed area studies; to a critique of the concept of "three
worlds";[48] to the argument that nomothetic analyses using data
from the United States and Western Europe were in fact extrapo-
lations from particularistic descriptions; to an open call for commitment, "the need for normative research," since in fact the work
of so-called value-free scholars was imbued with its own commitments.[49] When a U.S.-based area specialist of Indian origin, S.P.
Varma, keynoted a Workshop on International Relations and Area
Studies in India in the late 1970s, he adjured them:

> All area studies research is basically development oriented—
> the fundamental quest being how the various areas or regions,
> and I am thinking primarily of the developing countries located
> in different areas and regions, can be helped in their process
> of development. Area studies programmes, therefore, have got
> to be development-oriented and related with a continuous
> reassessment and re-evaluation of the theories, and strategies
> of development that have grown during the last 30 years.
> A revolutionary rethinking has been taking place during the
> seventies—particularly in the second half of the decade—with
> regard to the very meaning and purpose of development. The
> concept of development as related to growth in G.N.P. [gross
> national product] and rate of growth is no longer regarded as
> valid, and even linking up of growth with redistributive justice,
> which has been going on as the accepted development strategy
> within the World Bank circles, is no longer regarded as ade-
> quate. There is a greater talk now of Self-Reliance, Collective
> Self-Reliance and of Basic Rights/Basic Human Rights. Unless
> area studies are conducted under the continuous influence of,
> and as responsive to, the latest thinking on development, they
> will not be able to develop proper perspectives.[50]

The objectives of area studies, which still seemed clear in the 1960s, began to blur amidst a noisy and rather confused debate in the 1970s. In the end, however, more important than the internal debates about area studies itself was the emergence of a new form of "area studies" that did not call itself by that name. It was the sudden growth, particularly in the 1970s, of women's studies on the one hand and "ethnic" studies on the others (African American studies, Hispanic or Latino studies, Judaic studies, etc.). Two things characterized these various new academic enterprises. First, they were studying in large part the Western world and not the non-Western world, at least initially. It was the "Third World within" (or "oppressed groups" in core countries). Secondly, they insisted on linking these studies to the "Third World without": African *and* African American (or the black diaspora), Asian *and* Asian-American, Judaic *and* Israeli, women across the world, etc.

I call these academic enterprises variants of area studies because they too tended to group scholars from multiple traditional disciplines. And they too insisted that their subject matter could neither be studied ahistorically (pre-1945 ethnography and Oriental studies) nor be studied by simple application of nomothetic universalizing social science.

But these academic enterprises as social movements followed an inverse path from that of 1945–1970 area studies. Area studies, as we have seen, was a top-down enterprise. The Establishment (government agencies, university administrations, large foundations) sensed an academic void and encouraged new programs. Later, many (of course, not all) of the scholars attracted to the enterprise were radicalized, politically and intellectually, by the contact with the area. Women's studies and the multiple variants of "ethnic" studies had bottom-up origins. They represented the (largely post-1968) revolt of those whom the university had "forgotten." Theirs was a claim to be heard, and to be heard not merely as describers of particular groups that were marginal, but as revisers of the central theoretical premises of social science. To be sure, as time went on, the Establishment structures took note of the force of the claimants and sought to integrate their activities into less politicized channels. And to some extent they succeeded.

This is not the place to review the complex history in the last twenty-five years of these new forms of studies. I merely wish to claim that the creation of area studies laid the groundwork for their emergence, first of all by undermining the plausibility of traditional ethnography and Oriental studies, then by forcing the "Western" disciplines to take into account a larger range of data, and finally by questioning the sacrosanct divisions of the disciplines.

I also insist of course that these effects were unintended. Area studies programs got a big boost in the Kennedy-Johnson years. The same widened perspective of the U.S. Establishment led to such enterprises as the Peace Corps. Returned Peace Corps volunteers often went into graduate area studies programs in the 1960s. They were also among the first to occupy buildings in 1968 university uprisings. And later, they often went into the new women's and "ethnic" programs of the 1970s. For many scholars of a certain cohort this was an actual biographical progression.

Much then happened in the 1980s and 1990s: the general disillusionment with "development"; the collapse of many national liberation movement governments in Africa and Asia; the collapse of the Communisms; the Political Consciousness furor in the United States; the backlash against affirmative action. In the university, meanwhile, there has been a continuing explosion of new programs in a period of increasing financial squeeze. The structuring of the social sciences has been challenged not only by the blurring of the boundaries among them, but also by the emergence of a strong anti-Newtonian thrust in the physical sciences (with its emphasis on the arrow of time) as well as the spectacular expansion of cultural studies in the humanities (but also in the social sciences, particularly in anthropology).

The intellectual turmoil is real. What will emerge eventually is at present quite uncertain.[51] However, getting to where we are today is certainly not what the SSRC Committee on World Regions had in mind in 1943.

Notes

1. Social Science Research Council, Committee on World Regions, *World Regions in the Social Sciences; Report of a Committee of the Social Science Research Council* (New York: Social Science Research Council, 1943), 1–2.
2. Ibid., 8.
3. Ibid., 11.
4. Columbia University, "Preliminary Report of a Committee on Area Studies appointed by Dean George D. Pegram for the Joint Committee on Graduate Instruction, July 13, 1943," 2.
5. Ibid., 3.
6. Ibid., 7–8.
7. Cited in Lyman J. Legters, "Discussion," in T.H. Tsien and H.W. Winger, eds., *Area Studies and the Library* (Chicago: Univ. of Chicago Press, 1966), 15.
8. See Immanuel Wallerstein et al., *Open the Social Sciences, Report of the Gulbenkian Commission on the Restructuring of the Social Sciences* (Stanford: Stanford Univ. Press, 1996), for greater detail on these three cleavages.
9. William Nelson Fenton, "Integration of Geography and Anthropology in Army Area Study Curricula," *American Association of University Professors Bulletin*, xxxii, 1946, 699–700.
10. Ibid., 705–6.
11. Ibid., 706.
12. Robert B. Hall, *Area Studies: With Special Reference to Their Implications for Research in the Social Sciences* (New York: Social Science Research Council, 1947), 17–18.
13. Harry Eckstein, "A Critique of Area Studies From a West European Perspective," in L.W. Pye, ed.,

Political Science and Area Studies: Rivals or Partners (Bloomington: Indiana Univ. Press, 1975), 203.
14. Committee on Educational Policy, "Report of a Subcommittee on Languages and International Affairs," Harvard University Faculty of Arts and Sciences, November 12, 1945, 4.
15. Hall, *Area Studies*, 22–23.
16. Ibid., 24–25.
17. Ibid., 82–83.
18. Foreign Office, "Report of the Interdepartmental Commission of Enquiry on Oriental, Slavonic, East European and African Studies (Scarborough Report)" (London: His Majesty's Stationery Office, 1947), 5.
19. Ibid., 30.
20. Charles Wagley, *Area Research and Training: A Conference Report on the Study of World Areas*, no. 6 (New York: Social Science Research Council, June 1948), 1.
21. Richard J. Heindel, *The Present Position of Foreign Area Studies in the United States: A Post-Conference Report* (New York: Social Science Research Council, 1950), 2.
22. Jean B. Duroselle, "Area Studies: Problems of Method," *International Social Science Bulletin* IV, no. 4 (1952): 636–38.
23. Hans J. Morgenthau, "Area Studies and the Study of International Relations," *International Social Science Bulletin* IV, no. 4 (1952): 647–51.
24. See Wendell Clark Bennett, *Area Studies in American Universities* (New York: Social Science Research Council, 1951); see also Larry Moses, *Language and Area Study Programs in American Universities*

(Washington, D.C.: U.S. Department of State External Research Staff, 1964).

25. See Donald N. Bigelow and Lyman H. Legters, NDEA Language and Area Centers: A Report on the First 5 Years (Washington, D.C.: Office of Education, 1964); see also Lorraine McDonnell, with Cathleen Stasz and Rodger Madison, Federal Support for Training Foreign Language and Area Specialists: The Education and Careers of FLAS Fellowship Recipients (Santa Monica, Calif: Rand Corporation, 1983).

26. P.J. McNiff, "Foreign Area Studies and Their Effect on Library Development," College and Research Libraries XXIV, no. 4, (July 1963): 291–96, 304–5; Chauncey D. Harris, "Area Studies and Library Resources," in T.H. Tsien and J.W. Winger, eds., Area Studies and the Library (Chicago: Univ. of Chicago Press, 1966), 3–15.

27. Richard D. Lambert, Language and Area Studies Review (Philadelphia: American Academy of Political and Social Science, 1973), 1–2.

28. McDonnell et al., Federal Support, 7.

29. Lambert, Language, 2–3.

30. Wilfrid Cantwell Smith, "The Place of Oriental Studies in a University, Diogenes, no. 16, 1956, 106–111.

31. University Grants Committee, "Report of the Sub-Committee on Oriental, Slavonic, East European and African Studies (Hayter Report)" (London: Her Majesty's Stationery Office, 1961), 3.

32. Ibid., 63.

33. Hamilton Gibb, Area Studies Reconsidered (London: School of Oriental and African Studies, 1963), 10–16.

34. Ibid., 13, 15.

35. Denis Sinor, "Uralic and Altaic Studies," The Review of the College of Arts and Sciences of Indiana University (fall 1967): 1–8, 8.

36. Gibbs, Area Studies, 6–7.

37. Actually, there had been an earlier scandal. In 1965, it became public knowledge that, as early as 1955, a team of experts under the aegis of Michigan State University held a U.S. government contract to advise the South Vietnamese government of Ngo Dihn Diem, and to aid in the training of that government's secret police. See Robert Scheer, How the United States Got Involved in Vietnam (Santa Barbara, Calif.: Center for the Study of Democratic Institutions, 1965), 33–38; W. Hinkle et al., "MSU—The University on the Make," Ramparts IV, no. 12 (April 1966): 11–22.

38. Kalman H. Silvert, "Document Number 1," in I.L. Howoritz, ed., The Rise and Fall of Project Camelot (Cambridge, Mass.: MIT Press, 1967), 80–106.

39. Project Camelot, "Document Number 1," Rise and Fall, 47–49.

40. Johan Galtung, "After Camelot," Rise and Fall, 283.

41. Iriving Louis Horowitz, "The Rise and Fall of Project Camelot," Rise and Fall, 3–49.

42. Horowitz, Rise and Fall.

43. See Immanuel Wallerstein, "1968, Revolution in the World-System," in Geopolitics and Geoculture: Essays on the Changing World-System (Cambridge, U.K.: Cambridge Univ. Press, 1991), 65–83.

44. Johan Galtung, "After Camelot," 296.

45. Bigelow and Legters, NDEA, 61–62.

46. Lucian W. Pye, "The Confrontation Between Discipline and Area

Studies," in L.W. Pye, ed., *Political Science and Area Studies, Rivals or Partners?* (Bloomington: Indiana Univ. Press, 1975), 15.
47. Ibid., 20–21.
48. Carl Pletsch, "The Three Worlds, or the Division of Social Science Labor, circa 1950–1975," *Comparative Studies in Society and History* 23, no. 4 (1981): 565–90.
49. S.P. Varma, "International Relations and Area Studies," *Political Science Review* XIX, no. 1 (1980): 26–46, 40.
50. Ibid., 45–46
51. But see Wallerstein et al., *Social Sciences.*

(Ira Katznelson)

The Subtle Politics of Developing Emergency:
Political Science as Liberal Guardianship

"In the subtle politics of developing emergency, the elites are, for all practical purposes, the people."[1]

In the summer of 1968, I was invited to the office of the provost at Columbia University to be interviewed for a job in the Department of Political Science by David Truman, whom I had come to know rather well a few years earlier when I had been an undergraduate and he was the dean of the college. Truman was one of the country's most distinguished political scientists. His 1951 portrait, *The Governmental Process*, had proved a charter document for the postwar discipline, arguably its most important text. It had opened many pathways of empirical analysis while clarifying the normative goals and limits of the new political science. Cool in tone, realist in orientation, and behavioral in epistemology, the book sought to build bulwarks against what Truman described portentiously as "morbific politics."[2] The book described how interest representation actually worked and identified the institutional and ideological conditions required to keep American democracy stable and secure.

Truman also was the person who had called in New York's police to end forcibly Columbia's sit-ins three months earlier. Our conversation opened with his assurance that I already had passed muster with him as a potential colleague; would I mind talking about recent campus events? He uncharacteristically held forth for more than an hour, virtually without interruption, justifying his recent decisions by drawing a parallel between McCarthyism's assaults on liberal institutions, notably including the universities, and the aggressive stance of the late 1960s' New Left. At stake, he argued, was the fragile texture of assumptions and institutions that fortify liberal regimes against totalitarian depredations.

About Columbia and the New Left, we agreed to disagree. Truman then turned our colloquy to a retrospective discussion of *The Governmental Process*. Telling me he was considering an introduction to a new edition of the book, we talked about recent work in political science on barriers to collective action[3] and, not without irony, about the import of the movements of blacks and students for the stability of America's political system. At stake, he insisted with quiet passion, was whether the country's political class—the leadership elite responsible for managing the relationships linking citizens to their government and for safeguarding the systems liberal rules of the game—would be willing under conditions of crisis to protect the system. It was up to us, that is to those of us who were political scientists, he concluded, to develop and deploy a political science commensurate to this purpose. Our conversation had come full circle.

Truman's anxiety about the fate of liberal democracy, especially when stressed by mass political mobilizations, was not idiosyncratic, but emblematic of the project of postwar American political science. Like such estimable political sociologists as William Kornhauser and C. Wright Mills who feared the consequences of what they thought to be the atomization of America's population into an undifferentiated mass vulnerable to mobilization by undemocratic and demagogic elites, and like Samuel Stouffer and other students of public opinion who discovered very weak popular support for civil liberties,[4] these political scientists were concerned for the stability and capacity of liberal democracy in the United States. Distressed by the implications of the defeated fascist model, by the vitality of Communism abroad (and to a far lesser extent at home), by the growth of a strident authoritarian right-wing populism, and by the uncertain qualities of mass political participation, the country's principal political scientists sought to bolster and refresh political liberalism from the period just after World War II to Vietnam by harnessing their values to a theory-driven realist notion of science. In carrying out this project, they developed what Ludwig Fleck called a "scientific thought collective" whose members share questions, assumptions, and ways of working.[5] By the time they had achieved their disciplinary revolution, they had made very considerable advances in the conceptualization of political problems, empirical theory, and research methods. Certainly, the new American political science they fashioned was significantly more impressive than the prewar discipline. When Truman delivered his presidential address to the American Political Science Association in 1965, he had good reason to celebrate this history of scholarly regeneration and underscore the achievements of postwar political science.[6] He and his colleagues had carried through the project of creating a political science concerned with the dangers of mass politics and the terms of political participation based on the conviction that the country needed a political science to secure its liberal regime against external and internal adversaries.

There are many obvious ways American political science scholars were enmeshed in the cold war. Some developed close ties to the national state, including its emergent national security apparatus, building on the personal and institutional relationships forged between social scientists and government during World War II.[7] The subfield of international relations lost its idealist character and was reformulated on the basis of realism as an instrument of American purpose. Students of comparative politics and political theory sought to turn Mussolini's self-described "totalitarianism" into an analytical tool to provide a way to situate and compare the Bolshevik enemy. Political scientists also played a key role in shaping and directing the new multidisciplinary domain of area studies, created to provide information about far-flung parts of the globe suddenly important for postcolonial great power competition.

I should like to focus on the less obvious. Then as now, empirical studies of American politics defined the discipline's core. If we are to make sense of the impact of the cold war on the development of postwar political science, it is here, where its role was less transparent, that we have to look. The cold war, of course, is not a simple "cause," nor was it a unitary entity. It enters into the story of the progress of this part of postwar political science less as a mobilizing instrument than as a source of anxiety, a mobilizer of purpose, and a collocation of themes about liberalism, democracy, and the terms of political participation. The cold war deployed the urgent and threatening counterfactual of illiberalism at a moment when the capacity of liberal democracies to secure freedom and prosperity simultaneously still was in grave doubt in the aftermath of the post-1929 collapse of capitalism and the second of two unprecedented world wars. The American wing of political science, in this context, geared to secure the liberal option. This was not a new role; American political science, after all, had mainly developed as an aspect of work by the country's "new liberal" progressive intelligentsia at the turn of the century.[8] What was different, apart from the loss of American insularity, was the collapse of the benign and meliorist assumptions about human nature that had undergirded the pragmatist orientation to reform during the first three decades of the century. The manifest availability of mass support for fascism and communism and the absence of serious resistance to the murder of Europe's Jews in most places made naïveté unfashionable. If nothing else, the new political science was disenchanted.

Americanists working under conditions of anxious uncertainty about the liberal-illiberal antinomy during the heyday of the Cold War self-consciously reconstituted political science in the analytical space, to borrow Robert Dahl's phrase, "between chaos and tautology."[9] The specific efforts they made to build a bulwark against chaos by constructing an analytical science capable of transcending the tautological traps of concrete description were not so much determined in strong linear fashion by the cold war as shaped by it as a conditioning element. The cold war, I argue, set limits and exerted pressures on U.S.-focused political science. Unlike area studies or international relations, the cold war was located some-where outside the field of action in American studies. But its role was more than contextual. It also became inherently causal in the sense "in which the essential character of a process or the proper-ties of its components are held to determine [control] its outcome: the character and properties are then 'determinants.'"[10] The iden-tities of political scientists as producers of knowledge and as part of the guardian class for liberal democracy, the subject matter they chose to analyze, and the level and type of theory they developed, I suggest, were entwined with the cold war in just this way. The cold war thus helps account not only for key elements of their moti-vations, but also for the contours and content of their scholarship.

A New Politics of Science and Science of Politics

The story of the making of postwar political science usually is not told this way. The specific impact of the cold war epoch is masked because the two decades after 1945 are thought to fit inside a longer, continuous era. The conventional periodization discerns three broad overlapping periods: a founding era in the late nine-teenth and early twentieth centuries when political scientists focused on the study of formal-legal institutions; a positivist-behavioral movement that made its appearance in the 1920s and spanned World War II; and a postbehavioral era starting some-where in the middle 1960s marked by an epistemological plu-ralism, the independent momentum of separate segments of the discipline, and a loss of scientific and theoretical élan.[11]

By treating the history of political science almost exclusively as a methodological exercise, this traditional narrative significantly understates the distinctiveness of the postwar discipline. It under-estimates the singular qualities of the anxious political science shaped initially in the 1940s. The charged quality of this period's political science under conditions of concern for the security of America's liberal regime mark it as different from the more complacent and disinterested efforts of the prewar years, or those which soon followed. The period of crisis, of course, had begun well before the late 1940s. But only then, for the first time in nearly two decades, did the human and institutional conditions exist to support a coherent quest for a scientific and politically engaged discipline. Earlier, a high proportion of the country's most talented social scientists who subsequently proved to compose the leadership class of their disciplines, staffed the New Deal and served in wartime Washington agencies. With the demobilization of federal social science, this generation shaped America's universities as research environments independent of the state but supportive of the regime, and created powerful social science disciplines whose analytical abilities could be deployed to serve broadly liberal political purposes. These efforts proved remarkably successful, normatively and empirically; so much so, that critics inside the discipline, of which I count myself, have differed rather less from this mainstream than we sometimes like to think.

David Truman devoted his 1965 address as president of the American Political Science Association to the claim that something new and distinctive had happened to political science in the previous two decades. Breaking with the standard scheme of periodization (which, of course, then consisted of two periods, the legal-institutional and the behavioral), Truman's lecture assessed the attributes of postwar political science by deploying Thomas Kuhn's then fresh concept of the paradigm[12] to contrast "the restless searching that has marked the field since 1945" to the earlier discipline. Truman made a persuasive case for an epistemological break inside what we now usually think of as the middle period of the behavioral revolution. From the 1880s through the 1930s, he claimed both the initial abstract formalism of political science and the subsequent turn to behavioralism shared the optimistic, reformist faith characteristic of the Progressive movement. By the end of World War II, this orientation no longer met the tests of science or instrumental effectiveness. Suddenly, even when

238

up- to-date methodologically, it had come to seem old-fashioned, even beside the point. In consequence, members of his own generation ("whether as professionals or as citizens") had come to doubt the "uncritical optimism" of this inheritance, which bordered on the ridiculous in the face of the challenge posed by communism and fascism's "open and effective repudiation of the expectations and practices that underlay the implicit agreements of the profession." After the war, political life had come to be dominated by "the drastically altered character of world politics after Potsdam." Further, Truman observed, the transplantation of academic scholars to Washington during the New Deal and World War II (and, he might have noted, from European to American shores) had dislodged their parochialism and had brought them into contact with social scientists from other disciplines. The cumulative impact of these developments had made the discipline's old normal science obsolete and had provoked, if not a full-scale Kuhnian paradigm shift, the development of an ethos and set of agreements about how to proceed.[13]

Truman was devastating about the generation of his teachers (taking care to exempt his own "Chicago School" instructors as heralds of the postwar revolution). They had lacked a concern "with political systems as such, including the American system, which amounted in most cases to taking their properties and requirements for granted"; they had possessed "an unexamined and mostly implicit conception of political change and development that was blandly optimistic and unreflectively reformist"; they had neglected theory and, with it, had deployed "a conception of 'science' that rarely went beyond raw empiricism; and they had failed to place the American case inside 'an effective comparative method.'"[14] By contrast, he claimed post-1945 political science no longer took the properties of the American political system for granted; and it effectively deployed theory, guided by comparison and a realistic political psychology, to better understand the promise and perils of political change.

This new discipline, Truman made clear, was defined by the conjunction of two elements that previously had been kept apart.

The first of these was "a recommitment to science in the broad sense." By this he meant a positivist orientation that could move the empirical work of the discipline "cumulatively toward explanation, toward establishing relations of dependence between events and conditions" by aspiring "to explanations of classes of events...subject to the controls of empirical evidence and with sufficient systematic power at least to place its findings beyond complete invalidation by the day's events."[15] For Truman and his colleagues, methodical and cumulative empirical work remained the motor of the discipline. But, he insisted, it is not, and must not, be disinterested. Political science had to be a science of moral purpose and choice. Calling for a revival of the study of political thought as more than a polite gesture, Truman sought to incorporate its ethical and normative impulses as integral aspects of the discipline. Political scientists must not stop with description, however accurate, but must learn to marshal their emergent empirical and predictive capacities to clarify and assess the "probable consequences of proposals and events for the system and for the values implicit in it."[16] Truman's mixture of the recent history of his discipline with hortatory invocation insisted on the value of a political science, based on realist foundations, combining objectivity with explicit normative assumptions and goals.

Precisely this combination was deployed by the archetypal landmark works of the period to advance self-consciously this program; not only Truman's own *The Governmental Process*, but also such estimable books as Robert Dahl's *A Preface to Democratic Theory* and *Who Governs?*, and V.O. Key's *Public Opinion and American Democracy*.[17] Each showed how naive and crude elements of prewar political science restricted the discipline's ability to advance and protect liberal democracy against the challenges of other regime types. Each advanced what the sociologist Robert K. Merton called "theories of the middle range." Less abstract than grand theory, their program focused on particular subjects, committed to the consolidation of hypotheses and empirical claims capable of grounding comparative and normative evaluations.[18] Each defined a particular domain of American political life—

interest-group politics, public opinion, the policy process at the municipal level—and probed it in service of a better understanding about how key elements of the linkage between civil society and the state, the centerpiece of normative liberal theory at least since Locke, actually work in the United States. Finally, each assessed these sites and processes for their contributions to the health and security of American liberal democracy. Treating these texts as exemplary, I now turn to my central task: that of parsing and justifying the claim that the Cold War conditioned this new political science in an internal as well as an external sense of determination. I proceed with considerations of these texts' conception of political science as engaged social knowledge; of the implications of their choice of theory and subjects; and of their foreboding about threats to the liberal democratic polity, especially by a disorderly and unchecked mass. I close with a brief discussion of the omissions in their work.[19]

Realism and Guardianship: Another Theory of Democracy Elaborated[20]

Of course, this enterprise was not hermetically sealed inside political science but was part of a larger project by the period's liberal intelligentsia to retrofit liberalism in order to make it a capable instrument for dangerous times. Some of the most visible interventions by scholars as public intellectuals announced this undertaking to a wide and growing educated public in the period following the war. Three years before Truman published *The Governmental Process*, Arthur Schlesinger, Jr., had issued a bestselling manifesto that called for a break with soft-minded, fellow-traveling liberalism based on naive views of human nature. He favored a hard-edged liberalism to define a "vital center" and win the Cold War. Based on the darker philosophical anthropology of Reinhold Niebuhr, he described "our epoch as a time of troubles, an age of anxiety." He worried that the patrimony of the liberal tradition had rendered it incapable of fighting the battle "between free society and totalitarianism," adding that this "is a choice we cannot escape." He called for the extension and clarification of liberal ideas as "a fighting faith...drawing strength from a realistic conception of man." Lionel Trilling soon followed with his vastly influential critique of socialist realism in the humanities, appealing instead for an "active literature" and a deepening and thickening of American liberalism to recall it "to its first essential imagination of variousness and possibility, which implies the awareness of complexity and difficulty." To this end, Trilling sought a new realism, including a realism of human personality and motivation, turning for these purposes to Proust and to Freud, among others.[21]

The period's political scientists made equivalent moves, searching for sustenance for their own new realism outside their discipline's credulous and meliorist lineage, convinced, as Schlesinger was, that in the circumstances of the time "only the United States still has buffers between itself and the anxieties of our age: buffers of time, of distance, of natural wealth, of national ingenuity, of a stubborn tradition of hope."[22] The character and fate of America's political system, in consequence, was of more than local interest. Thus, Dahl thought it important that we discern without sentiment precisely how democracy, which he treated as rule by competing and overlapping minorities, differs from dictatorship, rule by a single, cohesive minority; and how America's liberal democracy, while "not for export for others" nonetheless operates as the archetype of "a relatively efficient system for reinforcing agreement, encouraging moderation, and maintaining social peace in a restless and immoderate people operating a gigantic, powerful, diversified, and incredibly complex society."[23]

This new realism, we will see, hovered between objectivity and normative politicization, encompassing both. It created a charged domain to make possible a political science that mattered by deploying its skills and knowledge to a political purpose. Yet, this determination to deploy the discipline to secure the regime's liberalism shaped and, at times, misshaped the science. It also created a striking and uncanny, though surely unintended, resemblance of the new realist liberal theories of elite and mass to Marxist-Leninist ideas about the "avant-garde" and "the masses" and to fascist ideas about the relationship between "elites" and "the masses."

But whereas totalitarian thought aimed at mobilizing the masses for aims defined by a party elite, the liberals sought to enmesh the population in institutions and ideas that would take the charge out of their political participation and permit a moderated democratic process to proceed. McCarthyism's immoderate demagogy was proof enough, they thought, that it could happen here.

There was reason, the postwar political scientists believed, to celebrate and cause to worry. They called on political scientists to identify and nourish those aspects of the political order that manage the connection of the citizenry to the state with the aim of moderating opinion and shaping the forms of political participation. But if there was cause for satisfaction, especially considering the alternatives, this generation of scholars certainly was not complacent. Truman concluded his volume with a discussion about prospects for "revolution and decay"; Key with a section inquiring about the "inevitability" of "indecision, decay, and disaster." For Dahl, even if America's polity was not "so obviously a defective system as some of its critics suggest," neither was it the kind of "pinnacle of human achievement … our nationalistic and politically illiterate glorifiers so tiresomely insist." This was not a group of conservative or complacent apologists. Its members soberly appreciated its positive attributes but never produced unqualified endorsements of the political system. In a dangerous and threatening world, they stared hard at the cruelties and hoaxes of the period's alternatives and emerged with a renewed appreciation for what Dahl called "the American hybrid." Most, after all, were New Deal liberals or strong egalitarians (Dahl, for example, was soon to show affinities for democratic socialism). Most opposed the war in Vietnam and supported the civil rights movement.[24]

Though neither apologists nor political conservatives, the postwar Americanists did assume the mantle of guardians of the liberal regime. "The great political task now as in the past," Truman wrote, "is to perpetuate a viable system." To this end, a political class, whose membership includes producers of systematic political knowledge, must play a pivotal role. "In the future as in the past, they will provide the answer to the ancient question:

quis cutodiet ipsos custodes? Guardianship will emerge out of the affiliations of the guardians." This was a task of obligation and accountability. As Key put it in his book's parallel last paragraph, "the masses do not corrupt themselves....The critical element for the health of a democratic order consists in the beliefs, standards, and competence of those who compose the influentials, the opinion-leaders, the political activists....The responsibility rests here, not in the mass of the people."[25]

In participating in this task of guardianship, this generation of political scientists found succor in some prewar studies of groups and power, notably those of Arthur Bentley, Charles Merriam, and Harold Lasswell, but also in scholarship written in a darker vein by such émigré figures as Karl Polanyi and Joseph Schumpeter.[26] Schumpeter's discussion of democracy, in particular, proved particularly influential because it provided the young postwar generation with unsentimental and hardheaded political foundations.

At the height of World War II, Schumpeter had agonized over the diminishing prospects of capitalism. Melancholic over what he thought was its inevitable dislocation by bureaucratic socialism, he had sought to salvage the prospect at least of a democratic socialism; but democracy of what kind? Not, he argued, the democracy of the classical doctrine grounded in the idea that the people decide on behalf of the realization of a common good. Government neither is premised on nor is a search for such a public interest; none exists. Rule by the people, moreover, is dangerous, because there is massive evidence against the rational capacity of the masses. "The typical citizen drops down to a lower level of mental performance as soon as he enters the political field....He becomes a primitive again. His thinking becomes associative and affective."[27] Without the props of a common good or a rational public, Schumpeter proposed the role of the people be limited to the act of selecting a government every four or five years. Then they should get out of the way to let informed elites rule.

It was this analysis of democracy Robert Dahl thought "excellent."[28] Its key elements—a special role for elites, distrust of the masses, stress on procedures, and a rejection of simple notions of the public interest—trace unifying threads across the major polit-ical science texts of the postwar period. But Truman, Dahl, Key, and their colleagues were not pure Schumperterians. They were committed not only to liberalism but also to liberal democracy, including its participatory elements. "At minimum," Dahl wrote, "it seems to me, democratic theory is concerned with processes by which ordinary citizens exert a high degree of control over leaders"; Key insisted that "unless mass views have some place in the shaping of policy, all talk about democracy is nonsense," and Truman focused on the play and conflict of interests in-between elections and outside of the electoral process.[29] They also understood that the quest for stable, effective, and legitimate lib-eral democracies would fail if political participation did not come to be anchored by effective institutions. Individuals and groups would not meekly go away between elections. Rather, they could be expected to express their dissatisfactions and fight for their inter-ests in ways that might threaten liberal values if participation were not managed and canalized in the zone between the state and civil society by appropriate institutional arrangements. Specifically, they thought it critical to deploy political institutions to produce publics rather than masses.

As liberal democrats and as institutionalists, this group of polit-ical scientists committed themselves to a particular kind and level of theory. Unlike their disciplinary antecedents, they insisted on the requirement of theory. "The non-theoretical bias of the earlier agreement within the discipline," Truman observed, "thrust the study of political thought out of the mainstream and retained it largely as a gesture toward polite learning." This "philistinism" was worse than regrettable. Because of the philistinism, the disci-pline was narrowed and cut off from the succor work on political regimes that philosophers from Aristotle through Locke and Mill could provide.[30]

But Truman and his colleagues did not simply counsel a renewal of traditional political theory. Rather, they wanted to con-nect the lineage of basic questions of governance to a new science of political behavior and institutional design. This would be theory of a new kind, neither exclusively "ethical in character" or solely "an attempt to describe the actual world,"[31] but both. This was their particular response to Merton's call for theories located in the middle-range between high abstraction in the manner of Talcott Parson's work on *The Structure of Social Action* or David Easton's attempt to develop an approach to political studies based on system's analysis, both of which were self-consciously disconnected from the configurations of particular times and places,[32] and a bare-bones wholly inductive empiricism.

More than an epistemological location, the new political science made a substantive commitment to liberal and democratic theory at the intersection of institutions and behavior. Taking the largest constitutional-regime rules for granted as stable givens, it sought to understand the systematic mutual impact of institutional arrangements on behavior and behavior on institutions in directing political participation and shaping political norms. "In the absence of standardized means of participation," Truman cautioned, mass "movements of the fascist type" threaten to develop, especially under conditions of significant inequality.[33]

Dahl's *Preface* was the most explicit of these attempts to "raise questions that would need to be answered by a satisfactory theory of democratic politics." He made explicit the widely shared conviction that these issues are not primarily to be "found in constitutional forms" but "in extra-constitutional factors."[34] Constitutional arrangements usher individuals and groups into the political process; once there, these patterning plans become permissive but are not determinative. Accordingly, political scientists must attend to the junction located between these grand regime features and political action, a space filled by institutions understood both as congeries of rules and as formal organizations.

Obviously, the new political science required a division of labor. Some scholars would focus on parties and elections, others on interest groups, yet others on the molding and deployment of public opinion. Irrespective of their topics, however, they would concern themselves with the sustenance of consensus about liberal democratic values and place their bets on the elaboration of theory geared to the two-way transactions between citizens and their government. This political science would identify and deploy the mechanisms that make effective, stable liberal democracy work as an appealing model geared to compete with its totalitarian adversaries. These tools include rules to protect the congeries of minorities who constitute the citizenry from the tight grip of control by a minority or by populist majorities (Dahl); an assemblage of linkage institutions (schools, media, parties), which shape and give cues to mass opinion (Key); overlapping interest-group memberships and identities (Truman); and a leadership group to operate these instruments (Dahl, Key, and Truman).

In spite of their diverse points of entry and emphasis, these authors shared in the project of elaborating on Schumpeter's insistence that we need a realistic alternative to the classical utopian theory of democracy. This entailed a rejection of "the people" as a meaningful category, not only, as for Schumpeter, because no such entity sharing common interests actually exists, but also because a populist orientation risks making the people available for antiliberal forms of political mobilization. Dahl's *Preface* turned on just these points. He situated his preferred regime type of polyarchical democracy as a more desirable and hardheaded alternative to two other democratic models. The first he described as Madison's system. This orientation is so concerned with the dangers of political participation and so distrustful of the people that it goes too far in the direction of preserving "the liberties of certain minorities whose advantages of status, power, and wealth," he thought, "probably would not be tolerated indefinitely by a constitutionally untrammeled minority." Madisonian democracy, he concluded, "goes about as far as it is possible to go while still remaining within the rubric of democracy." The second view Dahl labeled populistic democracy. Stressing the sovereignty of the majority, this model runs afoul of the fact that citizens do not care intensely and equally about different issues. Nor does this approach sufficiently take into account goals that might compete with political equality and popular sovereignty. These two purposes, he argued, "are not absolute goals; we must ask ourselves how much leisure, privacy, consensus, stability, income, security, progress, status, and probably many other goals we are prepared to forego for an additional increment of political equality." For Dahl, populistic democracy is flawed for more than this set of ethical reasons. Unlike Madisonianism, it violates the requisite that liberal democratic theory be empirical as well as normative. As a set of aspirations that cannot be put in action, "it tells us nothing about the real world" or about political behavior. Populist democracy also is naive. It fails to define membership in the political system (who will be admitted and under what terms) or to recognize that "every society develops a ruling class." Even more important, it is insensitive to the fact that political preferences develop over time within the political process or that majorities are not fixed entities.[35]

Dahl crafted an alternative by transcending the antinomy of the majority versus the minority. In seeking a balance between normative maximization and empirical description, he insisted that in a diverse and complex world of multiple interests and identities there are no majorities, only many minorities, even minorities within minorities. "Hence we cannot correctly describe the actual operations of democratic societies in terms of the contrasts between majorities and minorities. We can only distinguish groups of various types and sizes, all seeking in various ways to advance their goals, usually at the expense, at least in part, of others."[36] This central feature of America's regime is what makes it normatively attractive and different from illiberal competitors. It also is the mainspring of stability.

Dahl's goal thus was not abstract equality or the sovereignty of the majority, but an attainable and desirable "political system in which all the active and legitimate groups in the population can make themselves heard at some crucial stage in the process of decision." This, he hastened to add in his realist voice, does not mean "that every group has equal control over the outcome." Dahl's democracy is a system of endless bargaining in which "the making of governmental decisions is not a majestic march of great majorities united upon certain matters of basic policy. It is the steady appeasement of relatively small groups."[37] Dahl designed his next book, *Who Governs?*, to be an empirical investigation of just this system at work. In his community study site of New Haven, he found that inequalities were dispersed; majorities and coalitions were situational; intensities varied from issue to issue and from group to group; and the system contained enough slack so that those who wished to have influence could prove influential even under conditions of inequality in wealth, social position, and knowledge.[38]

Like Dahl, Key and Truman insisted on breaking up "the people" into its component elements, none of which constitutes either the whole or a majority of the whole. Key defined public opinion "to mean those opinions held by private persons which governments find it prudent to heed," but such opinion never is singular or undifferentiated. Nor does opinion directly shape the affairs of state as romantic democrats might wish. Rather, the properties and distribution of opinion divide the population into multiple publics. What Key stressed was how the links between these publics and the government are mediated by institutional transactions and how the commitments and actions of active and influential political elites determine whether American liberal democracy will thrive or degenerate.

Truman also insisted on the segmentation of the public into groups sharing similar views about specific matters under consideration. "The public is always specific to a particular situation or issue," Truman observed. Such publics seek influence through organization. The main vehicle is the interest group, which he understood not in terms of a priori categories, such as those of class or gender but in terms of behavior and interaction. "An interest group," he wrote, "is a shared-attitude group that makes certain claims upon other groups in the society. If and when it makes its claims through or upon any of the institutions of government, it becomes a political interest group." Truman's liberal democracy is an arena for the competitive play of these groups, not for the discovery of a common public interest. What keeps this system stable is the mechanism of overlapping memberships. The population does not divide along fixed lines. The system comes to be moderated because individuals are not wholly absorbed into any specific group and because they usually belong to multiple groups. They have compound identities, a complex array of interests, and many pathways and different degrees of participation. By way of this analysis, Truman replied to Madison's worries about majority domination and confronted the problem of differential intensity posed by Dahl's populists.[39]

This institutionalized competition of minorities, however, leaves the liberal regime vulnerable, Truman observed, because it is not self-equilibrating. Its stability requires two additional conditions: broadly shared values about the rules of the political game (especially civil liberties) and actors sufficiently committed to these values and the institutional arrangements which embed them. Norms and elites are Truman's necessary conditions for a steadfast and legitimate polity. He insisted that the institutional mechanism of overlapping membership on which he relied cannot cushion the political order at times of crisis caused by "disturbance in established relationships" unless the liberal rules of the game are widely supported by the population as a whole. Likewise, Dahl stressed the importance of precepts, arguing in his pivotal chapter on polyarchy that its most important conditions "can be formulated as a rule or, if you prefer, as a norm."[40]

But this condition cannot be taken for granted. Mass support for the values of liberal democracy is not a given. The population may be mobilized by demagogues as an undemocratic mass; or it may withdraw its support from liberal norms at key moments of change and stress. "The follies of the mass" may, "in a kind of Gresham's law," come to dominate political life, Key wrote. "What can we say about this melancholy process?" Like Truman, he turned to the role played by political influentials. "Mass opinion is not self-generating; in the main, it is a response to the cues, the proposals, and the visions propagated by the political activists." As a consequence, he continued, "democracies decay, if they do, not because of the cupidity of the masses, but because of the stupidity and self-seeking of leadership echelons."[41] Truman, we have seen, placed even greater emphasis on the custodial role of elites. Looking back from a post-1960s perspective, he elaborated on the last sentence of *The Governmental Process* "concerning the guardians and their affiliations" under conditions "of dissensus on the rules."[42]

Neither the closing sentence of *The Governmental Process* nor the pages that precede it assert that the system is self-corrective. On the contrary, the book contends that the essentials of the system are peculiarly in the custody of those in key governmental positions and those who occupy leading positions within the groups that make up the structure intervening between the government and the ordinary citizen. Such people are, in the technical and neutral sense of the term, elites. Given the ambiguity and dissensus on the rules, elite understanding and constructive action are essential to the continued vitality of the rules and to the survival of the system. "In the subtle politics of developing emergency, the elites are, for all practical purposes, the people."

These three versions of realist liberal political theory at the junction of institutions and behavior did not seek to exhort but to describe and design at a very fine-grained, situation-specific level. Dahl's *Who Governs?* is based on a rich historical and empirical rendering of party politics, coalition-building, and public policy about such matters as schooling and urban redevelopment in his university's hometown. *The Governmental Process* devotes some four hundred very dense pages to theoretically motivated descriptions of the ties between interest groups and public opinion, political parties, elections, the legislative process, the executive branch, independent regulatory agencies, and the courts. *Public Opinion and American Democracy* dissects the distribution, types, demographic basis, properties, and formation of public opinion, as well as its linkage to parties, elections, Congress, and interest groups. These bravura performances necessarily are bound to specific historical settings. Yet, the theoretical questions they raise, the way they situate their discipline, and their subsumption of methodology (in spite of their shared behavioralism) inside charged issues of ideology and moral purpose transcend their particular milieus.

The Cold War Optic

This joining of the local and general animates the continuing appeal and analytical power of this body of scholarship. Yet, if the anxieties of the cold war motivated the inscription of this political science, it also distorted and limited its emphases and orientations. These limiting effects were especially apparent when these works came face to face with deep-seated structural inequalities, especially those based on race, with social movements, and with the national security state. Of course, when Dahl wrote that "the full assimilation of Negroes into the normal system already has occurred in many northern states and now seems to be slowly to be taking place even in the South,"[43] putting a remarkably optimistic spin on the developments immediately following *Brown v. Board of Education*, he certainly was aware that Jim Crow and racism more generally were alive and well; when Truman ignored the role of the military in American life, he knew a great deal about NSC-68 and the issues C. Wright Mills soon was to make so central to his spirited analysis of the role of the armed forces in American life.[44] It was not, I think, mainly the ideological or ethical proclivities of this generation that pushed such key subjects into a zone of silence, although this did play a part, but the very theory they developed in their attempt to secure a vibrant nontotalitarian politics.

Some aspects of these theoretical limitations were noted effectively some time ago. By focusing on actual behavior and decisions, the political scientists of this generation underestimated the system's skewed capacity to set agendas (hence nondecisions), nor did they fully appreciate the biased qualities of actual participation along class lines.[45] But I think there is a deeper problem embedded in their theory. Its roots can be found in Schumpeter's effort, which they emulated, to find alternatives to the period's objective approaches, Marxist and otherwise, to stratification and hierarchy.[46]

This choice is clearest in Truman's work. At the outset of *The Governmental Process*, he distinguished two approaches to the specification of groups. The first, which he rejects, he labels categoric. In this approach, groups are "collections of individuals who have some characteristic in common." He dismissed this possibility with disdain: "In this sense the word is applied to persons of a given age level, to those of similar income or social status, to people living in a particular area, as Westerners, and to assortments of individuals according to an almost endless variety of similarities—farmers, alcoholics, insurance men, blondes, illiterates, mothers, neurotics, and so on." With this deft but glib move to make any objective classification of the social structure nonsensical, Truman went on to endorse a behavioral definition of groups based on "a minimum frequency of interaction....If the members of any aggregation of blondes begin to interact as blondes, alcoholics as alcoholics (or former addicts), people over sixty as aged —they constitute groups." Likewise, interests are not rooted in objective locations in the social structure; hence, there is no such thing as interests independent of cognition. Instead, interests are shared attitudes. By defining his collective units of political analysis based on relationships and interactions rather than on societal positions, Truman sidestepped the problem of providing an objective portrait of social inequality or choosing among alternative theories.[47]

His own text, however, reveals the costs of this move. When he turned, in the conclusion, to his fears of "morbific politics" and to the role shared values play in stabilizing the regime, he shifted to the problems posed by deep differences in values and political orientations that obtain when specific groups "arrive at interpretations of the 'rules of the game' that are at great variance with those held by most of the civilian population."[48] This unhappy circumstance is unlikely to arise, he observes, when citizens actually hold overlapping memberships in interest groups. After all, that is the purpose of this mechanism. He was forced to concede, however, that the distribution of group memberships in fact is not independent of social class or, especially, of race, and that as a result of deep-seated inequalities, many Americans are not integrated into the group system he so painstakingly had described. These unanchored, unincorporated citizens worried him a great deal because they are the most vulnerable, he hypothesized, to the appeals of antidemocratic ideologies and movements. Incredibly, Truman considered America's racial order (after virtually 520 pages of near-total silence on the subject) only through the prism of these fears. His prose is tortured:

> The appearance of groups representing Negroes, especially in the South, groups whose interpretations of the "rules of the game" are divergent from those of the previously organized and privileged segments of the community, are a case in point. Caste and class interpretations of widespread unorganized interests may be at least a ready source of instability as conflicts between more restricted organized groups.

The problem with the emergent civil rights movement (this, in 1951!) was that it threatened the political stability of the system because it challenged the existing "rules of the game." The value consensus required to keep the system on an even keel is "not threatened by the existence of a multiplicity of organized groups so long as the 'rules of the game' remain meaningful guides to action." But, of course, when excluded groups challenge their exclusion there can be no ready agreement on the status of the rules. "In the loss of such meanings," Truman cautioned with foreboding, "lie the seeds of the whirlwind."[50]

Two decades later, Truman did not back away from this passage. Indeed, he celebrated it for having heralded "the complex and swiftly moving politics of the Northern ghettos: the scorn of the black militant for the apparent vagueness and even hypocrisy of the white liberal, the appeal of the Black Panthers, the discarding of black leaders without whose ability to work within the system the court decisions of the past two decades and the civil rights legislation of the 1960s would not have appeared, and the ugly shadow of the backlash." Blacks had dismissed the rules of the game "as 'whitey's' rules."[51] The whirlwind had come. In the aftermath of these developments in black America, but also in the aftermath of

McCarthyism, the New Left, and the student movement, Truman insisted that "were I rewriting the book today I would give [this theme of elite responsibility in the face of the collapse of common meanings] considerably more prominence."[52]

For Truman and his colleagues it followed implicitly (certainly these authors explicitly preferred other values) that it is far better for the excluded to remain apolitical than challenge the dirty secrets of the regime. Their fear of mass politics and political disorder had become integral to their antitotalitarian program. Their theories treated disruption and protest as standing outside the normal process of legitimate political participation. Hence, they found it difficult to distinguish between the movements they hated, such as the anticommunism of the radical Right, and the movements whose goals they admired, such as the struggle for civil rights, because this type of collective action as such they constructed as the main threat to political stability.[53]

Nor were the substantive incapacities of the new antitotalitarian political scientists confined to class or race. Though it would be anachronistic to expect they would have been sensitive to the country's inequalities of gender, they did write when the nuclear threat was fresh, when the militarization of American society had become manifest, when such estimable figures as Truman's teacher Harold Lasswell were worried about the rise of garrison states and visible social critics such as C. Wright Mills bemoaned the ascendancy of the military to the top echelons of power.[54] Yet, with the exception of a short discussion of public opinion and foreign policy by Key and a cursory treatment of propaganda for foreign policy purposes by Truman, the landmark works I have been considering literally had nothing to say about the national security state. Perhaps this silence was the result of the highly plausible belief that it was a necessary evil under cold war conditions. I think the explanation is more integral to their theory. They literally had no place to put the illiberalism of congealed state power inside the relatively benign systems of political participation they sketched. Rather, it was placed out of view, hidden away in the basement of the liberal state.

Motivated by anxiety about illiberalism, the new political science of the postwar years did innovate brilliantly in theory, institutional analysis, and studies of political behavior. All political scientists who study the United States stand on their shoulders. "There is a need," Dahl's student Theodore Lowi wrote in the preface to his *End of Liberalism*, perhaps the first significant manifesto of a new generation, "to break the thirty-year moratorium on consideration of first premises that has characterized political science. Controversy must be opened on questions of theory and ideology, not merely on questions of methodology and practice."[55] This, I have argued, is precisely what Truman, Key, and Dahl in fact had been doing. Alas, Lowi's critique would be more apt today. Perhaps we might ask whether, after 1989, at a time when we are less vexed by antitotalitarian anxieties than at any time since 1917, political science might rediscover these possibilities to learn anew how the discipline could again matter as a powerful instrument deployed to strengthen and sustain liberal democracy—but this time, with the old silences transformed into vibrant subjects.

Notes

1. David B. Truman, *The Governmental Process: Political Interests and Public Opinion* 2d ed. (New York: Alfred A. Knopf, 1971).
2. Truman, *The Governmental Process*, 516.
3. Most notably, Mancur Olson, *The Logic of Collective Action: Public Goods and the Theory of Groups* (Cambridge: Harvard Univ. Press, 1965).
4. William Kornhauser, *The Politics of Mass Society* (Glencoe, Ill.: The Free Press, 1959); C. Wright Mills, *The Power Elite* (New York: Oxford Univ. Press, 1956); Samuel Stouffer, *Communism, Conformity, and Civil Liberties* (Garden City, N.Y.: Doubleday, 1955).
5. Ludwig Fleck, *Genesis and Development of a Scientific Fact* (Chicago:

Univ. of Chicago Press, 1979). The text was first published in Switzerland in 1935.
6. David B. Truman, "Disillusion and Regeneration: The Quest for a Discipline," *American Political Science Review* 59 (December 1965).
7. A useful overview is provided by Gene M. Lyons, *The Uneasy Partnership: Social Science and the Federal Government in the Twentieth Century* (New York: Russell Sage Foundation, 1969); see also the earlier *Effective Use of Social Science Research in the Federal Services* (New York: Russell Sage Foundation, 1950). The war proved a crucible for the development of empirical work on a large-scale and research that crossed disciplines, and an important testing ground for the institutionalization of

these impulses. After the war, not only the physical sciences but also the behavioral sciences were turned back to the universities.

8. For discussions, see James Farr, John S. Dryzek, and Stephen T. Leonard, eds., *Political Science in History: Research Programs and Political Traditions* (Cambridge: Cambridge Univ. Press, 1995).

9. Robert A. Dahl, *A Preface to Democratic Theory* (Chicago: Univ. of Chicago Press, 1956), 84.

10. Raymond Williams, *Marxism and Literature* (Oxford: Oxford Univ. Press, 1977), 85.

11. For instances, see David Easton, "The New Revolution in Political Science," *American Political Science Review*, 63 (December 1969); and David Easton, John G. Gunnell, and Luigi Graziano, eds., *The Development of Political Science* (London and Boston: Routledge, 1991).

12. Thomas S. Kuhn, *The Structure of Scientific Revolutions* (Chicago: Univ. of Chicago Press, 1962).

13. Truman, "Disillusion and Regeneration," 871, 868–86.

14. Ibid., 866.

15. Ibid., 872.

16. Ibid., 873.

17. Truman, *Governmental Process*; Dahl, *Preface;* Robert A. Dahl, *Who Governs? Democracy and Power in an American City* (New Haven: Yale Univ. Press, 1961); and V.O. Key, *Public Opinion and American Democracy* (New York: Alfred A. Knopf, 1961).

18. Robert K. Merton, *Social Theory and Social Structure* (Glencoe, Ill.: The Free Press, 1949).

19. Of course, these texts are not of one piece. But for the purposes of this essay, I underscore their similarities in spite of their differences,

knowing full well that they possess many differences in spite of these similarities.

20. The phrase, of course, comes from a pivotal chapter in Joseph Schumpeter, *Capitalism, Socialism, and Democracy* (New York: Harper and Row, 1952).

21. Arthur Schlesinger, Jr., *The Vital Center: The Politics of Freedom* (Boston: Houghton Mifflin, 1949), 1, 8, 243, 256; Lionel Trilling, *The Liberal Imagination: Essays on Literature and Society* (New York: Harcourt, Brace, 1950), vii, 284. For a thoughtful reading of this impulse, see Benjamin DeMott, "Rediscovering Complexity," *The Atlantic Monthly*, September 1988.

22. Schlesinger, Jr., *Vital Center*, 1.

23. Dahl, *Preface*, 133, 151.

24. For an important collection of criticisms along these lines, see Philip Green and Sanford Levinson, eds., *Power and Community: Dissenting Essays in Political Science* (New York: Pantheon Books, 1969).

25. Dahl, *Preface*, 150, 151; Truman, *Governmental Process*, 524, 535; Key, *Public Opinion*, 558.

26. Arthur F. Bentley, *The Process of Government* (Chicago: Univ. of Chicago Press, 1908); Charles E. Merriam, *Political Power* (New York: McGraw Hill, 1934); Harold D. Lasswell, *Power and Personality* (New York: W.W. Norton, 1948); Karl Polanyi, *The Great Transformation: The Economic and Political Origins of Our Time* (New York: Rinehart, 1944); Joseph Schumpeter, *Capitalism, Socialism, and Democracy*.

27. Schumpeter, *Capitalism*, 262.

28. With the caveat that he disagreed with the notion, as an empirical matter, that elections and party

activity are of little consequence in determining public policy. Dahl, *Preface*, 131.

29. Dahl, *Preface*, 3; Key, *Public Opinion*, 7.

30. Truman, "Disillusion and Regeneration," 873.

31. Dahl, *Preface*, 1.

32. Talcott Parsons, *The Structure of Social Action: A Study in Social Theory with Special Reference to a Group of Recent European Writers* (Glencoe, Ill.: The Free Press, 1937); Talcott Parsons, *The Social System* (New York: The Free Press, 1951); David Easton, *The Political System: An Inquiry into the State of Political Science* (New York: Alfred A. Knopf, 1953). Though Parsons stood astride his discipline of sociology in this period, Easton, though festooned with honors, never established for his trans-historical political science the hegemony he sought for it.

33. Truman, *Governmental Process*, 522.

34. Dahl, *Preface*, 134.

35. Ibid., 31,32, 51, 54.

36. Ibid., 131.

37. Ibid., 137, 145, 146.

38. Most treatments of this book have debated its empirical and pluralist portrait of New Haven without, in my view, paying attention to its tight linkage to the political theory of *A Preface to Democratic Theory*, nor to its realization of the larger anxious project of his generation of political scientists.

39. Key, *Public Opinion*, 5, 14; Truman, *Governmental Process*, 219, 237.

40. Truman, *Governmental Process*, 511; Dahl, *Preface*, 75.

41. Key, *Public Opinion*, 557.

42. Truman, *Governmental Process*, 2d ed., xliv.

43. Dahl, *Preface*, 138–139.

44. See Mills, *The Power Elite*.

45. The relevant literature is massive. For pioneering work along these lines see E.E. Schattschneider, *The Semi-Sovereign People* (New York: Holt, 1960); and Peter Bachrach and Morton S. Baratz, "The Two Faces of Power," *American Political Science Review* 57 (December 1962).

46. Schumpeter devoted the first section of his book to a critical, but not wholly unsympathetic, account of Marx's writings, announcing, in effect, that he wished his book to be understood as an attempt to develop a surrogate at the same level of analysis.

47. Truman, *Governmental Process*, 23, 24.

48. Ibid., 521.

49. Ibid., 523.

50. Ibid., 524.

51. Truman, *Governmental Process*, 2d ed., xliii, xliv.

52. Ibid.

53. As David Greenstone demonstrated in his incisive, though not unsympathetic, reexamination of Dahl's New Haven cases, this orientation hardly was unique to Truman. J. David Greenstone, "Group Theories," in Fred Greenstein and Nelson Polsby, eds., *Handbook of Political Science* (New York: Addison-Wesley, 1965).

54. Harold D. Lasswell, *National Security and Individual Freedom* (New York: McGraw Hill, 1950); Mills, *The Power Elite*.

55. Theodore J. Lowi, *The End of Liberalism* (New York: Norton, 1969), ix.

Contributors

Noam Chomsky is an Institute Professor in the Massachusetts Institute of Technology's Department of Linguistics and Philosophy. He is a Fellow of the American Academy of Arts and Sciences and the National Academy of Science and a recipient of the Distinguished Scientific Contribution Award of the American Psychological Association. Chomsky has written and lectured widely on linguistics, philosophy, intellectual history, contemporary issues, international affairs, and U.S. foreign policy.

Ira Katznelson is the Ruggles Professor of Political Science and History at Columbia University. His most recent books are *Paths of Emanicipation: Jews, States, and Citizenship* (edited with Pierre Birnbaum) and *Liberalism's Crooked Circle: Letters to Adam Michnik*. He is currently completing a book on the making and character of post-World War II liberalism in the United States.

R. C. Lewontin is the Alexander Agassiz Professor of Zoology and a professor of biology at Harvard University. He is the author of several books, including *Biology and Ideology*, *Not in Our Genes*, and *Human Diversity*.

David Montgomery is Farnam Professor of History at Yale University.

Laura Nader is a professor of anthropology at the University of California, Berkeley, where she has taught since 1960. Her previous books include *Harmony Ideology: Justice and Control in a Zapotec Mountain Village*, *Essays in Controlling Processes*, *Naked Science: Anthropological Inquiry into Boundaries, Power, and Knowledge*, and *Energy Choices in a Democratic Society*, a multidisciplinary collaborative effort of the National Academy of Sciences. She is a member of the American Academy of Arts and Sciences. In 1995, the Law and Society Association awarded her the Kalven Prize.

Richard Ohmann is a professor of English at Wesleyan University. His previous books include *Politics of Letters, English in America, Selling Culture: Magazines, Markets, and Class at the Turn of the Century, Making and Selling Culture* (editor). Ohmann also serves on the board of Radical Teacher.

Raymond Siever is a professsor emeritus of geology in the Department of Earth and Planetary Sciences at Harvard University. He is the author of *Sand* and *Sand and Sandstone, 2nd edition, Earth, 4th edition, Understanding Earth,* and over one hundred technical articles on geology, geochemistry, and oceanography.

Immanuel Wallerstein directs the Fernand Braudel Center for the Study of Economies, Historical Systems, and Civilizations at Binghamton University, and teaches at Ecole des Hautes Etudes en Sciences Sociales in Paris. His many books include *The Modern World-System, The Capitalist World-Economy, Historical Capitalism,* and *After Liberalism* (The New Press).

Howard Zinn is the author of *A People's History of the United States, A People's History of the United States: The Wall Charts* (The New Press), and a recent memoir, *You Can't Be Neutral on a Moving Train.* He is a professor emeritus at Boston University.